# BALLOON NOMENCLATURE

VALVE

RIP PANEL

NET

ENVELOPE
80,000 CU. FT. 52 FT. DIAMETER

FOOT ROPES

LOAD RING

PILOT VAN ORMAN

BASKET

BALLAST (30# SANDBAG)

PONTOONS (2)

WATER PROOF BASKET COVER

D1595979

*Wizard of the Winds*

# THE WIZARD
# OF
# THE WINDS

by

## Ward T. Van Orman

*World Champion Balloonist*

as told to
## Robert Hull

*Best wishes to my new friend, Lee !*
*Robert Hull*
*6/16/83*

**North Star Press**
**Saint Cloud, Minnesota**

Special thanks are expressed to Christine Beringer, age 16, a junior at Our Lady of the Elms High School, Akron, Ohio, for her gift of the title of this book, chosen from submissions of the journalism classes of Miss Lynda Culp.

Pen sketches: Patrick A. Dwyer

International Standard Book Number: 0-87839-032-4

*To my family*

# Contents

# Foreword

"A captive balloon bouncing in a roaring gale like a rubber ball, striking the earth and rocketing up the full height of its 290-foot tether, bouncing, bouncing, each time threatening to impale on an anchor stake the occupants of the frail basket . . ."

The near storybook description of Akron, Ohio journalist Helen Waterhouse introduced to a new generation of Ohioans back in July, 1941, the "Jack Armstrong" style exploits of Lorain, Ohio-born Ward Tunte Van Orman, Goodyear Tire & Rubber Company's multi-champion balloon adventurist and celebrated scientist, who still lives today in the Rubber City.

Those great skin-of-our-teeth capers poured out again these past months on that still strong voice of 82-year-old Van Orman, who I first interviewed in his spice-scented kitchen on Letchworth Drive as he nursed a glass of good scotch.

Tall and responsive as a cannon-blast, the man who won more international and national free balloon races than any other human stuck out his right hand like a punch and welcomed me to airship country.

He was attired in a fashionable jacket, flashy bow tie and crisply pressed shirt. The retired design engineer brushed back a huge wave of white hair and swirled his ice cubes. Drawn quickly to friends or strangers with a fondness for derring-do and a sweet compassion for the past, Van spun the old escapades on a voice charged with a poet's rhythms.

For years he had sought a collaborator and publisher for his tales of true-to-life encounters in an 80,000 cubic foot gas-inflated sphere—a permanent record for his children and grandchildren of an era that christened the great free balloons and airships of the world.

In a tattered paper-covered diary dated 1929, Van Orman chronicled this saga of balloons and airships as it first was and promised to be before the imaginative and dramatic lighter-than-air industry sank into despair in the ashes of the *Hindenburg* tragedy, the rise of Adolph Hitler and the breakthrough of sophisticated continent-hopping jet aircraft.

At 82, Ward Van Orman has turned to repairing neighbors' clocks. He directs an Akron glee club and the Lions Club chorus. He teaches the harmonica (a gift from the *Graf Zeppelin* commander) to any who will learn. He invites kids in at Christmas week to handle the controls of the big electric train still sprawled across the floor of the Van Orman attic.

But as one might expect, the Ohio adventurer's sense of romance returns frequently and with all the excitement of which memory is capable.

This is his story.

Robert Hull

# Author's Preface

Mark Twain wrote in the preface of his uniform edition of his books that he could not think of any good reason for such an edition other than the fact the "it pleased him."

"It is nothing," he confessed. "A cat could say the same of her kittens."

It is no different with this book. I am wonderfully happy it is out; happier still that it is over and done. Living one final time my whole life of ballooning thrills, thunderstorms, victories and crashes was almost too much at age 82. I almost didn't make it this time around. Yet this book is something that I have known for years I must complete.

The book is an illumination of early balloon racing in America and Europe, a narration of the hardships endured and some of the scientific challenges dealt with by the early pioneer balloonists. It is also a personal review of the incredible airship industry of Akron, Ohio, and of the magnificent union of German and American engineers who jointly dreamed and built there together—a part of American history too few Ohioans even know existed.

It is not a novel. It is a chronicle. It is truth as I remember truth to be, varnished over or honed a bit, perhaps, by the limits and cut of my personality and human fraility. It is mighty dangerous to expect Truth in any one book—even a review of balloons and airships. I urge any so inclined to further knowledge to seek additional information from the Balloon Federation of America, the Lighter-Than-Air Society of Akron, Ohio, the Goodyear Tire & Rubber Company, the Navy Museum at Lakehurst, New

Jersey, and the Smithsonian Institution.

I have attempted to underscore the scientific emphasis of otherwise romantic balloon adventures. Scientific testing, more than advertising, was the main thrust of everything the Goodyear Corporation did in the national and international balloon contests. What we learned, sometimes painfully, was directly applied to the construction of great airships because of the intimate physical relationship between free balloons and dirigibles.

The tragic balloon death of my dear friend Walter Morton in 1928, for example, directly contributed invaluable knowledge—knowledge which nobody knew then—as to the horrendous destructive power of the vertical air currents in a thunderstorm.

I am no daredevil. I never was. Don't believe in foolish risks. Perhaps it is my age that causes me to want to stop the Carl Thomases of the world from attempting trans-Atlantic flights in a balloon or to plead with today's hot air balloonists to pack sandbag ballast in their baskets.

No one in history has traveled the distance of the Atlantic in a balloon and there are numerous reasons why. I was never a suicide freak. For just that reason, I have urged that the one incredible danger of hot air ballooning is the crucial lack of instant reaction, underscored by the unnecessary repetition of powerline deaths reported annually.

The carrying of sand ballast, antiquated as the practice may seem by today's standards, would offer the amazing hot air sport its much needed margin of safety at a small cost in lifting power.

This book contains only the highlights of a life I have tried to consume to the fullest. Nor is it the complete story of ballooning in America or a-broad. But its episodes are faithfully characteristic of the efforts and problems everywhere in the early and mid-twentieth century, plus an added background of the beginnings of the art.

It is especially my personal thank-you to all those with whom I flew and for whom I flew. They were giants honed for the need and tempo of the times. You will meet them all in the pages to follow.

And because I believe that the opinions and reactions and testimonies of the public are as important to historical fact as statistical truth, excerpts from the media, credited where known, are presented at various places in the text to try to place happenings in some social as well as technical perspective, and, frankly, to make my presentation a bit more exciting.

Accordingly, my thanks are offered to Harold J. Taylor, former aviation editor of the *Akron Beacon Journal* and to *Journal* reporters Helen Waterhouse, Redford E. Mobley, C. W. Howard, Harry E. Harriman, Oscar Smith, Ruth McKinnney, Patricia O'Malley and editorial writer John

Botzum; to William T. Shenkel of the former *Akron Times-Press* and *Press* reporter Ruth Putnam; to the Akron Lighter-Than-Air Society; to V. O. Hodges of the *Associated Press*; to Irving Ramsell of the *Milwaukee World*; Julien Griffin, Frank Eblen, and James D. Hartshorne of the *Cleveland Plain Dealer*; to Captain W. E. Kepner, writing for the *Omaha World Herald*; to the *Case Alumnus Magazine*; to John T. Brady, *Boston Sunday Post*; to the *United Press Services*; to the *Lorain Journal & Times Herald*; to Thomas Wayling, Quebec, Canada; to Herbert O'Laughlin, N. A. N. A. Inc.; to Roy Greenaway, *STAR Newspaper Service*, Canada; to James Y. Nichol of the Toronto (Canada) *Star*, INS; to Art Arthur, *The Brooklyn Eagle*; to C. Roy Greenaway, USI, and the *Wingfoot Clan*.

I have saved for the last the highest tribute of all to the one in my life who was not only my constant friend and fan, but also my most positive and encouraging life force. Wherever I went to fly, facing unknown hardships and dangers, a telegram would be waiting from my late dear wife, Edith Van Orman.

The last sentence would inevitably read: "With my love you shall win."

Ward Van Orman

At the peak of his ballooning career, Van also enjoyed a casual homelife in between research for Goodyear and his annual air adventures. He is shown (above) picnicking with his late wife, Edith, and children Ward George and Edith Tunte.

Ward Van Orman, Fall, 1977, discussing the principles of ballooning with journalism class members at Our Lady of the Elms High School, Akron, Ohio. A member of this class, Christine Beringer, suggested the name of this book, *The Wizard of the Winds*.

# Author's Note

I make reference various times in this book to my four victories in the
James Bennett International Balloon Races, referring to the years 1925,
1926, 1929 and 1930.

At the same time the reader must note that the *official* victory in the
1925 race from Brussels was awarded not to me, but to the Belgian, A.
Veenstra, by the Aero Club of Belgium.

I have always believed in sportsmanship and the good loser. Countless things are more important than victory. Yet unfairness, either on the
part of participants or officials, cannot be tolerated. To the extent that in-
difference to bias and wrongdoing is tolerated—in any organization or
segment of society—the entire institution deteriorates in character and
importance to that precise degree.

A rule of the 1925 Bennett race forbade balloonists to descend into
the water under penalty of disqualification.

Having already flown the farthest distance, my aide and I found ourselves hopelessly over the Atlantic. Noting a tiny German freighter coming up on the horizon at night, we executed a nearly impossible maneuver
and landed bag and basket on its tossing deck, never coming in contact
with the water.

We were, nevertheless, disqualified.

On the other hand, the Belgian, Veenstra, who was declared the
winner, did, in fact, descend into the waves of the Bay of Biscay and was
nearly drowned.

Justice was not served in 1925. My aide and I abided by the letter of the

xvi • *Wizard of the Winds*

rules and flew the farthest. I have never conceded that victory on general principle in all the years since. The full story is told in Chapter 16, "Hundred-to-One Shot on a Tossing Ship Deck."

You may judge for yourself.

Ward Van Orman

Ward Tunte Van Orman
1894-1978

*Wizard of the Winds*

# · 1 ·

# *My Fingers Are Slipping!*

Sometimes our decisions are influenced by *something*—we may call it divine guidance, a sixth sense, or "a wee small voice." The first time I recognized such a guidance, I was hanging by my hands outside a balloon basket 500 feet above the ground with my strength ebbing quickly.

Ordinarily it would have been a simple matter to have pulled myself into the basket, but all sinew had been depleted by a long siege of typhoid fever. My arms no longer seemed to function to bear the weight of my body. I told myself it would be quite simple to let go—a quick drop, a dull thud, then oblivion.

My numb fingers were slipping when the *small voice* whispered, "Don't!" Given fresh strength, I looked up at the student pilot in the basket. His blanched face showed horrible fear.

"What shall I do?" he whispered desperately. And through my teeth there hissed one word—"Valve!"

The student jerked the valve rope opening the valve and the balloon slowly descended. I managed to cling to the basket to within two feet of the ground. Then I collapsed.

It was such a simple way in which my near-fatality occurred. In teaching the principles of free ballooning to future commanders of lighter-than-air ships at Akron, Ohio, the solo flight was a requirement. During World War I, instructors frequently terminated a flight with several students by making a landing with them, then replacing our own weight with sand or ballast, then sending them on their way alone.

This day, flying out of Akron's Wingfoot Lake, we had landed near Kent, Ohio. I stepped out into a wheat field and, in matter-of-fact fashion,

1

replaced my weight in the basket with ballast. The basket started up from the ground and believing it was a few pounds light, I grabbed the outside edge, intending to return it to earth. Much to my surprise, instead of stopping, as I added my weight to the basket, the balloon carried me air-borne.

The student, sick with fear as he saw me rising from the ground with him, forgot all he had been taught, and there we were high in the sky—a fever-weakened man dangling at the bottom of a basket, and a green pilot.

Later, this "wee small voice" again whispered, "Don't!"

We were in training for the final phase of balloon pilot's license requirements and three students and I took a balloon from our flying field, the Naval Air Station at Akron, and commenced what we had decided would be an exceptionally long venture, taking to the air two days before Christmas at ten o'clock in the morning.

The wind carried us due east from Akron toward New York City. The flight was of particular significance to me for in my pocket was a diamond engagement ring which I hoped to be able to present the young lady in my life on Christmas Day.

Our destination was indeed New York City, but the long afternoon and sub-zero temperature dampened our enthusiasm which was occasionally renewed by the picturesque sights of the snow clad mountains in western Pennsylvania. As darkness grew upon us, Joe Torrey, who was piloting, suggested that we terminate the flight because of the holiday traffic congestion in New York City, which would prevent us from reaching our homes.

Charley Roth, who was aide, seconded the motion and I, thinking of the ring, voted vigorous approval. We looked below us for possible landing fields, cities or railroads, but we appeared to be flying over absolute wilderness.

In addition to our difficulties, the lone flashlight which we carried developed a vexing habit of lighting only once every three or four tries. It is perplexing to navigate such a craft with the few instruments we carried without the aid of a flashlight, so I considered taking it apart and repairing it in the darkness.

I felt it would be a simple thing to unscrew the flashlight in the dark basket and locate the loose contact, but Joe and Charley, who seemed to sport no such confidence in my electrical repair prowess, vetoed the idea on the grounds that when I had finished, we would have no light at all.

Overruled, I acquiesced and offered a little prayer that the torch would not fail us at a crucial moment. It seemed to me we flew for hours over those snow-peaked mountains sometimes at five thousand feet, sometimes three thousand feet, and again just skimming the tops of the pine trees which projected imposingly through icy crusts. The wind whistled through the trees indicating very high speed and giving promise of a jolting landing.

By nine o'clock it seemed we would never find a spot suitable to land on. But as things looked their darkest, we slipped over the top of one of the huge snow white mountains and saw before us the lights of a town in the valley below. Then, too, our hopes were reinforced by the long scream of a freight train whistle, indicating transportation home.

Naturally my thoughts turned to my ring again and for the first time in several hours I was hopeful of delivering the gem on time. Our balloon swung down into the valley and leveled off about twenty feet above the longest, whitest field you ever saw—at least a half-mile wide and as far as we could see in the darkness of the night!

It was beyond all expectations. Here was a field that was better than any of the municipal landing ports in the United States today. It seemed we were running full length of this field which was at least five miles long and probably one-half or three-quarters of a mile in width.

So we cautiously valved a bit more gas and dropped down to within three feet of the touchdown. Joe was ready to pull the rip panel when the "wee small voice" whispered, "Don't." Terry released his grip on the cord as I dropped a sand bag weighing thirty pounds over the edge of the basket just to check the field. The missile crashed through the ice of what proved to be the Susquehanna River! The ice at this time was only a half-inch thick and a landing on it would have been disastrous.

Our balloon rose a few hundred feet from the buoyant effect of this sand bag I had dropped and both Joe and Charley realized how close we had come to a calamitous crash into freezing waters. Our winds followed the Susquehanna for at least two miles before the current in the valley carried us to one side. Here we managed a picture book descent into a clearing at one of the jack pine saw mills near Williamsport, Pennsylvania.

I might add that the ring was delivered safely, and on schedule.

In reality the ring represented one of my reasons for entering aeronautics. After graduating from Case School of Applied Science in Cleveland in 1917, I had the young lady very much in mind and was anxious to make a quick success in the world. Looking over opportunities available, I was confronted with two problems. A problem of patriotic duty and that of personal fulfillment. I felt the best opportunity of rapid promotion would be in a swiftly expanding industry.

I felt, on the other hand, that there would be no better way of serving my country than by training student naval officers to fly. So I accepted a position in Akron as a civilian instructor to student officers at the Naval Air Station.

As to all airmen, it seemed ages before I actually got off the ground the first time. I had nearly abandoned hope when the manager of the school, R. A. D. Preston, advised me I was to take my first flight in a free balloon going out the next morning. That notification kept me awake the rest of the night imagining all of the experiences ahead of me. At three that morning I was in the hanger looking over our craft in wonder and admiration.

The wicker basket was impressively rugged. The ropes running from the sphere to the basket seemed strong enough to hold any weight. Then the moment arrived. I could see the superintendent, who was also scheduled to make the flight with me, coming through the door. Following him was Commander Maxfield, commanding officer of the station, trailed by his airedale, "Blimp."

Blimp was the pet of the station. He had a peculiar aversion to dirigibles flying across the field. All day long he would race madly over the turf barking at the top of his voice and exhibiting his general displeasure at this noisy aircraft. As Hockensmidt and Maxfield approached the basket, I could see they were debating the possibility of taking the airedale along, but decided to the contrary.

The hangar crew balanced our balloon off in the hangar, the weigh-off, as it is known aeronautically, and carried the craft to the middle of the field. In the pre-dawn moonlight I could see that Blimp did not approve of the parting. Here was his master rising straight up to heaven in this strange craft and the beast moaned in the agony of absolute torture as a hound dog bays at the moon. One could almost see tears in the dog's eyes.

Once we had left Blimp behind us, I realized one of my life's foremost objectives had been achieved. It is not easy to describe the sensation of flying without engines—in virtual silence. In a balloon the moment you leave the ground you feel absolutely motionless. It is the earth that recedes from you downward and, according to the will of wind, in a lateral direction. You may be travelling at sixty miles per hour but you have no sensation of speed; there is no breath of wind in the face; the car hangs always vertically from the envelope.

It is only when you touch earth again that you realize your speed, for at that moment that the car stops you feel the wind; and if it be a strong wind your repose and quietude are rudely dispelled, and your balloon, caught by the wind, heels over and drags you about the ground.

Neither is there a sensation of height and none of giddiness. At an impressive height the earth has a concave appearance, but as there is no wall or line from you to the ground, the ordinary sensation felt when looking down a cliff is quite absent. At any considerable height also you are so far away from the ground that even if you are traveling at a very great speed it is difficult to see that you are moving at all.

It is the same when you are in an express train and your eyes are fixed on a distant part of the landscape. So slowly does the scene change that relative to the swift passage of nearer objects it appears to be going in the opposite direction to them and in the same direction as the train.

As the balloonist reaches the higher altitudes, the sky turns a deeper shade of blue or burgundy, and the sun appears like a glaring bright disc on a dark background.

Beautiful phenomena are seen by the balloonist. Halos around the sun and moon, rainbows, "glories" or "aureoles"—the coloured rings seen 'round the shadow cast by the balloon on the clouds—and splendid seas of rolling clouds above and below, reward his enterprise.

But the scenery beheld by the balloonist is an inexhaustible subject. No two voyages are like one another.

In the basket with the superintendent and Commander Maxfield, it was a bit disarming the first time out to feel not a wisp of wind brush by us as we almost instantly attained the speed of the wind currents carrying us in a westerly direction. I am no sentimentalist, yet the stillness impressed me and the beauty of the moon light over the sleeping farm houses filled me with utter tranquility.

We seemed monarchs of the winds, we three.

We had flown for an hour when Maxwell decided to descend lower to better view the countryside, and we did so until our drag rope skidded to earth. A balloon drag rope is an inch in diameter, 150 feet in length, and acts as a huge shock absorber as the inflated sphere swoops to earth, slowing the balloon's forward speed by dragging along the surface of the ground. It is a big thrill the first time you experience it as it produces violent jerks on the basket.

Nevertheless, Hockensmidt and I were enjoying every moment of it when interrupted by Maxfield's warning, "Watch this."

Just a few hundred feet ahead was a farm house and that long, heavy rope was about to collide with it. The hemp first touched the eaves of the porch, dragged and sawed over the tin eave troughs with the noise of a buzz saw cutting through thin boards. The rope plowed over the tin roof and slapped down on a tin porch in the rear with a terrific bang! When this occurred, Maxwell quickly poured over two bags of sand and we rose quickly to the heavens, lifting the unseemly cord with us.

We had ascended but two hundred feet when we observed a sudden light at the back door of the farm house. From the flickering of the light, we knew it was the farmer investigating the unexplained commotion that had terrified his family.

Maxfield whispered, "Be quiet." I suppose for fear the farmer might have a gun or a rifle in his clenched hands and more than willing to use it. To our amusement we watched this lantern circle around the barn and the house several times and finally stop at the back steps. We could visualize this farmer in his long nightshirt and slippers scratching his head, fingering his shotgun, totally bewildered by the disturbance.

We continued up two thousand feet, flew another hour, and finally landed near Spencer, Ohio. I was totally impressed with Maxfield's skill in bringing the balloon to roost. From two thousand feet we had settled as slowly as a snowflake and hit the earth practically without a jar.

On this first flight, I saw wonderful possibilities for studying air currents, meteorology, navigation and practically all those subjects needed in flying today. It was with this thought in mind that I considered it especially valuable to take the free balloon and use it as a working laboratory of the air.

Pilot Ward Van Orman in the 1920s

# 2

# Curing the Braggart

Airships such as the world's greatest dirigibles, the *Akron* and the *Macon*, were, after all, gigantic assemblies of free balloon units. These ships were simply huge duralumin cages in which were confined twelve balloons or gas cells, the entire assemblies being propelled by motors. Should the motors go haywire, the zeppelins would become nothing other than free balloons. Safety for ship and crew at that point would depend entirely on the free ballooning skill of the pilots.

This is precisely what happened on one occasion to the mighty *Graf Zeppelin* when all but one of its motors stopped over France and it was ballooned to safety by Dr. Hugo Eckener.

It was my job, therefore, to teach future pilots of these massive and majestic skyliners all the secrets I ever knew or heard of in regard to the art of free ballooning, gasses, wind and weather information.

And so we carried on our war training at top speed, running from five o'clock in the morning until ten and eleven o'clock at night in order to produce qualified airship handlers for World War I convoy escort and scouting missions.

And throughout that period of time the experiences we encountered and those brought back by the student officers, presented many strange aspects. For example:

One party of balloonists landed near Stuart, Virginia. Upon landing they were surrounded by an inquisitive crowd of spectators, many of whom were farmers. One of the audience, upon sight of the balloonists, prostrated herself upon the ground and shouted at the top of her voice that the Angel Gabriel had come again to this world. Precisely which of the balloonists represented Gabriel, I am to this day unable to say.

A flight I was on ended in the hills near Murfreesboro, Tennessee. In a very few minutes we found ourselves surrounded by two dozen mountaineers with squirrel guns pointed at our brains. I knew they might well have figured us for revenue officers out after their innumerable stills, and nothing in the balloonist books seemed to cover the situation.

I reached into the basket for the medicine kit and withdrew from it a bottle of excellent bourbon kept for emergency or extreme cold and handed it to the first man. The bottle traveled all the way around the circle and when it was emptied I said, "All right, fellers, let's get busy and get this balloon packed up!" Within fifteen minutes the bag was in the basket and we were on a farm truck headed for town.

Some of the students on their solo flights sent their equipment back to the station with the ropes of the basket entirely cut off. A close examination indicated a possibility that they were burned off. I at first refused to accept the excuse of the neophytes that their balloons had struck telephone wires in landing, but upon visiting the site I discovered for a fact that the ropes of a balloon basket sliding along a telephone wire between the poles can indeed be severed by the cutting or burning action of the wire.

Other student officers brought back strange tales of having to throw over their clothing to prevent hard landings. We believed some of these assertions for they came back minus their expensive leather flying coats of which they were so proud.

On one particularly cold winter morning with the thermometer standing well below zero, we were flying five hundred feet above the ground on the outskirts of Salem, Ohio. Someone called to us. We looked down and discovered a woman out on her back porch shaking out her tablecloth after breakfast. She was startled to see a balloon flying so low over her home on that morning but responded with an invitation for breakfast.

It being a particularly frigid morning, the thought of sizzling eggs and bacon could not be dismissed lightly. In but seconds our vote was unanimous. We proceeded over a woods and descended in the next field, tying our craft to a firm fence post. Filing single file into the little farm house, a more surprised woman never lived than the mistress of that abode. She quickly recovered her equilibrium, however, and in a very few moments plates of hot delicious breakfast came and disappeared with remarkable rapidity.

Occasionally the students brought back stories of their drag rope swinging in front of passing trains. As has been mentioned, the rope is about one hundred and fifty feet in length and when flying close to the ground drags along the terrain in the rear of the balloon acting as a very large brake and also shock absorber. It is a simple matter, then to picture the possibility of being caught by the train and snapping the balloon forward.

However, while such tales may have been true, I am not in a postion to vouch for their accuracy.

My next experience came as a result of a little plot afoot among the pilots at the Naval Station to give one of the student officers a real thrill. Before the first day of basic instruction had come and gone, the personality in question had already established for himself the unenviable reputation as a boaster and braggart. According to his own statements he had completed more airplane flights than any man— then, back in the days when not more than two hundred planes existed in the whole country.

He also claimed to have made more parachute jumps than any man in the United States—this in the days when the only parachutes available were aboard hot air balloons, used as life insurance by airshow pilots in red tights.

The yarn that especially grieved me was his assertion that he had dropped through the glass of greenhouses many times although he bore no scars from these experiences, which one had a reasonable right to expect.

Very quickly the instructing pilots reached an agreement among themselves that the next instuctor who took this "widely experienced flyer" with him would give him something to remember.

The instructor in question turned out to be me—and how I was to engineer *a flight to remember* I could not decide to save my soul. Nevertheless, I felt obligated to carry out my agreement.

We left the air station on a brisk west wind that carried us towards Youngstown, Ohio. The students and I had flown about an hour in an altitude of a thousand feet when I spotted Lake Milton ahead, and an idea flashed through my mind of a means to accomplish my obligation.

I remembered once talking to the late Leo Stevens, an old-time balloonist, and he told me a balloon basket would come down and you could strike the surface of a river or a lake and bounce right back into the air and make a big splash and have a lot of fun.

It immediately occurred to me that this would present the ideal opportunity to test out the bounce theory and at the same time give our most "widely experienced student" something to think about later.

So we started down toward the surface of Milton Reservoir and these student Naval officers became anxious and wanted to throw over ballast and I said, "No, we're going lower!" Seconds later they asked permission to throw over the coats to their uniforms. Again I said, "Oh, no! We're just going to descend a little further!" And we did.

We swung down until we were one hundred feet over the ground drifting toward the water at thirty miles an hour with the drag rope cracking through the branches of the trees. I was eagerly awaiting results of my dual experiment.

We hit the water with a startling smack, but instead of bouncing as I was told, we submerged into the ice water nearly to our waists. The only satisfaction that I had was that this fellow who bragged so much was even more scared than the rest of us.

He tried to climb up the rigging to get out of the ice water but I insisted he come down and take his chances with the rest of the crew.

I ordered the students to throw over eight bags of sand which were submerged in the water in the basket but the action had no effect on the balloon whatever. Ordinarily in the air this amount of ballast would have caused the sphere to rise three thousand feet, but submerged in three feet of water the effect was nil. As the next resource I cut off the drag rope but that, too, had no effect.

The student officer standing next to me wrapped up the coat of a brand new uniform and offered to throw it over. My reaction was that here was a real man who was willing to make any sacrifice to help us. I told him it was unnecessary, but insisted that everyone stand on the bottom of the basket in order not to force it deeper into the lake.

The spherical bag overhead now leaned thirty degrees ahead of us under the force of the wind. Our craft, a most undignified sight by now, continued to drift at about five miles an hour through the icy water. Our most widely experienced student seemed to be about ready to expire but I felt relieved to notice the other four seemed to be enjoying this unique experience.

The next problem confronting me was that of landing.

I knew that after throwing over two hundred and forty pounds of sand and a one hundred and fifty pound drag rope that the balloon would rise very rapidly upon leaving the water, which I felt would occur immediately upon striking the opposite bank. I also realized it would be almost impossible to make a safe landing in a thirty mile wind with no ballast and no drag rope.

The safety of the five students rested heavily upon me. I felt there was just one point where we should make the landing and that was immediately upon contact with the opposite bank which we were rapidly approaching. I had two officers grasp the rip panel which slits the top quarter of the balloon and the moment the basket touched the opposite shore, I ordered, "Rip!"

The basket gave one bounce out of the water, lifted all the water in it, as the gash produced by the rip panel plummeted the craft instantly to the ground five feet from the water's edge.

It is needless to point out that after this flight we were not bothered with the experiences of the most widely experienced student.

But I realized something else—that landing in the wild was for the birds. Something must be done about it. *What* could be done about it, I certainly didn't know, but when we got back to the Goodyear plant I designed some pneumatic pontoons about fourteen inches in diameter —L-shaped—to fit the bottom of the basket and up the sides in case we ran into a barn or stone wall, it would act to minimize shock. It also would keep our bodies out of the water in the event of an unexpected sea landing; still I felt it wasn't quite enough. I then took two of the L-shaped pontoons and connected them together—like a rectangle—and constructed a piece of fabric across the bottom.

Here was America's first life raft, a superbly improved version of which is carried on all overseas flights today. You can imagine my sense of satisfaction and bliss when my dear friend Eddy Rickenbacker drifted twenty-three days in the ocean and survived on a life raft closer to my original design during World War II. Multiply his experience by virtually hundreds of otherwise doomed bomber crews downed in the sea in combat operations and it is easy to see that my raft was a success.

I say this not in pompousness, but to point out that a little inspiration coming from an ice water bath did much to create a tool to save lives. Ironically, it may never have happened if I had not believed that story that a balloon basket will strike a body of water and bounce off it like a bedspring!

Photo was taken in 1919 during Van's fledgling days as a balloonist. He is shown in the basket (above right) as aide to Goodyear pilot Ralph Upson in the 1919 National Balloon Race out of St. Louis. This was the first balloon ever to use the L-shaped pontoons designed by Van Orman, which later, with a simple design change, became the familiar life raft. Upson was the second American to win the Gordon Bennett International Race, winning in 1913 from Paris, France, with a distance of 384 miles. Lt. Frank P. Lahm, an Ohioan, won the very first Gordon Bennett classic in 1906, also from Paris, with a distance of 402 miles.

Ward Van Orman putters in his basement workshop on a neighbor's clock or small appliance. However, his second-floor "balloon room," full of medals, trophies and honors from his adventurous past, is what guests ask first to see.

# 3

# A Lorain, Ohio Christening

If only because of the custom of such books to include the fact, I will say quickly and be done with it that I was born on the second of September, 1894, at two o'clock on a Sunday afternoon to Christina (Teen) and Richmond Guinnete Van Orman of Lorain, Ohio.

My earliest recollection of our home was the twinkling glimmer of the hard coal-burning base burner which heated our living room. To this day I can still visualize its cheery glow through the little isinglass window.

I recall venturing out of doors my first winter to gather a handful of snow. It was too cold for my hands so I put it under the base burner to warm it up. You can imagine my surprise when I found a puddle of water where my white treasure had been. It was my first scientific observation.

A few years later one of my friends gave me a water motor which operated on city water pressure, and, having that, I ordered a dynamo from Sears & Roebuck costing $2.98. It generated six volts and four amperes. My first installation was the placing of electrical plates on the stairway going up to the attic, which I connected to a high tension coil. It did not, of course, hurt them, but dozens of unannounced visitors literally got the shock of their lives if they trespassed my attic laboratory.

Similarly, I connected electrical charges to the clothesline outside (a bit of a dirty trick) and built a complete electrical railway under the eaves, with an automatic reversing switch at the end of the line. The motorized unit included a tiny electric bulb on the top of the car and I enjoyed thoroughly the hours invested in such railroad play.

I arranged my water motor so I could turn it on from this attic sanctuary where the belt to the dynamo ran through the inside of the wall, powering the train and electrical tortures alike.

I was somewhat feared in the neighborhood.

Clothes for an active young boy were a tough problem. My father was ill for two years and my mother supported the family by taking in roomers and hanging wallpaper. We slept on a folding bed in the kitchen and I would carry my mother's tools—a table and ladder—to her daily location on a wagon I had built myself.

I remember vividly the winter my shoes were open at the toes, perfectly useless. I tried to sew the toes shut. I remember looking in the Sears catalogue at a cobbler's outfit and quickly committed to memory the number of nails and lasts and consistency of sewing oil in the kit and dreamt of possessing the treasure one way or another.

But I never did get the kit. I kept sewing the toes of the shoes with black thread and as such, survived the winter.

One of my mother's customers, a party named Gawn, of Welch origin, presented me with a rooster which I taught to crow. Youngsters who ran through our yard were almost certainly chased by the big fellow. I remember so well his mate, the bantam hen, coming up into my playhouse which was on top of the chicken coop. She laid an egg and I had a can of boiling water there heated by an oil stove and I had a superbly fresh egg for my dessert.

My father was of Dutch descent and he had infinite patience, if also an insatiable restlessness. He first worked in a rubber stamp factory in York, Ohio, just outside of Medina, where custodial chores included stoking the morning fire to heat the shop. Next he was an apprentice to the machinists trade on the old Cleveland, Lorain & Wheeling Railroad, a branch of the B. & O., where he repaired locomotives. Then he went with the Bridgeport Brass Company, valve makers, who had a factory in Lorain. Later he built stoves and still later assembled automobiles before hiring on as superintendent of the Hoffman Hot Water Heater Company.

When mother died of breast cancer in 1908, I missed her terribly. I was fourteen but my younger sister took me under her arm and guided me through the rest of high school and then to college. Her name was Ella and she bought me a top coat at graduation to go with the tailor-made blue serge suit, a present from dad. The top coat cost sixteen dollars and was the most beautiful coat in the world, and I cherished it for years and years.

When mother died, we went to live with Aunt Ida who kept a boarding house for railroaders and firemen, and I would listen intently to the tales they spun, seeing myself a trainman.

After two years my father remarried and my stepmother was as fine to me as if she had been my real mother. She made shirts for me and helped me save money. Then followed two years' toil as a rail car checker for the Lake Terminal Railroad in Lorain making forty dollars a month and saving thirty-five of it to get into Case School of Applied Science in Cleveland.

Unfortunately a classmate told stepmother that I was doing poorly in my studies (an unwarranted accusation), and by graduation festivities she was beside herself with worry. When it was official I had passed, she and father (with a great sigh of relief) attended the graduation exercises at the old Beck Theater in Lorain.

I never discovered how the school board obtained such a notable commencement speaker. He was Dr. Russell H. Conwell who was then president of Temple University in Philadelphia and author of that magnificent essay, "Acres of Diamonds." I can see him yet coming to the center of the stage, looking the group over, saying not a word. Moments passed—still not a word—until I sensed the uneasiness of the crowd. Then the small, steady voice commenced. You had to move forward in your seat at first to hear. In two minutes' time he had every mind in that multitude drinking in every word.

And I remember yet, while he lectured I made a vow that someday I would equal Russell H. Conwell as a speaker on a stage entertaining the public. And it so happened that during my ballooning career I was forced into addressing luncheon clubs, church groups and other organizations and I gradually acquired the ability to hold my audience like Russell H. Conwell. I've often been thankful to that board of education.

Earlier in the year father had purchased a 2-cylinder Auto Car made by the makers of the Auto Car trucks. It looked like the 2-cylinder Renault taxi in Paris but didn't have oomph enough to take the Pennfield Avenue hill which was a pushover for a coaster wagon. Together, father and I spent the entire winter overhauling this car. The back wheels were so loose we had to put shims in them. The wheels were made of steel, though they looked like wood, and wore 28 x 3-inch clincher tires, the popular Ford size.

That summer vacation, father chose to celebrate our engine expertise with the announcement that we would all motor to Niagara Falls. Well, we started out merrily. I was to be chauffeur. We had reached Painesville, Ohio, when the engine clattered, then stopped with a bang. Father and I conferred, deciding it was one of the inlet valves which we had made new but of hardened steel. Its head had broken off and dropped into the cylinder.

Dad said, "I wish I had listened to you and taken the old inlet valve along." I said, "Well, I wish you had listened to me, too, because that's precisely what I need." Then I produced the can of spare parts I had hidden beneath the seat and gave a laugh. Dad could have *kissed* me!

We got the valve back in and resumed our journey, staying over night at Erie, Pennsylvania at an ancient stagecoach tavern. Rumbling about the streets of Buffalo, New York the next morning, the car's universal joint gave out, but fortunately we found ourselves stopped immediately in front of a machine shop. Father went in and turned a brand new part on a lathe, and that solved all of our problems beautifully. We had a glorious visit at the falls—my first, and we returned home free of troubles and with glowing colors.

Consideration of finding a job arose while still at Case Tech. My college classmate, A. G. Moranville, was a good friend and my checker player companion. He also built himself a run-about made of an old Franklin chassis and a Franklin air-cooled engine and it was a wonderful car. He had graduated the year before and gone to Goodyear who was then making blimps for Navy convoy patrol between America and England.

In the course of the war Goodyear produced 114 airships for that purpose, the Navy losing only one of them when its bomb rack jammed, necessitating a second run against a submarine. The sub put a well-aimed cannon shot through the gas-filled bag just as the aircraft loosed a death-dealing missile against the attacker. We traded one airship with no loss of life for one submarine and every soul aboard her.

In my junior year at Case I became very much interested in a girl named Edith Black. Edith Lucile Black was the daughter of the former mayor of McConnelsville, Ohio, who was also a judge in the local court there. I had met her at a dance and decided she was very, very interesting, enough so that I drove my 1-cylinder Harley Davidson 4 hp belt-drive motorcycle to her home in McConnelsville by way of the long, agonizing hill out of Mansfield up which I had to push the Harley for true love's sake.

In place of more trips on the motorcycle, Edith and I were married the following April and moved to Akron. She played the piano for silent movies at the Orpheum Theater to supplement our income. In time she gave birth to our children, Edith Tunte Van Orman, Ward George Van Orman and James Richmond Van Orman. Quite suddenly in 1932 Edith died of the flu. Her death took everything out of me. I recovered slowly, raised my children for sixteen years when I married Berenice Evelyn Davis who was secretary to the medical director of the B. F. Goodrich Company.

F. A. Seiberling had been company president when I joined Goodyear on June 6, 1917. I was experienced with motors, having served an apprenticeship both in assembling and testing automotive power plants on a part-time basis with the Willys Overland Company and also the Jordan Motor Company, both in Cleveland.

Such extra-curricular zeal came not so much from an insatiable urge for knowledge as it proved a comparatively painless way to earn dating money.

In the early days at Goodyear I taught a course in motor operation to student pilots. After the Armistice, I was put in charge of installing aircraft power plants. In time I was on a first name basis with all types of aircraft engines and expert concerning fuel consumption, so crucial to lighter-than-air.

That's when the letter came to Goodyear from the chief engineer of the Chester Shipbuilding Company of Philadelphia commenting on his steam engine design for airships. What he said he wanted was a once-over by the Goodyear brass.

It so happened I was in Philadelphia on other business and called the gentleman, explaining that Mr. Seiberling had referred the matter to me for further checking. I asked him to come to my hotel and we would discuss his steam engine.

He came, opened up the blueprints and showed me the design of his engine, and we came to the vital criteria of powerplants for lighter-than-air—which was the fuel consumption in pounds brake horsepower hour. I asked what his fuel consumption would be and he very proudly said, "43/100ths of a pound per brake horsepower." I answered, "Well, that's pretty good for a steam engine, but did you know gasoline engines used on our ships develop a horsepower hour on 39/100ths, and, therefore, due to your high consumption, it's not fair to hold out hopes to you for use of your steam engine to power dirigibles."

He left on what I thought cordial terms. But apparently not. He wrote to Mr. Seiberling the following day and told him how inconsiderate I had been in not giving him proper consideration. He did not choose to bother the Goodyear president with my arguments.

F. A. called me into his office. He asked what had happened. I explained to the chief executive that there wasn't any future in this infernal steam engine with fat fuel consumption. F. A. said, "Van, you should have taken the guy to dinner, bought him a few martinis and informed him you would give further consideration to his project—and not arrived at such an abrupt conclusion. I realize the conclusion was truthful . . . but remember, sometimes you have to be not so abrupt."

I said, "Yes, sir, Mr. Seiberling. I appreciate your kindness in not firing me."

But just imagine how bitter the guy was who desired me fired simply for being direct and honest with him! Nevertheless, in the years that followed I watched my "abruptness" more carefully. I learned through public contacts to avoid stating conclusions which are obvious. Abruptness *is* a precise characteristic of the scientist, of the researcher. You're seeking truth. Factual truth. And you endeavor to get right down to target without any embellishment. Well, the human race is so constructed that outside of that group, you don't shoot for target. You wander around a bit—*then* hit the bull's-eye.

During my Goodyear years I enjoyed a whole spectrum of experiences and I am still asked, "Which was more of a thrill to you personally —ballooning or research?"

It was always a difficult question. From an adventure standpoint I loved balloons and was therefore a licensed free balloon pilot, a licensed airship commander, an instructor in free ballooning. From a completely professional view, I was tickled to have been in on the engineering of blimps, the semi-rigid airship RS-1, and those twin sisters of flight—the largest dirigibles in the world—the *Akron* and the *Macon*.

Aside from these two queens, it of course was the great international James Gordon Bennett balloon race and America's own P. W. Litchfield Trophy balloon race (named after the second Goodyear president) that captured global attention in the early and mid-twentieth century.

We talked "winning" at Goodyear in the coldest winter months. A half-year away from next year's classic air duel, many minds at the big rubber company were still analyzing what had gone right at the previous Gordon Bennett, and, more importantly, what had gone agonizingly wrong. We were endlessly exploring new approaches.

Celestial navigation was a tremendous advantage to our balloon at a time it was considered with far less interest and importance by other pilots. Our radio compass bearings likewise pinpointed control and direction of our air voyages. Early in the experiments we hit upon a white fabric for our giant sphere to reduce the super-heat of the big bag. The new fabric produced a more stable balloon that used less ballast.

We even went so far as to develop a hydrogen *generating system*, using calcium hydride to generate hydrogen in flight, while its residue provided an excellent ballast. But I felt, after careful consideration, that it would give us such a tremendous advantage, it would not put us on an equal footing with other contestants. It would have put us so far ahead it would have taken all the sport out of balloon racing.

For a while, we were even considering adding a little light motor, something of a motorcycle type of engine, to produce up and down currents. Actually, one of the balloonists tried that and got his finger cut off in the gears. But that was one thing we never tried, just thought about. It was a little complicated and, again, we didn't feel it was quite fair—and washed it out.

Perhaps the most frequent question put to me today is, "Why can't these great international balloon derbies be reinstated today, perhaps as a fine world gesture of good will?"

The air has become cluttered with airplanes. That's a simple answer. Even in the 1929 contest, an airmail pilot almost collided with our balloon southwest of Cleveland coming in for a landing at Cleveland airport. Hot air balloon race rules today stipulate only daylight flying. There may yet be some special dispensation where you can fly through the night, but it's not safe. Airplanes are not what specifically stopped the Gordon Bennett balloon races, however. The last Bennett victory was earned by a Polish pilot, and, according to the rules of the race committee, the following year's big air epic would have been held in the homeland of the most recent victor—Poland.

But the tension in Europe due to Hitler's early boasts produced such fear that the Polish goverment felt it unsafe to hold the epic there.

So, in 1936, Adolph Hitler, by means of threat and boast, brought the James Gordon Bennett international balloon race series to an end for all time to come.

People still ask me about the possible return of dirigibles because of energy problems, pollution and the cost of fuels. Goodyear today has found considerable success in its fleet of airships—one in Europe, one in Miami, one in Houston, one on the west coast. In time of warfare, I feel myself that they are yet the logical craft for anti-submarine work and convoy work. As passenger-carriers for sightseeing purposes, they're ideal. For advertising purposes, they're superb.

But the airplane is well entrenched in all types of air transportation, over all terrains and seas. It would be difficult now to imagine airships entering that field again. As a freight-hauling machine there might be possibilities.

Before ending this chapter, I'd like to get off my chest something that has caused me to wince over the years as program chairmen by the score have sought to provide complimentary intoductions as I have talked lighter-than-air adventures from one part of America to the other.

The person introducing will say something like this: ". . . Now I'm talking about racing in a vehicle that has no engine. No wind. Races where each contestant has absolutely no idea as to the distance he will go, or the time it's going to take him to do it, or the direction he will fly . . ."

I of course continue to insist that the trained pilot has *considerable* control as to where he is going. In a thousand mile race, for example, I could forecast within 25 or 30 miles of where we would land. In the southeast quadrant of a low pressure area you will find surface winds running from the southeast, and as your balloon ascends, the winds will be shifting to the south.

The wind currents tend to swing in a clockwise direction from the southeast around to the northwest. So in a change of altitude, the balloonist *almost always* is presented a choice of direction. In a particular balloon race starting in Milwaukee, the winner flew to Lake St. John on a high speed current at 15,000 feet which lasted 14½ hours. When our basket went up, we flew in an *opposite* direction and landed at Fayette, Arkansas.

The balloonist has *reasonable* control over his destination and landing.

One midnight over the Atlantic in the 1925 race, I had to prove this premise or die trying.

But that story is for further on in the book.

Inflation proceedings at the National Balloon Races in Milwaukee, 1922.

# The Montgolfiers Observe a Bit of Smoke

When today's balloonists talk of their hobby as the "Sport of the Seventies," they don't mean everyone is rushing out to buy a balloon.

But they consider its fast-growing appeal is because it is such a delightful anachronism in our high speed generation; a gentle pastime practiced by people of romantic sensibilities.

Balloonists grope for eloquence when they describe the magic of their sport. One California engineer shouts the poetry of William Blake to the wind when he goes up. Others listen motionless to the tiny everyday sounds of earthbound life; dogs barking, doors slamming, children shouting. It's quite a lovely feeling.

The invention of the hot air balloon is generally and rightly credited to the Montgolfier brothers of the little French village of Annonay in 1782. But A. D. Topping, a veritable cornucopia of ballooning surprises and, indeed, the dean of the Akron Lighter-than-Air Society, believes it was invented before that. His source is Jules Duhem's *L'Histoire des Idees Aeronautiques avant Montgolfier*, published in 1943 in Paris.

According to Duhem and Topping, the discovery was made 73 years earlier, on August 8, 1709. The first successful balloon was demonstrated, they point out, to the King of Portugal by a 23-year-old Jesuit, Bartholomeu Laurence de Guzmaon (Gusmao in Portuguese; sometimes written Gusman or Guzman; Guzmaon is Dr. Topping's phonetic English version).

It consisted of a tray carrying combustibles, covered by a canopy of canvas or heavy paper. According to one story, it was seven or eight feet in diameter. The demonstration was indoors in a high-ceilinged room of the palace in Lisbon.

After Guzmaon had lighted the fire, the device rose to a height of perhaps fifteen feet, carrying the fire with it. It drifted against a wall, then fell, setting fire to some hangings and "everything against which it knocked." The king seems to have taken this mishap graciously, and another trial is reported to have taken place October 30th. An earlier one, August 3rd, was unsuccessful since the balloon burned without rising. Guzmaon seems to have been working on a larger version, intended to be dirigible (steerable), but the work was never completed.

Guzmaon is best known for his *Passarola*, a widely derided flying machine which Duhem suggests he proposed as a hoax to conceal his true plans. Gibbs-Smith, author of the paper, *Father Gusmao: The First Practical Pioneer in Aeronautics*, (Journal of the Royal Society of Arts, vol. XCVII), and also his book, *A History of Flying* (London, 1953) takes the *Passarola* more seriously, believing that Guzmaon's original is lost and that only unfriendly caricatures survive.

The extravagant claims made for the *Passarola* by Guzmaon—that it would travel 200 leagues in a day, carry cargo and be used to explore the world from pole to pole— were apparently taken in all seriousness by his contemporaries. As a result his actual accomplishment, remarkable as it was, was ridiculed by comparison, and Guzmaon, discouraged, dropped the whole project.

Three-quarters of a century were to pass before the balloon would come into its own.

Joseph and Etienne Montgolfier of France were first drawn to lighter-than-air experiments by watching smoke fly up a chimney. That set them to filling little bags with smoke to see them rise. Then they set to work in earnest.

On June 5, 1783, they held a public demonstration in the city of Annonay, using a linen globe 105 feet in circumference, filled with hot smoke over a straw-fed fire, and watched it fly over a mile.

News of the experiment spread like the wind. J. A. C. Charles, a physicist of Paris learned of the experiment and induced his brothers to build a similar apparatus which he personally filled with hydrogen. The bag was made of thin silk, varnished with elastic gum. It was thirteen feet in diameter.

On August 23, 1783, a little more than three months after the Montgolfier flight at Annonay, the hydrogen bag was set up in the Palace des Victories in Paris. Iron filings and dilute sulphuric acid were used to generate hydrogen, but it was a slow process. Bulletins were issued daily on the furtherance of the inflation. Crowds became so great that the partly-filled balloon had to be moved three days later to the Champ de Mars. But the fourth day after 500 pounds of sulphuric acid and twice that amount of iron filings had been used in generating the gas, the bag was ready to fly.

A sizeable crowd had gathered late in the afternoon as storm clouds moved over the city. A cannon was fired and the bag was released. It rose rapidly to an altitude of about 3,000 feet. Rain started to fall but the balloon's progress was not checked. The excitement was so great that the crowd of thousands stood in the rain watching the strange contrivance.

The Charles balloon remained in the air for three-quarters of an hour and finally descended about fifteen miles from the city. It so terrified the peasantry that it was torn to shreds by the time its builders could get to it. Thus the beginnings of the hydrogen balloon and the hot air balloon were separated by only a few months. They became quickly referred to as the "fire balloon" and the "air balloon" because hydrogen in those days was known as "inflammable air."

About a month later the Montgolfiers repeated their Annonay experiment in the presence of the King and Queen at the Court of Versailles. A new bag had been built and suspended below it was the first balloon basket—a cage that contained a sheep, a cock and a duck. The balloon was inflated and flew to a height of about 1,500 feet before descending some two miles away. Its live cargo was undamaged except for the cock which had been stepped on by the sheep before the take-off.

Later on, the insignia of officers in the lighter-than-air branch of the United States Army Air Corps contained tiny representations of a sheep, a rooster and a duck, in memory of the famous Versailles flight.

These early experiments were pretty messy. The Montgolfier brothers were convinced it was the smoke that caused the balloons to rise, as opposed merely to hot air. Consequently, early balloons were fired by piles of damp straw, old shoes and decomposed meat.

Well, you can guess the next question, "When would man be taken aloft?" It was answered just four weeks later in October, 1783. Jean Francois Pilatre de Rozier, a native of Metz and a young man of twenty-seven, became the Lindbergh of the day. He also became the first fatality. He went up in a captive hot-air balloon, taking with him fuel to feed the fire in the brazier that heated the air inside the bag. Ultimately, a spark from the brazier caught in the hydrogen envelope and pilot and craft dropped like a flaming comet into the English Channel.

It did not dampen world fervor. Balloons remained the sensation of the day. Thinking people of the time began to conceive some of the possibilities of flight. Benjamin Franklin in Paris witnessed one of the early ascents, pardoning himself from state meetings and boudoirs, to write home about it.

"Among the pleasantries that conversation produced on this subject," wrote Franklin, "some supposed flying to be now invented, and since man may be supported in the air, nothing is wanted but some light handy instrument to give and direct motion. Some think progressive motion on earth may be advanced by it and that a running footman or horse, slung or suspended under such a globe so as to have no more of weight pressing the earth with their feet than perhaps eight or ten pounds—might with a fair wind run in a straight line across countries as fast as that wind and over hedges, ditches and even waters."

"It had been fancied," Franklin continued, "that in time people will keep such globes anchored in the air to which by pulleys they may draw up game to be preserved in the cool and water to be frozen when ice is wanted, and that to get money it will be contrived to give people an extensive view of the country by running them up in an elbow chair a mile high for a guinea."

In time all kinds of balloon variations appeared. In 1863, a French photographer built a vast balloon that carried a printing office, a small photo lab, a refreshment room and a lavatory. Physicist Charles soon claimed the longest flight yet made in a hydrogen balloon, and to Charles goes the credit for the free balloon as it was later known with its valved released gas and its basket being held in place by a net.

Soon the English and Irish channels had been flown by free balloons and the problem of building bigger and better bags and finding some means of propulsion faced the inventors.

Vincent Lunardi in an early flight from England took with him oars to help propel bag and basket through the winds, but lost one in the ascent. Oars were found to be impractical. The era of "bigger bags" soon appeared with the construction of the *Flessalles*, a 500,000 cubic foot fire balloon that rose to an altitude of 3,000 feet with seven passengers, but quickly descended when the upper part of the bag was torn loose.

In the mid-1800s, an 85,000 cubic foot gas balloon was constructed which carried three Englishmen on a 500-mile flight. This bag was similar in size to the racing spheres of the early and mid-twentieth century. This was the famous Nassau balloon from which Robert Knockling was killed in an early parachute jump. Charles Greene, the best known British flier of a century ago was the owner of a Nassau, making him the sensation of the day by being carried aloft while sitting astride his favorite pony.

About twenty years later, Madame Poitevin made a similar ascent, but the Age of Victoria had set in and she was prevented from making a second trip by outraged public opinion.

Though certainly not much has been said of it in history, the second human to leave the face of the earth in a balloon was a youth living in the city of Baltimore, Maryland in 1784, a brief eight months after Jean Francois Pilatre in a captive Montgolfier balloon. Pilatre crashed and died. The Baltimore boy, 13-year-old Edward Warren, enjoyed himself and lived.

The following appeared in the *Maryland Journal & Baltimore Advertiser* on June 25, 1784:

> Yesterday, the ingenious PETER CARNES, esq. made his curious AEROSTATIC EXPERIMENTS, within the Limits of this Town, in the Presence of a numerous and respectable Congress of People, whom the fame of his Superb BALLOON had drawn together from the East, West, North and South, who, generally, appeared highly delighted with the awful Grandeur of so novel a scene as a large Globe making repeated voyages into the airy Regions, which Mr. Carnes' Machine actually performed, in a Manner that reflected Honor on his Character as a Man of Genius, and could not fail to inspire solemn and exalted Ideas in every reflecting Mind.
>
> Ambition, on this occasion, so fired the youthful Heart of a Lad (only 13 years old!) of the name of Edward Warren that he bravely embarked as a Volunteer on the last Trip into the Air, and behaved with the steady Fortitude of an Old Voyager. The "gazing Multitude below" wafted to him their loud Applause, the receipt of which, as he was "Soaring aloft," he politely acknowledged by a significant Wave of his Hat.
>
> When he returned to our terrene Element, he met with a Reward from some of the Spectators which had a solid, instead of an airy Foundation, and of a Species which is ever acceptable to the Residents of this lower World.

According to R. S. Block, past editor of Akron, Ohio's *Lighter-Than-Air Society Bulletin*, there is no account of Carnes himself riding the balloon that eventful day in Baltimore. It is believed that inasmuch as he had advertised he would ascend, Carnes probably found his weight too great for the lift of the balloon.

He had been advised before "to start as early in the day as possible . . ." as the power of his balloon "might suffer for the excessive external heat;" and also "that every European experiment of consequence, has been made in the cool seasons." Evidently the lift of the balloon was not too great on the occasion of the Baltimore flight. Hence fate singled out the young boy to become the first American to fly. Thirteen-year-old Warren evidently was a volunteer, for the hat was passed around the crowd for contributions for him.

The Carnes balloon was constructed of "beautiful, costly and richly varigated silks." At the bottom it had a "hoop which surrounded it, and to which it was attached by pieces of linen to prevent it from collapsing." From newspaper accounts there were a series of ascents made that day in Baltimore.

Being a captive balloon, that is tethered, with a line holding it fast to the ground so that it would not be carried away in the breeze, it could be pulled down to stoke its stove in order to maintain buoyancy, and thus make repeated ascents.

The balloon was a hot air balloon obtaining its lift with "a cylindrical stove of iron suspended at the bottom by which the air is rarified." Most likely, wood was burned, and it is evident that with the flammable silk envelope, this arrangement was certainly dangerous, especially in unstable or gusty conditions when the balloon might possibly oscillate.

One correspondent said, "He is particularly precautioned relative to his fire, and to let no temptation, no love of Fame, transport him to such enthusiastic ideas as to venture himself in the chariot of the sun lest the fate of the ambitious Phaeton should be his portion . . ."

What happened to Peter Carnes later is not known. He visited Philadelphia less than a month after the Baltimore first flight. There he made an unsuccessful ascent from a prison yard on July 17, 1784, when his balloon struck the side of a wall ten or twelve feet above the ground and jolted Carnes from the basket.

It then rose rapidly, caught on fire, and fell. Carnes evidently never built or at least flew another balloon, and no word of him was ever reported after this incident.

The fate of 13-year-old Edward Warren—the first American to fly on the first aerial flight in the United States—is also unknown. The Baltimore historian Ralph J. Robinson muses:

> What happened to Ed when he returned home, his pockets stuffed with money, undoubtedly flushed and excited, the admiration of his boy companions as he was of the city generally? Did his mother administer a sound spanking and send him to bed supperless as a warning against repetition of such a reckless deed?
>
> Did his father, throwing out his chest that evening in conversation with acquaintances, slyly intimate that Ed was a chip off the old block? One wonders. Also, and equally in vain, one asks who was this boy, who his parents, and what of his after life? No answer is now possible.
>
> Out of the unknown the lad came, enjoyed the spotlight for one glorious moment, and vanished.

Balloons, of course, were used for military observation purposes during the French Revolution and American Civil War. Likewise the Franco-Prussian War. They were effectively utilized in the two World Wars. During the French Revolution, French chemists set up a balloon flying school and taught generals and adjutants how to fly. More than their reconnaissance value, the balloons were found to splinter the morale of the enemy.

The North particularly used observation balloons in the American Civil War, a company being attached to McClellan's army. But the difficulty of generating gas by the crude methods of the time caused the giant globes to be abandoned before war's end.

By 1933, a piece of cloth which once was a piece of the silk gown of a southern lady and later part of a balloon used by the Confederates for observation purposes, had found its way permanently into the Army aeronautical museum at Wright Field, Dayton.

The memento is valuable chiefly as a reminder of the ingenuity displayed by the povery-stricken southern army in getting together makeshift equipment. The balloon may be one referred to by General Longstreet in *Our March Against Pope*.

> It may be of interest, (he wrote), to relate an incident which illustrates the pinched condition of the Confederacy even as early as 1862. The Federals had been using balloons to examine our positions and we watched with envious eyes their beautiful observations as they floated high in the air, well out of reach of our guns.
>
> While we sat there longing for such aerial stations, our poverty denied us, a genius suggested that we gather together all the silk dresses in the Confederacy and make a balloon.
>
> Soon we had a grotesquely patterned ship of many varied hues which was finished and ready for use in the Seven Days Campaign.
>
> We had no gas except at Richmond and it was a custom to inflate the balloon there, tie it securely to an engine and run it down the New York River Railroad to any point at which we desired to set it up. One day it was on steamer down the James River when the tide went out and left the vessel and balloon high and dry on a bar. The Federals gathered it in and with it the last silk dress in the Confederacy.
>
> This capture was the meanest trick of the war and one which I have never forgiven.

The cloth presented the Wright Field museum was a portion of a larger piece awarded the National Museum in Washington by the son of Professor Thaddeus S. C. Lowe. Professor Lowe figured prominently in the aerial activities of the Union Army.

And ballooning was hazardous enough, then and always.

Hydrogen is totally and explosively inflammable and the safer, somewhat less buoyant helium was too costly and often unavailable. In the United States, the only quantity producer of helium, the price for 1,000 cubic feet of helium was $104.00 as late as 1920. Fortunately for later American airship activity, the price per 1,000 cubic feet of the lifting gas, due to increasing production efficiencies, shrunk to $7.10 by 1933. By then the U. S. Government's Amarillo, Texas plant was capable of producing 37 million cubic feet of helium a year.

Inevitably, of course, the appearance of the airplane, which, from a technical point of view, offered everything the balloon could do and more, sent ballooning into a tailspin.

The development of tough, inexpensive plastic film resulted in scientific application of gas-filled balloons in the 20th century but it was not until the creation of an inexpensive new burner—together with a tough, cheap envelope—that the sporting possibilities of ballooning captured the fickle eye of the masses.

In 1945 a new type of heating apparatus was developed in this country and later the development of new materials made hot air ballooning even more feasible as a week-end hobby.

The man most credited with the revival is Ed Yost of Sioux Falls, South Dakota, the first man to cross the English Channel in a balloon. Yost developed a new hard-wearing envelope of lightweight calendered nylon which permitted the balloon to be used many times. In the 33 years since, sport ballooning has made impressive gains.

There are now four major balloon manufacturers and numerous schools across the United States where a person can train to become a licensed pilot. All balloon activities come under the auspices of the Balloon Federation of America in Washington, D. C. Prospective balloonists should write to the BFA, Suite 610, 806 15th Street N.W., Washington D. C. 20005 for the quarterly journal *Ballooning* which carries advertisements listing balloon flight training.

Once you're licensed, flying a balloon is not expensive—about eight dollars for four hours worth of fuel. But buying a balloon is a different matter. They start at about $3,000 and peak around the $10,000 mark.

Although it is unlikely ever to replace Monday night football, more and more of us are captivated by the art. There are more licensed balloon pilots in the United States—and, not surprisingly, more balloons—than in all other countries of the world combined.

The United States is the recognized world leader in hot air ballooning. It was here that ballooning interest revived after more than a century of near oblivion.

# I Pass My Test
# —and See a Parade!

What good fortune befell me in 1919! Ralph Upson, chief aeronautical engineer of Goodyear and a balloonist of international repute, challenged me to one of his little "tests" for selecting an aide in the upcoming National Balloon Race from St. Louis.

The test was disguised—cleverly so—as just a bit of fun.

But the deciding factor in this test was a little trick in navigation.

We mutually selected a time, hoping we would be able to fly to New York City to see General Pershing parade on his return from France.

It was a somewhat ambitious undertaking (considering that a free balloon drifts with the wind) to pick out an objective *four hundred miles* away and hope to reach it in a specified number of hours simply by selecting the proper air currents at varying altitudes!

We were, nevertheless, optimistic and invited Commander Hoyt, the Akron Air Station commanding officer, to accompany us. We used a 35,000 cubic foot balloon and stored in its basket all of our instruments, our scientific gear designed specifically for the approaching race.

We left Akron late in the day, had a marvelous flight over eastern Ohio, and after sunset found ourselves above the mountains of western Pennsylvania. We were fortunate in having a most gorgeous moon and the mountains were flooded with lemon-colored moonlight. In fact Hoyt and Upson were so enamoured with the scenery that they neglected their navigation completely.

The result was we simply skimmed over the tops of the mountains and coasted down the valley, devouring the scenery as we passed. It was hardly surprising then, under the circumstances, that the first light of dawn should find us lost. We knew we were *somewhere* over the central part of the state of Pennsylvania but could not be more specific than that.

Yet I assure you we had a method of navigation that surpassed celestial navigation, the radio compass and all the modern radar scanners since invented. This method of navigation consisted of shouting down to any convenient farmer, "Where are we?" And he would shout back, "You're twelve miles north of Scranton!" You would put your dot on the map and your navigation would be complete.

On this particular morning, there was the farmer in his farmyard milking his cows when we descended to some 200 feet above the ground. There wasn't a sound anywhere. Absolute quiet. When we got within hailing distance, I shouted down to the farmer, "Where are we?"

Instead of answering he gave a look all around. He couldn't make out what was happening. So a second time I cupped my hands and I shouted down, "Where are we?"

This time I got action! He got up off his stool, walked around the barn, opened the door and went in the barn, looked around, came back and stood in the doorway, took off his hat and scratched his head.

Then he started milking again.

By that time we were directly overhead. So I said again, "Where are we? Look up!" And he looked up and the minute he saw us his jaw dropped open. He was speechless. And then he said, "Boy, you can't fool me, you're right up there in that balloon basket!"

We already knew that.

We asked him the name of the nearest town which happened to be the groundhog center of Punxsutawney. We fixed our position and continued to fly over central and eastern Pennsylvania until twelve o'clock noon when a heavy sea fog rolled in ahead of us at an altitude of 6,000 feet to which I called Upson's attention.

He decided we must be near the Atlantic Ocean and also New York City according to recent checks on our position. We dropped down and landed beside the cut-off of the Lackawana railroad near Andover, New Jersey. We deflated our balloon and expressed it back to Akron.

We then proceeded the few remaining miles to New York City with the satisfaction that we had accomplished what is done most infrequently; that is, to fly a free balloon with the varying air currents to a definite objective. The officers of the Air Station as well as the students were highly elated over our success and especially so since we had landed so near our objective.

It certainly was a pleasure to witness General Pershing's parade on New York's Fifth Avenue—but we elected to come home by train.

# Victorious Descent on a Montreal Barn

In completing our training trip from Akron to New York City, we felt well prepared for the National Balloon Epic on October 1st, the first return engagement of the Great American Balloon Race since the war—and my own racing initiation.

We shipped our equipment to St. Louis and were so vitally interested in the race that we had our expert riggers follow the express shipment personally to see that it arrived there in plenty of time for the contest.

We inflated our balloon in St. Louis at the Missouri Aeronautical Reserve Corps Field at Grand Avenue and Merrimac Street, using a special quality of coal gas for the inflation. Ten balloons were competing in the race, all of 80,000 cubic foot gas capacity.

Ours was the finest balloon of the ten, being an exact replica of the one in which Upson won the international balloon racing sprint, voyaging from Paris, France to Yorkshire, England, except that the envelope used then was a yellow fabric one while this was silver. It was easily the prettiest bag on the field, made of 2-ply cotton with twenty coats of rubber between, and the outside sprayed with an aluminized composition to protect the rubber against light and heat which caused deterioration.

That brisk fall day in 1919, I had good reason to be proud of Ralph Upson, Goodyear II's international champion. It was he who had won the James Gordon Bennett race that was staged in Paris in 1913. In that great race all other contestants but the Goodyear crew (Ralph Upson and R. A. D. Preston) executed landings on the coast of France, fearing to venture out over the stormy Channel. Upson and his aide were confident that if they allowed their craft to go out over the ocean that they would encounter at a certain distance, winds that would drive them north to the British Isles.

They did so and traveled north to the Scottish coast. The landing was made and the great championship race and the trophy that went with it was theirs.

The day of the St. Louis race the weather bureau at Washington, D. C. wired the American Aeronautical Society warning of a "low" coming from South Dakota toward the Great Lakes and advised that no start be made because of the prospect of turbulent storms.

With this advice fresh in our minds, we left the ground at 6:15 pm.

The other balloons went up light, carrying only necessities. But Upson, the crack dirigible navigator, went equipped with everything for a pleasant voyage including a hammock for resting and reading, electric lights, an extra-heavy drag rope, maps, cold cream for his complexion, axe, shotgun, fishing tackle and implements galore.

He took at least 100 pounds of equipment more than any of the others in addition to 40 bags—30 pounds each—of ballast.

Of the great spheres leading us, one seemed to be leaking badly and having considerable trouble maintaining a required altitude. We later learned that the balloon landed near Chicago. Extreme leakage ultimately forced it down at midnight.

About 9:15 pm we had a magnificent view of the Aurora Borealis in the north, appearing to us in fan-shaped lights golden in color and flaming upward. They disappeared as faint orange-colored shafts of luminosity.

Upson decided to catch a little sleep at this point and so turned the responsibility of flying the balloon to me.

To the west there appeared a series of lights which fascinated me and to which I gave careful attention. I studied these flashes as they appeared and after much deliberation concluded that far off to the west the thunderstorms about which the weather bureau had warned were making their awesome approach.

I knew no alternative than to wake Upson and draw his attention to the situation. I shook him vigorously several times and he reluctantly sat up. I informed him that the lightning was moving in on us from the west and asked what we ought to do about it. He got up from the hammock, looked over the basket to the west, gazed at the flashes for a few moments, said nothing, and climbed back into the hammock.

My first reaction was one of utter amazement. What kind of a man could look at the serious picture as I have described it, and give so little thought to it? It was obvious he considered the phenomena not worth the interruption of his precious sleep.

This was a consoling thought indeed. From then on I merely kept one eye on those flashes. The haze increased and we appeared to be sailing in a world all our own, twelve hundred feet above sleeping towns, villages and farm houses in western Illinois.

About midnight we were thirty miles to the south of Chicago veering slightly to the east, when Upson took over. I went for a little rest. The sensation was really luxurious. Not a sound to break the stillness—not even a breath of air rushing by us. We were a part of the air itself. It seemed I had been asleep for just a moment when I was awakened by the most mournful sound imaginable. A low moaning came from beneath us. I jumped from the hammock and asked, "Ralph, what's happening to us?"

The slow moaning sound continued to greet my ears and I was really alarmed. Ralph, observing me with a half smile, replied, "Well, Van, we're about 500 feet over the middle of Lake Michigan." He said it so quietly that I was instantly reassured. Yet that doleful sound kept greeting my ears and as I peered over the edge of the basket I could just make out the outline of the crest of the waves as they broke.

It was fascinating flying over Lake Michigan and for the rest of the night I stayed up, watching the altimeter carefully for fear we might suddenly sink into the waves.

Shortly before daybreak we sighted a light which appeared to be bouncing along the surface of the water. As we approached we could make out the silhouette of the shore and evidently a human who was carrying a light which was intermittently cut off from our view by the movement of the man's legs as he walked. We came closer and shouted down the usual question, "Where are we?" We could see the light stop and the man who was carrying it was evidently aghast that a voice from the darkness should hail him thusly. Then he suddenly saw our craft and shouted back, "Where are you going?"

We replied, "Where are we?" He responded again, "Where are you going?" As long as we were within hailing distance we tried to find out where we were and this chap tried to find out where we were going.

Dawn found us flying low over the sand-covered forests of central Michigan. We were skimming the tops of the trees; as the sun gave birth to morning our gas expanded and we ascended to 4,500 feet. At this altitude small billowy clouds formed beneath us, appearing to move rapidly backwards. I called Upson's attention to this observation and he laughed again and ordered me to lower the sounding device and then said, "Van, I'll show you why those clouds are moving backwards."

We dropped our sounding device down until it touched the strata of these clouds and much to my surprise this sounding device was carried rapidly backwards until it seemed to be dragging behind us.

I said, "Why, Ralph, we are going much faster than the lower clouds." He replied, "That's right. We're making excellent speed here." This condition continued until the clouds formed solidly beneath us.

As near as we could estimate about eight o'clock that morning we passed over Lake Huron near Saginaw. Our elevation had gradually increased until at nine o'clock we were maintaining an altitude of 6,000 feet. We could not see the lake under the cloud cover and we felt that we were monarchs of this new domain. Off to the south we noticed a large black mushroom push its way through the top of the strata. It dropped back down several times but on each upward ascent it appeared to grow larger.

It was fascinating to witness this strange apparition develop, and finally with a tremendous upward rush we saw it develop into a competitive balloon! Studying it closely through the field glasses we decided it was none other than our most formidable competitor Captain H. E. Honeywell!

Then the race commenced in earnest. Here was tangible evidence of other competitors in the air making every bit as good progress as we were. It was up to us to outdistance him! Indeed, the incentive of having our most accomplished rival in view was tremendous. Off to the west of us we could see the sky was dark and threatening. We appreciated the fact that ahead of us everything seemed to be clear and promising.

We continued our flight over Lake Huron until 11:30 am when the lower clouds began to break up, and at twelve noon we were passing over the tip of Cape Hurd, which is the junction point of Georgian Bay and Lake Huron.

We had climbed to 10,000 feet by this time, and through the holes in the clouds we could see the little steamers on Georgian Bay bouncing on the waves and lashing the bay into a fury.

I noticed that Upson had closed up the balloon's appendix. This is the safety valve, opening the balloon's interior to atmospheric pressure by means of a long tube at the bottom of the craft. He felt it best to conserve a little gas by allowing the pressure to build up in the sphere, not only conserving the gas but also increasing the stability of the balloon.

The manometer now registered an inch and a quarter of pressure. Upson suggested I get a little sleep. Before turning in I asked him what pressure the balloon would stand before it burst. He said it would stand one and one-half inches of water pressure. I also had noticed that he was allowing the balloon to work up gradually and the pressure continued to increase.

Ralph noted the alarm written on my face but reassured me that the balloon would soon check its ascent.

As I crawled into the hammock, the manometer was reading an inch and three-eighths and I frankly wondered if the man had gone mad to allow pressure to build up within one-eighth of an inch from bursting force while we were still flying over the waters of Georgian Bay.

I did not want to comment on this method of handling the bag for I felt in my heart that he must surely know what he was doing (Regardless, it was hardly within my jurisdiction to criticize). Yet one might easily appreciate my alarm when I knew the bursting pressure to be close and the balloon still inching skyward!

I had lain long moments in the hammock, feigning sleep, when the long-expected happened. A terrific crash! A rustle of fabric! I *knew* the balloon had burst! I literally could feel my hair raise up—my helmet seemed to stand on the very ends of this straightened hair. I leaped from the hammock, not even wanting to look up, but rather looked down to see how far from shore we were going to strike as we plunged with our burst balloon into the choppy waters of Georgian Bay.

Ralph must have appreciated the mute appeal in my glance for he fairly choked with laughter. Only then did I dare gaze up at the bottom of the huge bag and discovered to my great relief that the string which was used to tie the appendix shut had merely broken under the pressure. The terrible crash that I had imagined the explosion to be, and the rustle of fabric had been produced by the sudden opening of the appendix.

It was then that Upson, with great amusement, assured me that the inch and one-half pressure which he had informed me was the bursting pressure of the sphere was merely the *safe* operating pressure and that the true bursting point was much closer to four to five inches pressure.

About 3:30 pm we passed over the eastern shore line of Georgian Bay near Parry Sound, Ontario. Drifting over the wilderness we could make out the cliffs around us as we left the bay. It was gratifying to note our speed holding so well. We were making around fifty miles per hour almost due east. About three hours' flying time took us over this Canadian wilderness before we approached the outskirts of civilization again. Before passing into the night, Ralph Upson felt it highly desirable to obtain a location fix. We started down from our altitude of 13,000 feet to within 500 feet of the ground. Again we shouted to a farmer shocking corn, "Where are we?" and he replied, "Two miles east of Athens, Ontario!"

It is interesting to note that at this particular point Honeywell saw us start down and decided we were going in for a landing. So thinking, he felt that in order to win the race himself, he would merely stay up about a half-hour longer, travel a few miles further and have the race in the bag.

But instead of landing, we bounced back up to 6,000 feet and sailed eastward with a fast current bearing us rapidly toward the Atlantic Ocean near the coast of Maine.

Darkness of the second night in the air drew on and by eight o'clock we found ourselves crossing the St. Lawrence River near Cornwall. Again my attention was directed to the north where I could see flashes of light again appearing and studied them most carefully. I considered it might be a trolley line paralleling the St. Lawrence River. Closer observation indicated it was the thunderstorm which had pursued us all day and had worked around to the north of us.

Clouds were rapidly fencing us in. Upson ordered an ascent to the higher altitude to escape the lightning and to seek yet faster currents at the same time. Up we darted to 13,000 feet and broke through the last cloud shelf into one of the most resplendent panoramas I have ever observed in the moonlight.

Beneath the top of these billows of white we beheld clouds occasionally tinted with crimson which we knew were produced by the lightning. It seemed a relief to rise up into calm and peaceful air once more with the knowledge that we were clocking excellent speed and were free from the hazard of those dangerous bolts!

Our joy proved extremely short-lived. In a few seconds, a huge cloud developed from nowhere and enveloped us in its grasp. A sudden squall hurled us earthbound at a terrifically fast rate of speed. The lightning became more evident and the concussion from the bolts most pronounced. At each concussion our craft would shudder as if some giant hand were wringing the life from it.

We hurled downward 10,000 feet. We then checked our speed by tossing overboard most of our precious ballast which we had hoped would carry us towards Maine to break the American distance record and give us victory. Instead we now used it to combat the weight of the rain which was spearing us into the ground.

But we slowed appreciably from 3,000 feet to within 500 feet of the earth. We broke through the clouds once more only to be dismayed by the wind whistling through the unlimited forests which appeared to stretch miles in every direction. It seemed again that we were caught over the Canadian wilderness with a forced landing imminent at any moment and no place to land but in the trees.

Then a happy thought occurred to me that the best way to find civilization in a case like this was to land near some road. I expressed the thought to Upson and he said, "Fine." Within the next minute a flash of lightning ahead of us illumined a long white streak ahead which we knew to be a road. By making a quick estimate of our speed and the distance to this road, we knew we could land fairly close. So at the proper time in utter darkness we pulled on the valve to drop our balloon the remaining 500 feet and it responded by slowly sinking. I had the flashlight over the edge and in the next moment I saw a roof of a barn literally rise up to meet the bottom of our basket. Actually we had descended on the roof of a barn, bounded off it into a farmyard, departed the craft and deflated our balloon.

It was now pouring torrents of rain and absolutely black but we felt renewed confidence after twenty-seven hours in the air, flying over vast bodies of water and wildernesses to be on the ground near civilization. About a quarter of a mile down the road we could see the lights of a farmhouse and Upson suggested that we go there and spend the night.

If we had thought accurately, we should have appreciated the fact that there would also be a farmhouse near the barn we struck, which was the case, one being directly across the road not a hundred yards away. But in the dark of the night we could not see it, and so we set out down the muddy road in quest of a place to sleep in shelter from the rain. A short time later we walked to the door of the distant farmhouse and knocked vigorously.

A sleepy farmer in his nightshirt and bare feet answered us. We told him the whole story of the balloon race and asked him if he had a place for us to sleep that night. From the quizzical expression on his face we knew we had made a mistake in telling him the truth about flying a balloon from St. Louis.

He told us very brusquely that all of his rooms were filled with company and recommended a hotel in the village a mile and a half away at Stanbridge East. Both Upson and I were bone weary from fatigue and the strain from our long endeavor, and decided that in some cases one could afford to be a little more reticent about conveying the truth of a matter. As we plodded the mile and a half through the rain, this view was strengthened.

We arrived, soaked to the skin, at the little village hotel at Stanbridge East, walked into the bar where the proprietor was shooting pool with some of the village characters, and simply asked for a room. He looked at our clothes and sized us up and decided that since it was a public hotel he probably could afford to take a chance on us and give us a bed, but being curious to know how we had gotten in this condition, he insisted on the facts and we told him.

He cocked his head back and howled and went downstairs to join another lot at poker. About twenty minutes later, evidently after the crowd had talked the matter over, he came up to our room and told us that there was a chap downstairs who had two dollars to bet that there was no balloon down the road and asked us if he should take it. I told him to bet his money and if there was any more money to be bet we might put up a little ourselves.

We then turned over and tried to go to sleep. The strain of twenty-seven hours and the first race was a little too great. I could hear them downstairs hitching up their horses and buggies at 1:30 in the morning to verify our statement.

The next morning we returned to the balloon. A crowd had gathered, eyeing the great machine draped over the barn roof, but many willing hands assisted us and helped us pack our equipment for shipment back to Akron. We had made 1,050 miles in twenty-seven hours and had won the National Race. It was inspiring to me to see the skill and accuracy with which Upson piloted the balloon to victory. I felt also that here was a real man's game in which many of the sciences could be employed to aid the objective.

In our hour of victory we were saddened to learn that the thunderstorm of which the weather bureau had warned, had claimed two victims from our midst. Captain Carl W. Damon and Lieutenant Edward J. Verheyden, flying the balloon *Wichita*, representing Wichita, Kansas, were killed by the storm which had followed us over Lake Huron. The storm had driven them into the crashing waters of that rain-hammered lake.

The *Wichita* was merely an hour behind us in crossing the water, but that time lag was sufficient to have put them into the most turbulent path of the cloudburst. Captain Paul McCullough and Bernard Von Hoffman, representing the city of St. Louis in the balloon *84* landed during the storm in the wilderness just east of Parry Sound. After three days the pair made their way to the town of Waubannik where they made their overdue report to the race committee.

We were disappointed in not breaking the American endurance record, but felt gratified by our splendid speed under such trying conditions.

# Labrador in 40 Hours!

Our victory in the National race from St. Louis gave us such a feeling of confidence that when we entered the National contest the following year at Birmingham, Alabama, we felt it would prove a fairly simple matter to force our craft to triumph.

Accordingly we shipped our balloon to Birmingham and prepared our craft for inflation on the field beside the Sloss-Sheffield Steel Plant, half a mile north of the city. There were ten balloons entered again representing the army, navy and civilian balloonists of the United States. We had excellent preparation and excellent gas supply so that as our balloon filled, we gained increased (and, as it turned out, unjustified) confidence.

The front page of the Birmingham *Age Herald* read:

The great balloon race starts today and should their final landing place be Cuba or Canada, oh, prohibition! Where is thy victory? Oh, death! Where is thy sting?

Twelve balloons are ready for flight today and the army has made a covenant at last with the navy, army pilots giving their sworn statements that they will not take a mule to tow them in should they land in the sea if the navy bag will forego the use of a boat should they find themselves at the finish in the heart of the great American desert.

Saturday afternoon, September 26, 1920, our little traveling baskets or "boats" were packed and ready for the start. The baskets measured 4 x 6 feet and besides the two pilots and the standard shotgun and fishing tackle, most included canned tuna fish, tongue, cheese, chocolate, malted milk tablets. Packed in was all kinds of fruit, five thermos bottles containing coffee, tea, chocolate, anything else to drink the pilots could get hold of—hard boiled eggs, bouillon cubes, quantities of water, baked beans—all needed supplies.

Food could be heated and prepared at any altitude from 1,000 to 20,000 feet with the aid of a bucket of unslaked lime. Dear housekeepers, just think of having to cook a meal in a basket measuring 4 x 6 feet and suspended from a bag full of gas 11,000 feet in the air. It might almost lend a charm to cooking.

Pilots were provided with diminutive cooking vessels which can be inserted in a bucket of lime and heated by pouring a little water on that lime. Any food can be brought to the boiling point in about ten minutes. The unslacked lime, when wet, gives out a tremendous heat so that even at a very high altitude the pilot and his aide are able to keep warm and cozy in their small basket.

By 1920, thanks, in part, to the war experience, science offered controls to ballooning. We carried a thermograph of a specially made thermometer to show temperature, a hydrograph to show moisture, a compass to indicate direction, a manometer to show gas pressure in the balloon, a vertimeter to show speed up or down, an altimeter to read altitudes and a statoscope to tell upward and downward motion. Perhaps most important of all, each racing balloon was provided maps which indicated many things, including high voltage lines in all the eastern and southern states.

Perhaps the most prolific chronicler of the 1920 National was Helen Bethea of the Birmingham newspaper.

Up in the air for a thousand feet or more (she wrote), and off on a trip in a little boat drifting with the will of the winds for 100 miles or 1,000 miles and down again in different places—surrounded by new scenes and faces. What could be more grand and glorious? Nothing could make the average person feel more free unless it was getting the rent all paid at one time.

The 12 balloons which will start from Birmingham today at intervals of five minutes each after the first one takes the air at 4 o'clock sharp in the afternoon will have as their official objective, "Labrador in 40 hours!"

That will be the objective, but with the ever present possibility that the landing will find some of them reposing in the Everglades of Florida with the Indians and alligators, others brushing the ice off the north pole and still others hovering about the outskirts of our own Jefferson County. The last may sound far-fetched but Alan R. Hawley, a former president of the Aero Club of America and American balloon racing champion, states that cross-currents in the winds make it extremely possible in this race.

"What do they expect to accomplish?" is a question which had been going the rounds. There are a number of things it can accomplish, it seems. None of the pilots have been very definite yet but then Columbus in a spirit of adventure proved once that the earth was round—and, incidentally, discovered America. The young balloon pilots point out that they have not explored the moon yet, nor Mars either, for that matter.

Commercially speaking, also, how many are there who would like to sail up in the air 6,000 feet, wait 12 hours and come down in China? Well, you don't have to do it, but it all depends now on the development of suitable oxygen bags or containers for the canning of good breath and the feat is accomplished!

Just give the inventors time. They will do it.

There was, I recall, a distinctly human touch in the farewell scenes that afternoon as one after another of the balloon crews shoved off. The parting of the young bride, Mrs. Burt, from her husband, the pilot of an army balloon; the enthusiasm of the young northern lady, the fair sponsor of the *Elsie Delight*, as she showered the pilot, the veteran A. Leo Stevens and his aide, Mr. Weston, wealthy Chicago paper manufacurer, with kisses and an armful of American beauties; the youthful Von Hoffman and his fellow student from the University of Missouri who flung over sand without stint in their effort to be away and accomplish something worthwhile for their alma mater; the spontaneous ovation given to the Navy when Lieutenants Emerson and Sloman with their bag of tricks brought up the rear of the departing fleet.

These were a few of the incidents in the afternoon of thrills—but nothing, perhaps, thrilled the emotions of the crowd more deeply than the crew of the bag, *Ohio*. Mr. Rasor, the veteran balloon builder and his young ex-soldier son, like buddies had toiled together from early morning in the face of labor shortage and had come through on time and in good humor. As the big basket which would house them for the next two days or so began to surge upward, there was a spontaneous burst of applause mingled with kindly words of encouragement. Until the lonely voyagers passed beyond the treetops fringing the northwest corner of the field, now tinged with the reddish gold of the setting sun, the applause did not diminish.

Thousands of eyes followed them sympathetically and thousands of hearts pulsed faster in the hope that in Monday's reckoning they would mark a credible score.

Twenty thousand persons witnessed the hop-off at the field adjoining the Sloss-Sheffield plant. The people came by streetcar, on foot, aboard motor trucks and in limousines. All afternoon the huge crowd swarmed onto the field. When Warren Rasor, veteran aeronaut of Springfield, Missouri, and his son-aid, took the air at 4:54 o'clock, the field, the surrounding streets, trees and roofs of buildings literally were alive with surging, cheering humanity, struggling to catch an initial glimpse of the first National balloon race ever staged in the south.

As the first balloon sought its element, it glistened blood red in the flow of light from the westerning sun, but when the final bag shot into the air, it floated into a sea of amber and crimson and rose pink—an ocean of clouds tinged by the last dying gleams of sunlight. Golden and shining silver, the huge globes of silk and rubber caught and held the attention of the watching thousands from the moment the spectators thronged onto and about the field—until the last floating bag glided out of sight.

The 1920 National contest was the most closely mapped and forecasted race in the history of ballooning to date. C. W. Andrus of the government aerological station at Leesburg, Georgia, having investigated weather conditions, calculated that the balloons would float over western Tennessee, over Missouri, over Illinois sometime Sunday before noon—possibly sailing over St. Louis by way of Springfield, Illinois, traversing to the Chicago district Monday morning.

He said air currents were calculated to take us over the Great Lakes, the Michigan peninsula and into Canadian territory somewhere between Sault Ste. Marie and Parry Sound.

He added, "Best conditions will be obtained at 1,000 to 1,500 meters (3,000 to 4,500 feet) altitude during the first twelve hours. At 1,000 meters the wind will be about ten meters per second (25 miles per hour) from the southeast, increasing after passing into Tennessee. Every effort should be made to make all possible speed during the first twelve hours in order to drift into the faster moving winds nearer the low."

Andrus told the newspapers he expected the winds to land the balloonists at least at the nearest Great Lakes point, a distance of some 600 miles by early Monday morning, and probably around Chicago.

"If all goes well," he concluded, "and they follow the weather forecast, maintaining the altitudes we have suggested, I firmly believe some of them will clear the entire Great Lakes region and land somewhere in Canada. They may not reach Labrador—this year's target, but they will certainly be headed that way."

Upson and I stepped into the basket at 5:24 pm starting sixth in a northwesterly direction from Birmingham. Immediately on leaving the field, passing over the Sloss-Sheffield Works, we were surprised at the wilderness of northern Alabama.

Our speed seemed painfully slow—ten to twelve miles an hour—but we again were hoping to find the higher speed as we progressed north. We read the official weather forecast several times. Ironically, our problem was almost identical to that of the St. Louis race. We would first fly north gaining speed as we approached the storm area, then turn easterly and eventually land northeast of Birmingham.

With this reassuring report checked over again we felt increased confidence as we sailed over the northern Alabama forests in the moonlight. Beneath us the only sounds breaking the stillness were an occasional rustle of the winds through the trees and the croaking of the bullfrogs in the swamp land.

The night drew on and we flew almost without incident up until midnight when we passed over a little sleeping village where we shouted down for our location. It was Corinth, Mississippi. From that point our course seemed to straighten as we started over Tennessee, passing east of Memphis and Nashville during the night. We found ourselves early the next morning over the hills of Kentucky, flying very low—in fact, at times the drag rope trailed the ground.

I was standing looking over the edge of the basket when suddenly a shot rang out and a bullet whined by our balloon. The marksman was not in sight but as a precaution against further shots and possible dire consequences, I took the prerogative of leaning over the basket and shouting several terms which came to mind that are not suitable for print. The effect produced was satisfactory and we heard no more shots fired until much later and by then we were out of range.

It seemed quite natural for a mountaineer to brush the dust off his squirrel gun hanging over the mantel piece and draw a bead on our balloon. Possibly he thought the aircraft a new form of transportation for revenue officers, but I think it more likely that the mountaineer simply considered the little dots in the sky toy balloons and sought to improve his marksmanship.

About noon, Upson pointed out that the winds were dropping and we were in a very unstable condition. In any event we were simply bouncing up and down, using a considerable amount of ballast in doing so, and making no distance whatever.

We spent the rest of the afternoon up until 4:00 pm in this fashion when we finally managed to get across the Ohio River just east of Evansville, Indiana. Towards evening the wind picked up a little and we were again making from twelve to fifteen miles an hour now in a northeasterly direction. Our ballast supply was painfully low and at best it did not seem possible to stay in the air a second night.

We did pass the critical point, however—the evening contraction which usually takes a considerable quantity of ballast to counteract the effect of cooling the gas. But as darkness grew, we discovered ourselves caught in a vertical current which was flinging us skyward for thousands of feet. I watched Upson to see whether I should attempt to check the terrifying thrust by valving the balloon, but he was intent upon watching the instruments. Still higher and higher we shot; past 11,000 feet, 12,000 feet, 13,000 feet. Then Upson opened the valve slightly. The balloon checked itself at 15,000 feet.

The temperature had quickly dropped from a balmy, summerish seventy degrees to below freezing. Then the balloon started down again.

Although I asked no questions, I could imagine what was going through Upson's mind as he looked at the five lonely bags of sand in the corner of the basket. I knew that ordinarily a descent from 15,000 feet should require from ten to twelve bags to check. This situation I felt positive would require the use of those five precious bags and necessitate a landing long before we desired to terminate our flight. But good fortune rode the edge of our basket for instead of plummeting downward, we simply settled slowly through the air, so slowly that the motion was hardly perceptible, and it took us just an hour to descend the 15,000 feet which we had made previously in eighteen minutes.

As I could see ground approaching in the moonlight and the five precious bags of sand still in the basket, I felt reassured and knew Upson felt likewise that we should at least be able to make an effort to stay aloft the second night.

Our craft seemed to check itself automatically at a level of 150 feet above the ground. Here we entered a splendid current running northeasterly at a speed of twenty miles per hour towards Ohio and probably into Canada. The effect of the altitude during the day seemed to have been less pronounced on Upson than myself, for I felt utterly exhausted and Upson urged me to get a few minutes' sleep. I lay down in the bottom of the basket while floating just over the tips of the trees. I slept quite soundly for several hours with a sand bag in the middle of my back.

By early morning we were approaching Wakeman, Ohio, still flying northeasterly, headed for Lake Erie and Canada. Then Upson asked what I thought about crossing the lake. I knew at the time that in order to win the race we should have to get into Canada and put Lake Erie between us and Birmingham.

But my better judgment told me that with the International Race less than two weeks away, we should have to think about that, also, and it would likely take time to regain our equipment from Canada. I felt it better to take second or third (which we felt we had won) and be sure of getting into the James Gordon Bennett contest the following month with full equipment. On that basis, we stayed up until we reached the southeast shore of Lake Erie near Lorain, Ohio, and landed at 6:15 pm in the lovely little town of Amherst, 629 miles from Birmingham.

One of the military balloons in the race, piloted by Navy Lieutenant Rolfe Emerson, made an intermediate landing in Kentucky. Over Spruce County, Indiana, the pilot basket was cut away and from that time on the pilots clung to the rigging above the load ring, a simple circular hoop just two feet in diameter.

The maneuver, a brave if somewhat foolish act to lighten their load, might have proven successful except for a tremendous storm which arose as the balloon approached Sandusky Bay, cutting off its approach to the Canadian coast. Forced to traverse Lake Erie lengthwise if they proceeded, and with insufficient ballast to compensate for the downward force of the driving rain, the crew elected to land. Lieutenant Emerson did so by ripping the balloon in the air a few feet over a hayfield three miles east of Grafton, Ohio.

Aboard the two-foot load ring, clinging only to balloon netting, Lieutenants Rolfe Emerson and Frank Sloman rode for *thirteen hours* across Ohio. One can imagine the discomfort—indeed, the *agony*—of the two men enduring a storm-tossed flight of such duration aboard a twenty-four inch circular hoop! Their basket cut away meant of course the loss of all navigational instruments, all clothing, food and water.

Nor did the telegram received by Dr. Cortney W. Shropshire at race headquarters in Birmingham tell the whole story. In the wire, neither navy man dwelt on the hardships they must have endured, or bemoaned the fact that their efforts were all in vain. Despite their heroic fight against the elements, our *Goodyear II* balloon exceeded their distance, nosing them out of even third place.

Another of the military balloons left Birmingham in such haste that the pilots forgot to take their food and drinking water with them. After flying for twelve hours they decided they were in great danger of running into the Atlantic Ocean and made a hurried landing. When they could check their location, they found they were near Lewisport, Kentucky, about the central part of the state, and in absolutely no hazard of the ocean whatever.

Simply an error in calculation.

Still another balloonist, I was told, carried with him a jug of stimulant which he felt was absolutely crucial for flying. His aide told me he made splendid mileage up until 2:00 am of the second morning when the contents of the jug were completely exhausted. Immediately upon reaching this state of dryness, the pilot lost all interest in flying and made a quick descent into western Ohio.

But by now Lieutenant Richard Thompson, piloting *Army No. 1*, and Homer E. Honeywell, piloting *Kansas City II* were receiving congratulations from every quarter of the North American continent, following their landings on Canadian soil.

Lieutenants Thompson and Weeks landed near Richmond, Ontario, 1,040 miles from Birmingham and Honeywell at Thamesville, Ontario, near Chatham and across from Detroit, Michigan, about 750 miles, direct measurement, from Birmingham.

Both crews were to represent America in the upcoming Gordon Bennett rivalry—as would we, the third-place winners.

*Army No. 1* passed over Alabama, Tennessee, Kentucky, Illinois, Indiana and Ohio, sailing over Lake Erie between Fremont and Sandusky, flying seventy-three miles across the water and landing in the field of Roy Johnston, five miles east of Howard Township, Kent County, Ontario, Canada.

"When we landed," Lieutenant Thompson reported, "Mrs. Johnston was alone in the house and would not open the door. She was convinced that the balloon which had *U. S. Army No. 1* on it was the first arrival of the United States Army marching on Canada to attack the country. We had a time convincing her but finally persuaded her that we had no warlike motives."

"When that was accomplished, she and her neighbors were most hospitable. The Canadian papers were full of the arrival of the balloon and for several days the name of Birmingham was an oft repeated word among the people of Kent County."

When *Army No. 1* reached Madisonville, Kentucky early in the race, the wind had died down and it was necessary to go very high," according to Captain Weeks.

"The pilot threw out most of the ballast and ascended to 30,000 feet, the highest altitude recorded in a National Race. The atmosphere at that altitude was very calm, but beneath they could see a storm raging. It was because of this storm that the other two Army balloons were forced down. The sky was clear but all about the 30,000 foot altitude, Lt. Thompson and I could see what looked to be the edge of the universe— clouds piled in every imaginable fantastic shape. There were dogs and cats and human beings—the same kinds of cloud pictures every child in the world has seen in the sky, only these were much more impressive and much larger, and they gave one the feeling of standing in a hall walled with blue and lined with alabaster statues."

While at that altitude, Captain Weeks attempted to lift a bag of sand weighing 40 pounds and found it nearly impossible to nudge it from the floor of the basket, its weight being equivalent to about 250 pounds at sea level. The two pilots were so weak and drowsy they had to drink hot tea and sniff aromatic spirits of ammonia to keep awake. The rarity of the atmosphere had a trying effect on their physical system.

On the other hand, as the pilots flew over Lake Erie, their drag rope was allowed to skim the water and they were but a very few feet above the tops of the boats they passed. The crews on the boats and the balloon alike caught the giggles as the deep bass signals of the big boats were answered by Captain Weeks' little toy tin tooter he had found in his pocket.

# . 8 .

# Cockroaches in Our Basket!

The story of America's participation in the first International James Gordon Bennett Balloon Race has been told often yet is not popularly known.

In 1906, the stylish James Gordon Bennett, citizen of the elegant turn of the century world, a prototype international multi-millionaire, was very much the romantic, dashing, exceedingly popular figure on the doorstep of the Age of Wonders. Bennett was called the Commodore because of his love for yachting. His own yacht was manned by a crew of 100 men. He also skippered the *New York Herald* newspaper, a gift from his father. Later Bennett took up residence on the continent after fighting an unpopular duel.

Perhaps ironically, Bennett's races were never organized to produce headlines. Thus there was a great curiosity, a paradox about this whimsical, eccentric man.

Today his name is remembered primarily in connection with motor racing. This started with the Gordon Bennett Automobile Contest in 1900 which was the very first Grand Prix formula race, and extended to motor races with which he had absolutely no association.

Bennett himself disdained anything mechanical. He preferred riding in a coach and four, even in the twentieth century, and never witnessed any of the automobile races which bore his name.

The Gordon Bennett Balloon Race series began in 1906 and lasted through 1935, sixteen years after his death. They were always his favorite.

Only those truly devoted "balloonatics," it was said, could tell one competing balloon from another (something of an exaggeration) so there was no commercial overtone; and the fact that the balloonist had no idea where he would come down (a worse exaggeration) provided just the sport which Gordon Bennett relished.

The first Gordon Bennett race was born quite by accident during the period of brass bands, national anthems, top hats and dust clouds. Some saw them as considerably more spectacle than competition.

The Gordon Aviation Cup for airplanes was distinct from the Aeronautical Cup for balloons and was not instituted until 1909. The main rule, which Mr. Bennett himself influenced for both competitions, was to limit the number of contestants from any one nation to three. In addition, *three* consecutive wins by one national club would retire the trophy which would then become the permanent property of the winning club. All nations were invited to compete which held membership in the Federation Aeronautique Internationale.

The 1909 Gordon Bennett which was the very first airplane race in history was held at the champagne city of Rheims, France, above the plains where Joan of Arc had camped. It was won in a tremendous upset victory by an upstart Yankee, Glenn Curtis, flying at 47 miles an hour!

Three years earlier the first James Gordon Bennett Balloon Race was started from Tuileries Gardens in Paris on September 30th under the auspices of the Aero Club of France. From the United States, Great Britain, France, Belgium, Italy, Germany and Spain, sixteen cities entered balloons. Being the very first such race, it was considered an event of considerable importance and attracted one of the largest crowds ever assembled in the Tuileries Gardens—over 250,000 spectators!

Ohioan Frank H. Lahm was in Paris during the planning stages of that spectacle. The U. S. had yet no entry and Colonel Lahm, then past sixty years of age, bought a balloon and learned to fly it in order to represent the United States in general, and Akron, Ohio, in particular. Word of the expected exploit reached his son, Frank P. Lahm, a young army officer just out of West Point, who made a hurried trip to Paris, some say to protest. Little is known of their discussion. What *is* known is that young, inexperienced Frank took the balloon away from his father, flew the race and won the first Gordon Bennett victory!

After that, American balloonists flew victoriously in nine of the first nineteen international contests.

Lahm's victory started the Akron winning succession. His knowledge (amassed rather quickly) was passed along to Ralph Upson. Upson later became a professor at the University of Minnesota, long after notching the great world race of 1913 from Paris. After that racing balloons was up to me and I had mammoth boots to fill.

For example, that incredible race of the younger Lahm in 1906 . . . When that race started from Paris, the wind seemed favorable for a fairly long distance flight over the continent. But seven hours after the start the wind made a sudden change in direction and carried the balloons toward the English Channel. Lahm, piloting his father's balloon, *United States* found courage to attempt to cross the vast channel, leaving the shores of France at about midnight and not reaching the English coast until dawn.

Once there, his course carried him up the coast of England and at two o'clock in the afternoon he was forced to land due to a sudden wind shift veering off to the northeast, carrying him over the North Sea. He landed in a hurry at Flying Dales, 410 miles from Paris—the winning distance.

Victory by the United States in the first international contest put the responsibility of the next year's classic up to the Aero Club of America. On October 21, 1907, the second race for the Gordon Bennett cup was started from St. Louis. There were nine entries—three from Germany, two from France, one from England and three from America.

Over 300,000 people saw the start of the heat. *Erbsloh*, one of the German entries, won the race by landing at Asbury Park, New Jersey, a distance of 872 miles. This flight broke the American distance record for balloons which had stood since 1859 when Professor Wise made his flight from St. Louis to Henderson, New York.

For the third meet, held in Berlin, October 11, 1908, there were 23 entries from eight nations, the largest number of balloons ever to enter the Gordon Bennett competition. The race victory that year was earned by Colonel Schaack, representing the Swiss Aero Club, and he set a would duration record, staying in the air 73 hours and flying 753 miles.

During one year's celebration, a story has been told of the American who went ballooning with a foreign entrant. When the foreign aide was injured and unable to take part in the race, neither man knew the other's language. They had been up all night and had been using their drag rope to conserve ballast. When the rope became tangled in a tree, the foreigner dived into his luggage aboard the basket, muttering curses, and pulled out a stick of dynamite. The man jumped onto the webbing of the huge balloon as the American stood frozen with fear.

What he feared most was that disappointment had temporarily deranged his companion, for within a few feet of the basket was a bag filled with 80,000 cubic feet of highly inflammable hydrogen! Nevertheless, the foreigner hurled the dynamite downward with a practiced flip. It landed in the tree and did its job cleanly and neatly. The balloon was freed.

It was in the 1908 race out of Berlin that the Americans Forbes and Post lost much of their ballast in a take-off accident and the balloon went skyrocketing to 300 feet where it burst. While hurtling to earth at breakneck speed, Forbes cut ropes, allowing the bag to form an improvised parachute inside the netting. This broke the fall somewhat but they crashed through the roof of a house, stopping suspended above the dining table of a dignified German couple at lunch!

The fourth race was held at Zurich in October, 1909, and for the second time the U. S. took the honors. Edgar W. Mix's flight ended with a landing at Warsaw, 690 miles from where he started.

This brought to America the hosting of the fifth international distance race which started from St. Louis, October 17, 1910. This contest created considerable stir as a number of the contestants were not heard from for days. The *America II* crewed by Hawley and Post, was given up for lost. If they had not fallen somewhere in the Great Lakes, it was reasoned that they likely came down in the endless forest area of Canada. Professor Broch of the Dominion Survey said he had little hope of their ever being found.

Large rewards were offered for their recovery. It turned out that *America II* landed just north of Lake St. John. After tramping in underbrush for five days, and very close to exhaustion, the two met trappers who guided them to St. John where they received the good news that they had won the race. They had kept aloft 46 hours and traveled 1,172 miles in a direct line, thereby establishing *another* world's record.

The sixth international race was held at Kansas City, October 5, 1911, with France, Germany and America competing. This struggle was won by Lieutenant Hans Gerick of Germany who landed at Ladysmith, Wisconsin, a swift flight of 468 miles.

The balloons of the following year rose from Stuttgart, Germany on October 27, 1912. Twenty balloons were engaged in the contest which was won by Maurice Bienaime of France who landed near Moscow after traversing a distance of 1,358 miles—still *another* world's record!

But it was an all-American affair back in Tuileries Gardens in Paris in 1913, the same setting as the first Bennett classic. Ballooning in Paris was by now so popular that the race attracted more than half a million persons including all kinds of authorities—sporting, political and military. The U. S. A. won both first and second places.

The big cup went to the *Goodyear* balloon piloted by Ralph Upson. Second place went to the *Uncle Sam* balloon of pilot H. E. Honeywell of Kansas City.

Aeronauts Upson and R. A. D. Preston in the *Goodyear* crossed the English Channel, as Frank Lahm had done before them, and landed near

Bridington on the Yorkshire coast some 400 miles from Paris, a somewhat nervous though brilliant flight of 43 hours and 20 minutes.

A veteran European balloonist expressed admiration for the way the two took advantage of certain atmospheric conditions, the value of which the other balloonists failed to recognize.

The balloons started from Paris in a southwesterly direction, but then veered around to the west. As this would carry them out over the Atlantic, all balloons but the *Goodyear* landed when they reached the coast. Upson and Preston, however, saw that the wind was making a clockwise movement that would swing them around to the northwest and finally to the north, hopefully depositing them in England. So sure were they of their knowledge of these meteorological conditions that they more or less calmly allowed their craft to drift out over the raging Atlantic, even though at the time they were traveling due west, a direction that would miss the southern tip of England.

But the winds *did* veer clockwise just as the team had anticipated. The current carried them north over England and finally veered to the northeast so as to bring them to the very doorstep of the North Sea. At that time they were flying high and the visibility was so poor they did not notice they were approaching the sea itself until practically over the shoreline. The Yanks pulled their balloon valve wide open and came down at a dangerous speed, landing only a few hundred yards from the high bluffs that drop a sheer hundred feet or more to the sea below.

This victory for the fourth time again brought to the United States the honor of hosting the International Race. It was scheduled to be flown in October, 1914, but because of the war the race was not held again until October, 1920, when the host city was Birmingham, Alabama, the heart of the deep south.

After our experience in the National Race that year, Upson and I felt well prepared for the effort. Yet a tinge of regret came upon me as I anticipated this contest, for it represented the parting of the ways for Ralph Upson and myself. He was leaving our organization after this race and I could no longer look forward to flying with him. With a most heavy heart I went forward with the race preparations.

We were pitched against the most famous balloonists in the world. Representing Italy was Major Valle and Major Leone with one balloon and Major Madori and Lieutenant Pirazoli with another. From France there was Captain Hirschauer and Lee Nathan. Flying for Belgium, was the famous Lieutenant Ernest DeMuyter aided by Lieutenant M. Labrousse. Of all the foreign contestants, Lieutenant DeMuyter was probably the most outstanding and interesting balloonist—a seasoned veteran and expert with sea planes, airplanes, dirigibles and free balloons, a career commencing at the age fourteen. Italy's Major Valle, skipper of the *Audens*, had won the Olympic championship in free balloon flying *for perfection of flight* that very year at Antwerp. The Olympic race was for a distance of 25 miles and the balloon landing nearest the designated point was deemed the winner. Major Valle missed the mark by only 500 yards. Contrary to the ideas of the American public on Italian complexion, Major Valle was the possessor of light skin tone, blond hair and keen blue eyes. I sensed in his professional attitude that he was, above all things, accurate and would be a formidable opponent.

Valle was a distinguished figure throughout Europe, having been decorated in the war ten times, seven times for valor in action. The major was among the first to reach the front after his country declared war on May 26, 1915, taking part in an engagement in Ampola. He had piloted a P-4 dirigible balloon loaded with bombs and other high explosives. For this he was noted as saying, "I'd defy death to save a day!" He also piloted the V-2, M-9, M-10, M-14, F-5 and M-19 balloons, flying over the enemy's war camp and dropping explosives on railroads and supply depots.

In spite of his record for destruction, Major Valle was not a man of violent appearance. He was quiet—extremely quiet—and his manners were those of a polished gentleman.

Major Madori, pilot of the *Trionfale VI*, had spent four years at the front during World War I in a branch of the Italian Army commanded by his Highness, the Duke of Aosta. Madori had been wounded at Brest, France. His experienced aide, Lieutenant Pirazoli, had spent four years at the front with the Italian second and third armies; was in twenty big engagements and had been commended for bravery.

Major Valle, when asked if he expected to win the 1920 international race, replied, "That is what I came for. I don't expect to, but I believe I can and I mean to."

The weather bureau again sent the meteorological expert C. G. Andrus from Washington and every weather indication pointed to a long distance contest. In studying our maps before the flight, it looked very much as if we would have conditions comparative to our long flight from St. Louis. The storm area moving in over the Great Lakes would draw us first north from Birmingham and later northeast with the final run easterly towards the state of Maine.

A rough guess on my part indicated that we should land somewhere near Schenectady, New York.

Upson and I left the ground at 4:54 pm, October 25th, just before dusk. Shortly after leaving the field near the Sloss-Sheffield Company plant, we started north over the pine forests of Alabama, passing fifty feet above the Italian balloon of Majors Valle and Leone.

The first night passed without serious incident except that we were overrun by a most peculiar pest. It happened that in storing our balloon, our drag rope which was coiled in barrel-shaped form had become literally infested with cockroaches. They first appeared as I bent over the chart table working out our speed and direction calculations. I was forced to stop frequently to snap one of the little fellows out into space and then continue my work.

Upson watched these interruptions with some degree of patience, but finally said, "Well, Van, we simply must work as if these insects weren't here." I replied, "All right, Ralph," and watched him as he started doing computations while I flew the balloon. True to his agreement he let the first insect march across the paper without interruption. With the passage of the second, he appeared more perturbed. As the third roach skated across the chart it was evident he was restraining himself with effort. At the appearance of the fourth he broke all promises and commenced snapping the rascals off the paper into thousands of feet of space.

As the night wore on, we were enamoured with the beautiful moonlit forests of northern Alabama and southern Tennessee, flying slowly but surely towards the north to gain closer contact with the storm area over the Great Lakes.

Early the next morning we encountered a little rain squall which pattered down on the top of the balloon for ten to fifteen minutes but we soon drifted beyond this. Daylight revealed a strata of clouds forming at five or six thousand feet, giving us perfect protection against the heating effect of the sun upon the gas of the envelope. It was really a remarkable day's flying which we put in, hovering almost in perfect stability at from five to six thousand feet, which is almost unknown in balloon racing. We passed over Herron, Illinois about noon and by five o'clock in the evening we were swinging over Champaign, Illinois.

We noticed at that time a very peculiar phenomenon. Beneath us the smoke on the ground was blowing directly south while we were drifting with the upper currents due north. We really should have placed more importance on this curiosity for it represented a turning point in our race. We were careful to pick out northerly currents and that evening we found ourselves over the corner of Illinois, Indiana and Michigan.

Upson and I kept the balloon at an altitude of from five to six thousand feet that night and noticed that the lower currents beneath us ran very rapidly off to the east and southeast. This, too, was of singular significance. Yet we desired to travel as far north as possible to obtain the high speed of the storm area moving in on us. The night of the 26th passed without much effort and we were delighted to find that we had forty bags of ballast left out of the sixty with which we had started from Birmingham. We felt sure we could not only break the American distance record of 1,173 miles, but also the endurance record of 48 hours and 23 minutes as well.

It was with a feeling of renewed confidence that dawn of the following morning found us over Hillsdale, Michigan. For some peculiar reason, however, we seemed to hover above the village of Hillsdale for an hour or more.

Upson decided that something was amiss. He took careful calculations of our speed and found we were only making eight to ten miles an hour and that seemed to be in circles. According to our studies of the weather map, we should have been making from forty to fifty miles an hour at that very moment. In the face of that fact, Upson decided to take a drastic step and go for altitude in search of a high-speed current.

We threw over several bags of sand and as we ascended Upson urged me to quickly get direction readings so that we could calculate our course above the clouds. But the effect of the rapid rise of the balloon produced a very marked rotating motion due to the diamond-shaped meshes of the net with the result that the compass continued to spin rapidly and I was absolutely unable to acquire a direction with it. The compass we used was the dry type and it was then I resolved in future contests to use the liquid type compass which is less liable to spin in such cases.

We were much perturbed in not resolving our direction readings for at 6,000 feet we entered a dense cloud formation which persisted until we acquired our maximum altitude of 20,000 feet.

There was a marked change in weather conditions from 2,000 feet over Hillsdale with its warm, balmy temperature to 20,000 feet with the thermometer reading below zero. We also were handicapped by lack of oxygen. At 20,000, we seemed to be skirting the uppermost edge of the cloud mass and snow sparkled in the sunlight all around us. I noticed Upson acting peculiarly as he sat before our controls studying the instruments while I stood in the corner, gasping for breath.

His head seemed to drop forward frequently, finally coming to rest upon his chest. I then realized that he was unconscious from lack of breathable air. I pounded him vigorously on the back and as a result he wakened, shook his head and continued studying the instruments with glassy eyes. Then his head dropped over on his chest again.

It was only by breathing as deeply and as rapidly as possible that I was able to remain conscious myself. Occasionally I had to throw over a bag of sand to keep the craft at this altitude where we felt we were making excellent speed. We did not *know* our speed, of course. Being above the clouds and having no sextant with us, we were at a loss to know our exact velocity and direction.

In short, we were flying blind.

My own strength was giving out. Ordinarily at the lower altitudes it is a perfectly simple matter to pour over a thirty pound bag of sand, but at this altitude it seemed impossible to lift this weight from the bottom of the basket to the edge. Upson continued to have difficulties staying conscious. I seemed to have even more trouble keeping cognizant. By sheer persistence we fought to maintain this altitude for four hours.

By the afternoon of the second day we had run so low on ballast that we knew we would soon be forced down. We had insufficient ballast to check this descent and realized it would represent our final landing one way or another. There was a good possibility that we were over Lake Erie. We had risen to this high altitude only one hundred miles west of that body of water and believed ourselves to be flying in an easterly direction which would put us somewhere over Lake Erie near the mouth of the Detroit River.

I knew Upson had come through some tight places and my hope and prayer was that he would bring us through again. As we descended through this bank of clouds, we could hear the reassuring sounds of train whistles beneath us which buoyed our morale considerably! But at 8,000 feet a most melancholy note reached our ears—a *boat whistle!* It was disconcerting to again believe ourselves headed into the waves. Coupled with our physical exhaustion, I felt we could put up no great battle against the water. It was really with fear and trembling in my heart that *Goodyear II* dropped through the lower edge of the cloud strata at 5,500 feet—where we viewed a large island directly beneath us, the center of which had been cut out for the passage of boats.

I instantly recognized the geography as Lime Kiln Crossing which I had seen under construction years before. The lower air currents were carrying us towards the American shore when a reversal of the current carried us across the river where we were forced to throw over part of our equipment and clothing to check the now rapidly falling bag. Our basket came to rest a few miles from Amherstburg, Ontario, on the extreme western end of Lake Erie.

We were fortunate, indeed, in our landing, for a few moments more flying would have plunged us into the whitecaps!

When the final report of this International Race reached us in our little hotel at Amherstburg, we learned that Lieutenant DeMuyter in the balloon *Belgica* had landed in Lake Champlain near Hero Island, winning the race for Belgium. Captain Honeywell came in a close second, landing on Tongue Mountain near Lake George. Major Valle won third place, landing near Homer, New York, and we, with a most conscientious effort, had won only fifth place in a race of seven balloons.

It brought very forcibly to my mind the necessity for even more careful study of the weather conditions, for in reality we had underestimated the speed of the storm area by which we had hoped to win the race. And, too, further regret was added to a parting of the ways for Upson and myself. I had hoped to be his assistant in victory in our final race together. But this merely served a dual purpose to strengthen my confidence in Upson's ability as a scientific balloonist, and also an obligation seemed to fall on my shoulders to recover the Gordon Bennett Trophy for America which Upson had won and which now was being carried back to Belgium.

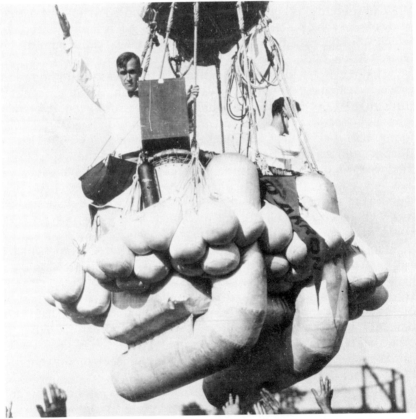

Looking more like some medieval weapon of war than an efficient racing craft, the basket containing Van Orman and his aide, slowly rises above hordes of well-wishers, filled to the brim with several days' rations, weapons, survival gear, a bottle of good scotch and the most modern meteorology equipment in the world. At this point hope is high for a several hundred mile journey into Boston, Canada or Nova Scotia.

# We Surprise the Cunning Honeywell

The next year my business was again in Birmingham for the 1921 National Race. Ralph Upson was this year pilot of the *Birmingham Semi-Centennial* balloon. How strange it was indeed to face him as a competitor!

Nevertheless, with the assured obligation of winning the International Race for America resting on my shoulders, it was necessary to enter the National preliminaries and place among the first three positions.

Our difficulties increased for in addition to the problems of racing which ordinarily confronted us, we were confronted also with the problem of financing the contest. Goodyear at that time was undergoing a financial depression which necessitated getting help from civic sources. The Chamber of Commerce came to our rescue, and with Willard F. Seiberling (son of Goodyear's F. A. Seiberling) as aide, we left for Birmingham with hopes high.

Weather bureau reports indicated a very slow race. The best possibilities seemed to be in endurance rather than speed to gain maximum distance from the starting point. Balloon inflation was delayed by a lack of gas capacity and at the start we were about two hours behind schedule. Each balloon had been provided with a sponsor from the Birmingham schools. The last act on the field was receiving kisses and the purple and white colors of Bessemer High School, sponsor for the *City of Akron*, from teenager Ethel Williamson, a student there. It was not disagreeable.

Once off the ground, Willard and I kept our eyes fixed on the manometer. We were flying our balloon with the appendix (the bottom opening) tied shut and allowing pressure to build up inside the balloon to assist in checking our ascents which we would encounter in the race. This particular craft was capable of standing one and one-half inch water pressure or about eight pounds per square foot. With a full balloon, this corresponded to pressure produced by a rise of about one hundred and sixty feet.

I glanced at the altimeter, watched it pass the one hundred foot mark and was astonished to see no indication of pressure registering on the manometer. Glancing quickly at the bottom of the balloon, I was similarly distressed that it was tightening up to a tautness of a drumhead.

It was obvious to me that within a rise of twenty-five feet more, the pressure building up in our balloon would exceed even the slightest margin of safety. Something was terribly wrong with our instruments!

It was a hazardous situation, having on board over a ton of sand with the possibility of our craft bursting overhead. We both realized that should this occur, the envelope would not have sufficient time or space to form a parachute to check our fall and drastic steps should be taken.

Without further conversation, I grasped the valve rope and valved vigorously, which allowed considerable gas to escape from the top, relieving the pressure and likewise starting us rapidly descending. Since we were only 150 feet in the air, we were forced to throw over three bags of ballast most hurriedly to check this drop. Immediately we started to rise again—fast! Disregarding our instruments entirely, at the first indication of tautness in our balloon I valved it again and *again* we fell.

We repeated this cycle several times until we had attained an altitude of one thousand feet and had the satisfaction of seeing the bottom of our sphere extremely slack, indicating the absence of pressure.

At this time I opened our instument case and was astounded to find that the tube which connects the manometer with the balloon had been pulled off and simply extended through the top of the instrument case with absolutely no connection to the manometer.

I might again attribute the warning to the "wee small voice" which whispered in my ear, "Valve!"

We made extremely slow speed the first night, passing over Florence, Alabama, and by the moonlight along the Tennessee River we could see the outline of Mussel Shoals. Willard seemed remarkably enthusiastic over this race and all through the night he fretted over ways to speed up the *City of Akron.*

The next morning, dawn found us south of Nashville swinging over a hill to the south of that city where we noticed a yellow balloon come up from behind us. We studied the craft carefully, saw it drop a few hundred feet into a faster current, and, to our dismay, pass us a quarter of a mile to the west. As it passed, we could see it was our most formidable competitor, Captain Homer E. Honeywell. We, too, sought the same current, but for us it did not exist.

Willard was terribly discouraged at the thought of Honeywell's passing us, but I said, "There is just one way to beat Honeywell, and that is to stay up longer than he does!" We passed over Nashville at 9:00 a.m. Here a change of wind carried us northeast and then east, and by 11:00 a.m. we found ourselves actually becalmed near the city of Lebanon, Tennessee.

Making no speed whatever, we decided to try out the higher altitudes. About a mile to the north of us, Honeywell had observed our actions and evidently thought it would be well to try the same move. He, likewise, started up. We rose fairly slowly until we reached 11,000 foot altitude, but Honeywell was going still higher. I studied conditions over the clouds, continued testing the fickle currents and concluded there were no winds above us of any value and that our greatest hope lay in getting back close to the earth to take advantage of the ground breeze.

We did this but had only enough ballast to travel five miles, towing our drag rope through the woods, across farms, over telephone lines. We dropped to earth four miles east of Lebanon. This final move enabled us to make five miles greater distance than Honeywell. The official record of the finish of that contest gave us 187 miles against Honeywell's 182 miles, and also the privilege of representing the United States in the International Race in Brussels that year.

Failing to emerge victorious for the Goodyear Company, I was at least thrilled that Ralph Upson took the cup as pilot of the *Birmingham Semi-Centennial* balloon, landing ten miles west of Stuart, Virginia, a flight of 423 miles. Second award went to young Bernard Von Hoffman in the *Riverview Club of St. Louis* aircraft for a flight of 201 miles, landing fifteen miles northeast of Carthage, Tennessee. We took third.

It turned out to be one of the closest balloon contests in the Gordon Bennett series for even the ninth place balloon, the U. S. Navy craft piloted by Lieutenant Commander L. G. Roth, flew on our heels for 118 miles, coming down eight miles east of Lawrenceberg, Tennessee.

Perhaps more than any other question, I am asked what we *talked* about in that little basket during so many hours aloft? Well, I recall no frivolous conversation. It was strictly business. No woman talk at all. We were there to make miles. I cannot recall a *word* that wasn't strictly business! We'd discuss the clouds. We'd discuss our speed, our objective, our navigation, how long we could stay aloft and all of that. We'd talk thunderstorms. We'd time the bolts of lightning, estimating their distance. We were up there to go far, to make the miles. Every bit of our equipment was chosen to make miles and in my last races I never even

carried a camera because a camera does NOT produce miles!
We gave it everything we had. And it hurt when we lost.

Ward Van Orman always loved the crowds that inevitably gathered before the start of the international balloon races. He is shown above in a snapshot taken in the 1920s.

## • 10 •

# *An Unscheduled Bath in the Irish Sea*

After winning a place in the International race, we were again confronted with the specter of financing our European flight. We were forced to call upon the citizens and newspapers of Akron for financial support, which they gave most generously. In many cases, families who depended upon incomes from investments only found themselves deprived of these incomes and were actually in want, and yet in the face of this condition the response was most generous.

Before leaving Akron, Willard Seiberling and I gathered together barely sufficient funds for the trip to Brussels, but how we were going to get home was another problem. We left on this assurance of Major Thomas S. Baldwin, airship pioneer, that if we required money to cable him. We sailed for Antwerp on October 23rd on the S. S. *Finland*, studying navigation under the captain of that boat as we crossed, in the hope of applying marine methods to the contest upcoming. We found this method to be very satisfactory, but it required further study before we could use it accurately.

Arriving in Antwerp, we hastened to Brussels where we inflated our balloon in Solbush Park near the spot where the martyred English nurse, Edith Cavell, had been executed during the war. The inflation was a nightmare. First, the gas supply was very low and finally required thirty-six hours before we could get sufficient gas into the big sphere to start the race. During this time a terrific ground wind had whipped our craft around, causing the balloon to shift in the net. The top of the balloon at the valve, being tied at the net, did not shift and this produced several folds of fabric directly under the valve.

Any attempt to leave the ground under this condition would have been most hazardous and being a firm believer of safety first in flight, I crawled up one side of the net over the top of the balloon sixty feet in the air as it swayed wildly about in the gusts. Willard stood beneath with the rip cord in hand with instructions to rip the balloon, which would deflate it instantly in case of any danger of its breaking away while I was on top of it. Somehow I succeeded in keeping my footing as I untied the net from the valve, shifted the fabric to its proper position and smoothed out the folds.

During inflation, our work also was hampered by heavy squalls of rain which soaked us and the equipment.

As ascension started, considerable commotion centered around the Italian balloon, for when leaving the ground the pilots held huge bouquets of roses in their arms, the offerings of their wives or sweethearts who came with them from Italy. They were obviously intent on making one of the most magnificent starts ever made in an International Race. But as they left the ground it was evident to onlookers that they had not thrown over a sufficient quantity of ballast to clear a row of trees adjacent to the field. The crowd, sensing a collision of balloon and trees, shouted in French and Flemish to throw over some sand! The Italians, not understanding French or Flemish, interpreted this as an outburst of applause on the part of the spectators, and bowed very low to the crowd beneath them. But the spectators, seeing the inevitability of the collision, shouted even more vigorously in French and Flemish, "Throw over a sack of sand!"

The Italians, due to this second outburst of applause, assumed that they certainly must be making one of the most *superb* starts ever made in the history of the sport, and bowed so low that they almost fell out of their basket to be gracious to the crowd.

However, the next moment their basket struck the top of the trees. The Italians were thrown to the floor of their little car, their feet protruding in the air, and instead of their bouquets of roses, we now witnessed their balloon bouncing back from the row of trees with branches draped around the pilots' feet. In a few more moments, with no further bows to the crowd, they were finally on their way. I made a mental note to be extremely cautious about magnificent starts.

One of the other balloons leaving later also ran into difficulty due to the confusion of language. Lieutenant DeMuyter, winner of the previous year's Gordon Bennett Race, was balancing off his balloon with a squad of Belgian soldiers who spoke only one language, Flemish.

Lieutenant DeMuyter, who spoke only French, was giving instructions and at the proper moment shouted the usual order, "Lachetz tous!" which means "Hands off!" One of the Flemish soldiers who misunderstood this order still kept close to the basket, and as the balloon rose from the ground, the anchor hook, which DeMuyter carried on the outside of the basket, caught in the soldier's belt and carried him into the air like a flaying dog.

Again the crowd, seeing that the additional weight would soon pull DeMuyter into the same trees the Italians had struck, shouted, "Throw over a sack of sand!" DeMuyter obeyed almost automatically although he did not know why he should be forced to throw over additional sand when he had balanced off properly.

The next scene was the soldier frantically grasping the edge of the basket and pulling himself up into it. The moment the soldier's head appeared over the basket rim, DeMuyter, who was now sixty feet in the air, appeared visibly shaken as he grabbed the soldier's shoulders and pulled him into the car, simultaneously ordering his aide to throw still more valuable ballast to the winds.

At about the same time, Bernard Von Hoffman seemed also to be having difficulty with *his* balloon. It was a brand new yellow globe, a thrilling sight to behold, of the varnished type, but it seemed to be leaking gas at an alarming rate. As the inflation progressed, it was evident that Von Hoffman's craft could not possibly stay up for any great length of time.

Willard and I were seriously concerned over this condition, especially in view of the fact that the winds would doubtlessly carry the balloons out over the southern edge of the English Channel. We were certain that under these conditions it was foolhardy to fly a balloon leaking as rapidly as Von Hoffman's seemed to be, over such dangerous waters.

With as much entreaty as I could muster, I endeavored to persuade Von Hoffman to land before he reached the English Channel but he seemed quite reluctant to promise definitely that he would do so. It was therefore with considerable anxiety that we watched his departure from the ground in his bright yellow balloon, hoping quite desperately for the best for him.

We learned later that he not only succeeded in flying across the edge of the English Channel, but also across England—then attempted to fly the Irish Sea! Unquestionably he might well have made it, too, except for the fickleness of the winds.

It seems the leakage of their balloon was far more of a problem on the ground with the winds blowing over the surface of the sphere than in the air. This is the apparent explanation of their endurance aloft.

Nevertheless, Von Hoffman was caught over the Irish Sea with a dying wind and was finally becalmed some twelve miles off Cork. It was a particularly trying situation as he later related to the overseas press, as follows:

> Mr. McKibben and I drifted to a point some five miles off the Irish coastline. Suddenly the wind shifted north in spite of all our attempts to find a current heading inland. There was nothing we could do but go northward with the wind and away from dear Ireland. Ballast was running short and we threw over everything including rations and water to postpone our watery immersion as long as possible.
>
> About 5:30 Monday afternoon, we passed two ships and flashed our distress signal. One of these stopped, and, after turning around, much to our astonishment proceeded on its way. We ultimately concurred that our slim hope lay in staying in the air as long as we could, trusting to drift over one of the islands east of Dublin. By eight o'clock Monday night, we had used all our ballast except for one bag. We cut away all parts of the balloon that were unnecessary and eventually cut away the drag rope which was 300 feet long and weighed 199 pounds.
>
> So we were in an alarming predicament over the sea. At 9:00 pm we sighted the ship which we discovered was the *Thistle*, coming from the west. We dropped down close to the water and signalled for the third time that day just how bad off we were. Thank God, the ship's engines stopped at once and a small boat put over the side.
>
> As our basket hit the waves, my assistant pilot McKibben was stunned by a blow from the load ring and fell into the water. Sudden release of his weight sent the balloon spiralling upward out of the sea at a terrific pace. At 500 feet up I ripped out one of the side panels of the balloon with all my strength, sending the craft like a rocket back to the deep. The lifeboat had already picked up McKibben and was heading for me, entangled in the rigging and wreckage of the *City of St. Louis* sprawled in disarray on the surface of the Irish Sea.
>
> Indeed, I fear the balloon is lost altogether. I would like to try to save it but have no idea of how to accomplish that. When I left St. Louis I was presented two flags of the city and given definite instructions to save the flags at all cost. "We don't care a toss about the balloon, it's the *flags* we want to save!" my own father assured me. Chief Steward Whittington on the *Thistle* assured me that he would look out for the flags on the wreckage when he returned to Ireland last evening.

Back to the fate of the *City of Akron*, we had drawn last starting position in this contest and left the ground at 6:10 pm with thirty-eight bags of ballast. Ahead of us stretched out in a line towards the northwest, we could count ten of the thirteen balloons in the contest and a casual glance at the map showed that we would have to cross the North Sea, the English Channel, and, if we were luckier than Von Hoffman, Ireland.

We dropped our sounding device fifty feet below us and watched its movements very carefully. Whenever it would veer off to the north, we would alter our altitude so as to take benefit of that particular direction, as we wanted to get as far north in England as possible in order to strike down in either Ireland or Scotland.

By most careful checking of air currents, we found the best altitude at around 2,000 feet. We were vitally concerned as to our direction for as I drew a line from Brussels along the course which we were following, we noted that the line ran along the southern coast of England with only a few miles to spare. This we referred to as the "dead line," and decided we did not dare swing to the south of that line before crossing the English Channel or we would miss England entirely and come down in the Atlantic Ocean.

With the sky very overcast, we could not see the ground plainly enough to distinguish the landmarks and could not identify one village from another. We relied entirely upon our compass for our course. And even with this instrument, we seemed to be having a great deal of difficulty. In checking over our equipment at the field at Brussels, we found that the compass which we had brought from America had become demagnetized and it had been necessary to purchase another instrument in Belgium.

This instrument seemed quite satisfactory on the ground but once in the air it developed a most vicious habit. The needle kept jumping off the pivot at the crucial moment. It became necessary then to slip out a ring, remove the glass, and place the needle back on the pivot with our fingers, then put back the glass and ring. This was nerve-racking, especially since we were flying a compass course with only a few degrees of safety to spare.

According to our compass readings, we thought we should sight the lighthouse of Dunkirk within the hour. Willard kept busy studying the ground with binoculars to see if we could pick up the flashes ahead of us. Apparently we had been riding in a thin layer of clouds which barely concealed it, for the next moment it came upon us with a blinding flash. We both took out our stop watches and I began timing the intervals between flashes, which ran two seconds, a half second and seven seconds.

Independently, Willard obtained the same results and a hurried reference to the *Admiralty Light List*, which gives the location and interval of the flashes of the lighthouses along the North Sea and English Channel, indicated that this light was Dunkirk. For further check I said to Willard, "Look towards the north and see if you can locate another lighthouse." Willard looked and there it was flashing at an even five second interval.

"That's fine," I said, studying the list. "It is Nieuport. That checks our compass course as being absolutely correct."

With the coast line only five minutes away, we quickly decided to fly across the southern tip of the North Sea and the Channel. At 8:50 pm we passed directly over the lighthouse at Dunkirk and on across the water. It had taken us just two hours and forty minutes to reach the coast, and by measuring our distance from Brussels to Dunkirk, we found we had averaged about twenty-eight miles per hour.

Flying conditions over water, particularly at night, are always very stable. It was no longer necessary to continually watch the instruments, dispensing sand meagerly or generously as the case necessitated to keep our craft at established altitude. I suggested, as we had gone without lunch and dinner and it was 9:00 pm that we prepare some food. The bare mention of the suggestion made us both realize we were practically famished.

Willard opened one of the cans filled with lime and partially dipped dipped in it another can filled with water and coffee essence, and poured additional water on the lime. Soon the lime was sending up a cloud of steam and in no time we had boiling hot coffee. The coffee was horrible but the heat seemed just what we needed. After a short recess for supper consisting of fruit and sandwiches, we again began concentrating on our immediate problems.

Beneath us we could hear the waves rolling in the thirty mile wind which stirred up the channel, and the foghorns of the lightships bellowing beneath us. It was a simple matter now to check our location simply by listening to the time interval of the blasts of these lightships and check them back against our *Admiralty List*. After an hour and a half's run in that most perfect equilibrium, we could see ahead of us the lights of the English coast and could identify both Dover and Folkestown.

Coming closer we made out in the distance the chalk cliffs of Dover, but were again dismayed suddenly to find our course veering off to the south. Now we were running nearly parallel with the coast. Willard dropped the sounder lower and we picked out another current which carried us forward to within a thousand feet of the chalk cliffs. Here we found ourselves in a reversed current and actually started to backtrack *away* from England toward the continent!

We shifted our altitude still again, going higher to 1,800 feet where we again found the winds to deliver us across the English coast line. We crossed the shore at 11:25 pm and it seemed reassuring to have land beneath us again. After crossing the shore line, we continued at the 1,800 foot altitude until shortly after midnight when we dropped down and shouted down to occupants of a horse carriage we could hear rumbling over a small English bridge, "Where are we?"

We were informed we had arrived over Tunbridge Wells. It was evident from this bit of news that we were *not* getting as far north as possible for a clear shot at Ireland. We thus investigated the various altitudes and found the most satisfactory current at 4,500 feet. When I say satisfactory, it is hardly true in the full sense of the word, for even with that current the best possible distance we could make from Brussels would be Lands End, the most westerly tip of England.

Ireland was out of the question.

At 2:45 am we passed two miles to the north of Portsmouth and at 5:30 am we passed over Southampton with the waters of the Channel in plain view. We were drawing ever closer to the *dead line* and it seemed that the race might be cut short at any moment due to the hazard of sailing out to sea.

Shortly after passing Southampton, we passed over a clear expanse of level, treeless land which we learned afterward was Salisbury Plain. At the center of the plain we were surprised to see a circular formation of rectangular shaped stones, each at least twenty-five feet high—these, relics of the druids, a religious sect, who, by viewing through certain stones, could compute the calendar and the constellations of the heavens. Our reaction was one of sheer awe, perhaps best expressed by the poem by Siegfried Sassoon:

> What is Stonehenge? It is the roofless past:
>   Man's ruinous myth; his uninterred adoring
> of the unknown in sunrise cold and red;
>   His quest of stars that arch his doomed exploring.
>
> And what is Time but shadows that were case
>   By these storm-sculptured stones while centuries fled?
> The stones remain; their stillness can outlast
>   The skies of history hurrying overhead.

On leaving that eerie plain we ran into most trying conditions. Layers of mist began to form at the altitude which we kept for best direction. In order to keep away from the coast we had to stay in the clouds and fly blind. This was particularly nerve-racking as we were forced to drop below the clouds frequently to check the coast line. With the sunrise our difficulties increased for the heat of the sun penetrated through the clouds, making the air conditions very unstable.

We would no sooner get the balloon in equilibrium at one altitude which was best for direction than the balloon would go higher due to the heating effect of the sun. To bring it down we would be forced to valve a portion of our precious gas, and then probably drop below the desired level and for the moment be carried toward the Channel.

We even tried drag roping on the ground for a time, but still could not find a satisfactory answer to our problem. Both Willard and I felt like we were walking a tightrope, and any slip might mean disaster.

Indeed, even with luck it looked as if we would have to land near Bridgeport, yet by careful maneuvering we managed to get by that city where the coastline curves slightly southward, and once again we felt reassured of the possibility of reaching Land's End. We were sure that if none of the other balloons made Ireland, we would win the race, making the greatest distance from Brussels.

The thought buoyed us up, but as we approached Exeter, our hopes were dashed for the dozenth time, for the wind faded into an absolute calm. At all altitudes even the clouds were at a standstill. We had only six bags of ballast left, and so we began to throw away part of our equipment in hopes of staying up the remainder of the afternoon and that night making Land's End on a change of wind direction.

We cut off all spare rope around the basket and in the rigging, the inside lining of the basket and even sacrificed a portion of the week's supply of canned goods carried in case we landed in the sea and had to wait for a boat. We got down to our life preservers, cut them up and dropped them over. We finally poured over the drinking water when a final check showed nothing remaining in the basket except one lonely bag of sand. We went so far as to put our clothes and other necessary paraphernalia into our knapsack to drop just before landing in order to check the fall.

While Willard was sitting on the floor of the basket preparing this knapsack, I said, "You had better get it ready for immediate use." The next moment we were caught in a vertical current and started up rapidly. By careful valving, for we had only one bag of ballast with which to check our fall, we knew we should not rise above 2,000 feet. We ascended to 2,900 feet, nevertheless, and when we started down, we both knew the race was over and it was simply a question of surviving the landing.

As we broke through the clouds we viewed beneath us a large estate, and we were heading terribly close to the manor house. Frankly, we hadn't thought it possible to descend from such an altitude without a severe landing, but by careful use of the emergency ballast, we balanced off so that we just settled down. The local farmers actually plucked us out of the air without a bounce.

We had landed on the estate of Squire Byrom, the squire of that county, approximately six miles north of Exeter where the late Walter Raleigh departed for the Colonies. A crowd of fifteen or twenty farmers soon gathered and were most helpful in deflating and packing our equipment. While we were thus occupied the butler from the Manor house appeared, bringing us an invitation to tea. Tired as we were, it seemed too good an invitation to refuse. Although we were ashamed of our appearance we took this opportunity of being entertained in one of the large English country houses, in fact the largest of any of the manors we had seen in our flight.

When we reached the manor, the butler entertained us at tea with an account of the family fortunes. We were then conducted to the conservatory where the Squire's maiden sister and housekeeper received us. She asked us where we came from.

"Akron, Ohio."

"From where had the Gordon Bennett race begun?"

"Brussels."

"Where were we going from here?"

"London."

With that she quite politely indicated the conversation was over.

We caught the next train for Exeter and on to London where we found that we had won sixth place in the International race. Lieutenant Armbruster of Switzerland had won, landing on a little island off the coast of Ireland. My friend Upson had been becalmed over the Irish Sea and finally drifted back, landing on a similar patch of earth off the coast of Wales.

A postmortem of the race showed that of the last few balloons which started, we had made the best distance. In other words, the contest had divided itself into a northerly and southerly group. After the ninth balloon had left, a shift in the wind had carried the remaining balloons a little further south and of this group we had been most successful.

It was consoling to learn that DeMuyter was likewise caught in this group, and we had outdistanced him by fifty miles. But even that consolation did not overcome our disappointment at being unable to bring the Gordon Bennett trophy back to America. We felt that with the next year's contest we should be able to compete even more scientifically, and perhaps with increased experience prove victorious.

Returning to America, Willard and I booked passage on the *Olympic*, sailing from Southampton on a Wednesday noon. The first few days we had a remarkably smooth voyage.

I had always been desirous of experiencing a heavy storm at sea. When Sunday morning arrived, the weather looked as if my wishes would be fulfilled. By noon the waves were running thirty and forty feet, producing a considerable motion of the ship and by evening the gale was lashing the Atlantic into a fury.

Most of the passengers had retired to their cabins but Willard and I paced the deck until eleven o'clock, fascinated by the storm. It was an inspiring sight and we both felt it a suitable night for a shipwreck at sea. Willard preceded me into the cabin and I followed shortly after.

I was just climbing into the upper berth with my hand on the light switch when I heard the swishing of the water on the cabin floor. Glancing quickly downward, I was amazed to see six inches of water rushing into the space between the cabin floor and partition. Sensing, of course, the possible damage to the instruments which were in our baggage and also the cameras which would be ruined by the salt water, I jumped to the floor to salvage our luggage.

Willard at this time was half asleep and looking over the edge of his berth to see what was happening. By then I had the luggage safely piled onto the upper berth. The water had now reached a depth of about a foot and was extremely cold on my bare feet. I told Willard that if the water rose much higher we would have to move to an upper deck and proceeded immediately to find out the cause of the *Olympic's* problems.

Opening the cabin door I was greeted with another rush of water six inches higher than the level in our cabin. Every roll of the boat would alternately clear our cabin and then fill it to a depth of eighteen inches. Glancing down the hall I was astounded to see several stewards scooping up the water in pails. My first reaction to this was of the utter uselessness of trying to bail out a ship the size of the *Olympic* with water pails, and the second reaction was that if they were actually attempting to bail out the ship with water pails, the situation certainly did not point to a disaster.

I called down the corridor to the stewards asking the cause of the trouble, and was very calmly informed that someone had left the bathroom faucet running earlier in the evening and also allowed the tub to overflow. In time the bathroom was flooded to the point where the door burst open, spilling torrents of water into the hallway.

Willard and I felt this would probably be the nearest to being shipwrecked at sea that we would experience.

Aide Walter Morton (left) shown with Van Orman prior to Morton's untimely death in 1928 when the Goodyear balloon was struck by lightning after its ascent at Pittsburgh. Van Orman escaped with a broken ankle. The tragedy led to Van's concentrated research on lightning protection for airplanes and balloons.

## · 11 ·

# A Few Trinkets for a Path of Smashed Wheat

In order to compete in the approaching International Race which was to be held in Geneva, Switzerland, we were again forced to go through the usual procedure of an elimination contest or National Race held in Milwaukee on May 30, 1922. We used the same equipment we used in the previous International Race, the heavy two-ply balloon which was extremely serviceable, yet quite heavy for racing purposes.

Our standard equipment list this year included two flashlights for use in a night landing, maps showing the magnetic declination, a compass, canned food, unslaked lime, a speed indicator, shotgun and ammunition, a hand axe, hand pump for pumping up the pontoons of the basket, two life preservers, portable seats, water, distress signals lights, a lighthouse chart, dark glasses to protect against snow blindness, matches in waterproof boxes, a waterproof cover for the basket, a first-aid kit, a stop-watch to record speed, and a special instrument case in which there was a varograph, vertimeter, manometer, statascope and barograph.

We did not carry sleeping bags for should it have become necessary to spend the night in the woods, the balloon itself would have answered the purpose admirably. My partner, a fellow claiming a charmed life, was Walter Morton who first contracted lighter-than-air fever during his association with Major Thomas Baldwin.

Morton had helped Baldwin assemble and fly the first dirigible successfully flown in America. Then Walter went with Roy Knabenshue, another pioneer of the art and the first man to tour America giving dirigible exhibition flights. Those were the days when the car under the big gas bag was as long as the bag itself and consisted of a steel network in which the pilot had to cling while in flight.

Not finding dirigible navigation exciting enough to suit him, Morton interested himself in free ballooning and joined Edward R. Hutchison, on of America's most famous exhibition balloonists. But even this did not give him the thrill he wanted—he found that thrill when he made his first parachute jump from a balloon.

"It is just like stepping off the world into nowhere when I get out of the balloon basket with a parachute harness strapped about me and trust to potluck that the big umbrella-shaped parachute will open," laughed Morton.

Walter kept up his parachute work for three years completing several hundred successful drops.

I had employed several aides over the years as partners in these races. In making such an important selection, I always considered a man who had sufficient confidence in my judgment to enable him to cheerfully take certain risks. When Walter came to Goodyear in 1916, he was an expert at splicing rope. I thought that with his background and experience he would contribute much to our chances for victory. The man was absolutely fearless.

Once when picking berries as a boy, Morton had been shocked by a lightning bolt and knocked to the ground. Experiencing horrendous storms as we did, it must have been a real agony for him, for one never outlives the awesome memory of being struck by a bolt, but he never uttered a word of complaint. The whole episode would be brought painfully to mind again in three short years.

In 1922 Morton and I inflated our race balloon in the baseball park at Milwaukee. Due to a legal difficulty between the race committee and the gas company, all spectators were excluded from the field. It was most unusual to have over a hundred thousand spectators outside the gates clamoring for admission.

Before the start of the race we went over the weather conditions with the U. S. Weather Bureau representative, Vincent Jakyl, an expert on upper air currents. Briefly, there was a fair weather area covering the New England states and a very extensive fair weather area covering the states west of the Mississippi River. Between the two, on the early morning weather maps of May 30th, a very long trough-like storm area existed.

Soundings of the currents aloft indicated that this troublesome movement was rapidly approaching the northeast and would be highly problematical if it were upon us at the time of the start. Mr. Jakyl strongly urged that if we wished to travel up the St. Lawrence valley, we would immediately, on the start, have to ascend to the unusual altitude of 15,000 feet. But this condition presented a serious dilemma, for if we ascended to 15,000 feet with our heavy balloon it would be questionable whether we could survive even the first evening's contraction when the sun set. On the other hand if we stayed low the first evening we would unquestionably start southeast, gradually changing to the south and southwest.

The accuracy of Jakyl's forecast was further strengthened by the rising barometer a few hours before the start and by the dampening of the winds from the north.

Quite logically, then, since we were starting in the next to the last position in the race, we decided to fly the lower altitudes particularly since we were handicapped with the heavy equipment. We left Milwaukee shortly after 5:00 pm and ascended to 1,500 feet. Our direction now was towards the southwest and we soon left land fall swinging out over Lake Michigan. We flew down the Lake Michigan shoreline passing the Great Lakes Naval Training Station, Waukeegan, then swung towards the south, cutting for shore just to the west of Chicago.

Chicago's millions of lights glowed beneath us as we searched the winds aloft to find those which would give us the greatest speed towards the south. Several times during the night we sighted the lights of other balloons. A general clearing of the clouds indicated we were rapidly moving out of any influence of the storm area. Nevertheless, about 2:30 am a vertical current hurled us down, and we struck the ground and rebounded somewhere in the western part of Illinois.

Daybreak found us crossing the Mississippi River and below we could see the large areas of farmlands which had been inundated by recent spring floods. Even farmhouses were submerged to the roofs.

About nine o'clock that morning a high speed wind seemed to develop very close to the earth. As usual when flying close to the ground during the day we found the air very rough and unstable. This meant we had to throw over our ballast quite frequently to counteract the eccentricities of the winds, and likewise we often were forced to valve our precious gas to prevent going too high.

By 11:30 am it became evident that although we were making satisfactory speed at the lower altitudes it was a terrifically expensive proposition, and our ballast supply was diminishing at an alarming rate. We felt positive that in order to win one of the first three places in the contest we would have to fly through the second night. In other words, to conserve our ballast supply we would have to ascend to a higher altitude to obtain smoother and more stable air conditions. This entailed a temporary sacrifice of speed and distance.

To obtain the desired stability we ascended to 9,000 feet about noon.

We were making only three or four miles per hour when we noticed off to the north of us a silver balloon rapidly overtaking us at the lower altitudes. Much to our dismay we found it was *again* Captain Honeywell! With this, I turned to Morton and lamented, as usual, "There is only one way to beat Honeywell and that's to stay up longer than he does!" It was really heartbreaking to see him pass us as though we were anchored fast! But we knew we would not have sufficient ballast to descend to the faster currents with him and therefore played the waiting game of stalling at the higher altitudes until sunset produced more settling air conditions.

Even at the higher altitudes our ballast supply diminished, and by 6:00 pm there was a question in my mind as to whether we could even survive the second night in the air.

By 7:30 pm we had exhausted our ballast and were throwing parts of our equipment over the side. Our canned goods were the first to go. Next our ammunition. It was curious to note that a box of shotgun shells, dropped from an altitude of 2,000 feet, failed to explode on impact with the hard earth.

By 8:00 pm it was evident that we required at least forty-five pounds of ballast to get through the evening contraction. We only had thirty pounds of equipment available and as this went over the side we hoped against hope that somehow we'd view tormorrow's dawn in the air. I noticed Mort gripping the sides of the basket as if he wanted to hold it up in the air, but eventually we had to face the inevitable.

Ten minutes before the contraction was completed we were entirely out of ballast and were forced to make a landing as best we could a mile and a half south of the little village of Fayette, Missouri. We made an excellent landing in a wheat field, deflated our balloon, packed it up and shipped it home.

The following morning, as was our usual custom where we had damaged the crops, we asked the owner of the wheat field what the damages were to his crop and in the true American spirit he answered by saying, "The wheat was thin where you landed, but I wonder if I could have that bottle of olives for a souvenir." We tried to persuade him to accept some remuneration for his damaged wheat, but he was quite insistent that the *wheat was thin* (which was not the case) and we compromised with several souvenirs which we carried on the flight.

That day we learned from the Associated Press dispatches that the race had been won by Major Oscar Westover of the United States Army Air Service, and true to our expectations, Captain Honeywell came in second with Lieutenant Reed of the United States Navy third. Major Westover had ascended to 15,000 feet at the start of the race and after only fifteen hours in the air had traveled northeasterly 750 miles, landing near Lake St. Johns, Canada.

Captain Honeywell traveled 550 miles in a southwesterly direction, landing near Springfield, Missouri. Lieutenant Reed in the same direction traveled 440 miles. Both balloons stayed in the air over forty-two hours. We came in fourth with 380 miles, our flying time slightly over twenty-six hours.

It was a splendid victory for both Major Westover and Captain Honeywell, both of whom flew meteorologically opposite courses. And as far as Mort and I were concerned, we were consoled with the thought that we had done our very best. We resolved in future races to secure lighter equipment more adapted to racing purposes rather than for long and rugged service.

Ralph Upson, my old friend, had been caught in the same way we had, with the same weight balloon, only he had attempted to reach the higher currents, was prevented from doing so by the sheer weight of his equipment, and was forced to land near Painesville, Ohio, finishing fifth.

The press was much interested, as always, in the National Race of 1922. One reporter, Irving Ramsdell, filed the following dispatch with the *Milwaukee Journal*:

> Captain John Berry of St. Louis, in the Air Pilgrimage which started here Wednesday, came down in Monticello, Illinois, after a 280-mile journey lasting more than twenty hours. We passed Racine, Wisconsin at a 500-foot altitude about an hour after hop-off.
>
> I use the pronoun 'we' because I also was aboard.
>
> Captain Berry was jockeying for a good wind. I looked over the side and saw Lake Michigan about a half-mile beneath us and apparently rushing upward at what seemed a mile-a-minute speed. When we had dropped to within fifty feet of the water I yelled and we struck.
>
> The basket was immediately half-filled with water. The balloon skipped from wave to wave, drenching us. The Captain was floored by the crash so I grabbed an axe and began chopping away the sand ballast bags. The balloon, released of its weight, leaped upward. We were in a haze until we reached Chicago when we suddenly swooped down, tearing off a piece of the roof of a house. Sometime later a freak wind shot us into an air eddy and half the covering of our basket was torn off when we scraped a haystack in a field.
>
> We huddled in the basket shivering for the rest of the night. Soon after dawn we purposely dropped low and learned we were in Indiana about 100 miles south of Chicago. We were forced to release all ballast and baggage to stay up. About 11:00 A.M. yesterday we were caught in a squall and then a treacherous wind ended our journey. Three times we were nearly spilled as we whirled back and forward.
>
> I threw over everything but the big bag shot downward at what seemed at least forty miles per hour. 'Duck!' yelled the Captain, just before we hit ground, but in the next two minutes we covered more than a mile,

bouncing along, tearing down fences, trees and telephone wires with Captain Berry vainly trying to get hold of the ripping cord to let the gas out to stop us.

The next thing I knew we were both thrown sprawling in an oatfield. Both of us were bruised but not seriously hurt.

It is a rugged sport for visiting reporters!

H. E. Honeywell (bareheaded) was Ward Van Orman's fiercest competitor in the U.S. He is shown here greeting race officials and dignitaries in Brussels, Belgium in 1925, the year the Belgian, A. Veenstra, won the race with a flight of 836 miles. U.S. Ambassador Phillips (with derby and cane) is second from left.

## . 12 .

# Our Dismal Showing
# and Winners Who Died

In our search for lightweight equipment for the 1923 National Race to be held at Indianapolis, July 4th, the only equipment which I could find available was a single-ply that had been used at Kelly Field during the war for training army officers. This equipment had been severely handled and had been shot and pierced in flights over Mexico. The balloon was in rather poor condition. Lieutenant Von Thaden had secured the equipment and asked me to pilot his craft for him.

We spent considerable time in repairing this thing, fixing up several holes and tears in the balloon until we felt it was in reasonable shape for racing purposes. We laid out the bag inside the brick speedway at Indianapolis. As usual we were deluged with rain even before the gas was turned on.

Our balloon was laid out on a low spot inside the track and the rain pocketed in the top of it, weighing it down to such an extent that the gas would not flow into the sphere until the water had been drained off. In order to do this we had to pick up the balloon fabric between our fingers, raise it up sufficiently high to drain off the water, and thus handled it much more severely than usual.

To check for possible damage we made still another inspection before inflation and found everything apparently satisfactory. As we inflated our balloon it seemed gas tight, but during the balancing off period, appeared to be leaking gas at a very appreciable rate. We made an excellent start from the racetrack, hoping to run northeasterly over Lake Erie, Lake Ontario, and land somewhere in New York state.

As usual, during the evening contraction we expended a considerable quantity of ballast, but felt positive that when the sun finally went down we should ride in equilibrium the rest of the night with practically no further expenditure of ballast. Both Von Thaden and I concentrated on our problem of conserving the ballast. Much to our consternation, after the sun finally sank in the west, we found we had to *continue* to throw ballast, making a very appreciable inroad in the remaining supply.

In fact it soon became evident that we would have to work strenuously just to survive the night in the air. By 10:00 pm we had used all of our twenty-eight bags of sand and had started in on our canned goods and supplies. By 11:30 pm we were cutting up the drag rope in an effort to stay in the air just a little longer. At midnight we had only thirty pounds of equipment left at an altitude of 2,000 feet, with the knowledge that a midnight landing lay moments ahead of us in a 30-mile wind and with very inadequate flashlights and no drag rope to absorb the shock.

Both Von Thaden and I peered anxiously over the basket into the darkness beneath us hoping to pick out a suitable field to land on. After seemingly ages of this tenseness, our flashlights finally lighted a cornpatch. To avoid the shock of striking the ground with no drag rope, we made an effort to land our balloon on a row of trees immediately adjacent to the corn. We threw over the last thirty pounds of equipment to cushion our plunge.

The basket finally skidded down the branches of the trees until we hit ground just inside the fence of the cornpatch. After valving sufficient gas to compensate for his weight, Von Thaden stepped out of the basket and pulled the balloon back into the field where we proceeded to deflate our machine. When the top of the balloon near the valve reached the ground, we discovered an eight-inch slit in the fabric which accounted for our unusual loss of gas and ballast which had forced our humiliating showing.

Hearing a commotion in his field, the farmer came out to investigate the noise and found two stranded balloonists, Von Thaden and I, dismally viewing our leaky goods. He invited us to spend the remainder of the night with him.

The results of this race were most unsatisfactory, indeed. We had won next to last place, making slightly over fifty miles from Indianapolis, being forced down at Hartford City, Indiana. The only reason we were not in last place was that the balloonist who came in last had a craft which leaked more than ours.

As we lay in the little farmhouse near Hartford City, Indiana, I proceeded to promptly forget that race and turn my attention to the National Race one year away. I was especially interested in radio equipment for receiving weather reports, and deciding upon the general characteristics of the radio receiving sets while at this farmhouse. Also the balloon for the coming race would be gastight and particularly lightweight.

In reality we were more fortunate than we knew for in the subsequent International Race starting from Brussels, the American balloonist encountered terrific winds and thunderstorms. Captain Honeywell's craft at Brussels was wrecked by the high ground wind. Lieutenant Lawrence of the United States Navy was forced down with a terrible thunderstorm in Holland, and Lieutenants Olmstead and Shoptaw of the United States Army were killed by the lightning.

Two other balloonists were fatally injured when their balloons were struck with lightning, and it was only after this International Race that we realized that we had actually been fortunate in not winning that terrible night over Hartford City, as embarrassing as the defeat had tasted.

This radio set designed and built by Van Orman was carried in his basket in numerous races. It was over this set that he received a special message from his wife as part of an all-night special broadcast over a Cleveland station, featuring the Goodyear Metropolitan Orchestra and other company talent. It inevitably buoyed and encouraged Van to win.

TOP PHOTO:    Ward Van Orman (top, with cap) directs securing procedures as the fully-inflated balloon lifts against the strength of several men who have yet to secure sandbags to basket. It is the 1924 National Race from San Antonio, Texas.

BOTTOM PHOTO:    Ward Van Orman makes final tests of multiple instruments before flight.

## . 13 .

# A Radio Show at Fifteen Hundred Feet

For the next National Race to be held in San Antonio, we had prepared our equipment—instruments, radio and balloon—to the point of maximum possible perfection. For two years I had worked on a radio receiving set which now was capable of receiving signals over a distance of 2,500 miles. By actual test I had received a Los Angeles station seventeen out of twenty attempts. The set itself, using Westinghouse WDll tubes that worked on a dry battery, was simply a four-tube superheterodyne set with push-pull amplification, reflexed back upon itself. The antennae system consisted of two wires, each 200 feet long, suspended from the equator of the balloon.

I had arranged with radio stations all over the United States to broadcast weather reports once every hour of this race. That was the beginning of the weather broadcasting system in this country. It was very helpful, indeed, to receive these hourly weather updates.

Before the start of this race, my Goodyear friends had gone up to Cleveland where they took over the WTAM broadcasting station and sent out over the airwaves a special program for my aide, C. K. Wollam, and myself in the balloon. It included Smith's Metropolitan Orchestra, messages from Goodyear executives, and the live voices of Mrs. Wollam and my dear wife Edith, who wished us well and related important messages regarding weather and sightings and progress of other balloonists. It is quite difficult to describe the thrill of hearing your wife's voice come out of the thin air at 1,500 feet at 1:00 am in the blackness of early morning flying over the plains of Texas.

The program was indeed an enjoyment and a thrill and it lasted until dawn of the next day when we lost radio contact.

We had been given an absolutely free hand in the designing of our balloon and we constructed a single-ply envelope of rubberized fabric which weighed three hundred eighty-five pounds or less than half that of our original racing craft. Even the basket itself was fifty pounds lighter than the conventional balloon basket.

Wollam and I inflated our balloon at Kelly Field, using a mixture of natural gas and hydrogen. When the starting time arrived we were mighty anxious to break the American distance record of 1,173 miles which had stood since 1909.

It seemed, indeed, that our time had come.

We left the earth at 5:40 pm with *eighty-six* bags of ballast—more sand than had ever been carried in any free balloon of this size. Of course this was partially due to the excellent lifting powers of the gas mixture.

We started off in a northerly direction and I looked up into the appendix of the balloon, through which the valve line and rip cord passed, to make sure they were clear and saw a most disheartening picture in the top of the envelope. Evidently during inflation due to the wind's rolling the fabric of the envelope in the net, a large fold had formed in the top of our balloon and was hanging down immediately adjacent to the valve.

It appeared obvious that should we open the valve the normal distance this fold of fabric would drop into the opening and cause a very high leakage of gas. I felt that even on the *first* opening of the valve, the race would be considerably shortened for us and that we would be absolutely unable to make a satisfactory showing with our splendid equipment. To be sure, after a full year's preparation we felt beaten just that quickly, but would not admit it. We both bowed to fight it out and to avoid opening the valve until absolutely necessary.

Ahead of us we could count five of the other balloons in the race, and to our rear, the last balloon. Army planes convoyed us for half an hour, after which we found ourselves flying over the vast plains of central Texas. At 7:15 pm we turned on the radio set and were able to receive station WOAI at San Antonio which advised us that no weather bulletin was available at that time. This represented the first service of our radio equipment, although not yet rewarding, needless to say.

At 7:30 pm we passed over Friona, Texas, and from then on until midnight we successfully received important weather information from stations WDAF, WOC, KHJ, and ultimately WTAM in Cleveland, 1,100 miles away.

It is impossible to depict the thrill which was in store for me. Our craft near 1,500 feet altitude drifting silently over central Texas with not a sound to break the stillness of the night. I could not believe my ears when from out of that quietude came my wife's voice broadcasting a message of "God's speed" from the Willard Storage Battery station at Cleveland. I can only state that the miracle of the radio in bringing Edith's voice to me over such a distance caused the shivers to run up and down my spine.

For a period of four delightful hours WTAM entertained Wollie and me with this beautiful program put on by the Goodyear Radio Club which encouraged us towards victory.

The next afternoon we were flying directly over the Kansas City broadcasting station and our alert Goodyear manager, seeing some free time on the air, went down to the radio station and wished us luck and Godspeed wherever we were. If he had been alert, he would have just looked up in the sky. We were directly over the radio station and he could have saved himself all that trouble by just shouting up in the air.

Shortly after the midnight broadcast, our balloon crossed the Red River near Byers, Texas. At 7:30 am the next morning we sighted another balloon one and a half miles to the east of us, evidently Von Thaden. We were making excellent speed, having covered 300 miles in fourteen hours, and felt confident with the storm area to the northwest of us that our acceleration would soon materially increase.

The remainder of the morning we flew through heavy clouds, finally getting a bearing near Middleburg, Oklahoma. During this period we received several weather bulletins from stations WOC in Davenport, KDKA at Pittsburgh, and KSD at St. Louis.

At noon due to a slight fracturing of the cloud cover, our gas expanded and we were carried up and up to an altitude of 15,000 feet. At this elevation the temperature dropped to twenty degrees above zero and we encountered several snow flurries. Wollie and I also noticed the lack of oxygen. We had endeavored to secure bottled oxygen in San Antonio but were forced to ascend without it, and had now reached the altitude where we needed oxygen.

There was a consolation in our present dilemma that helped neutralize the lack of oxygen and that was the fact that we were accomplishing a strategic meteorological maneuver. The morning's weather reports received over the radio had indicated that the storm area, which was carrying us to the north and northeast, would probably stagnate over Minnesota within twenty-four hours and the race ultimately would be terminated by making a circle around this storm area as the center.

It was evident then, as a simple problem in geometry, that the balloonist at the farthest position from the center of this storm area would be able to make the greatest distance from the starting point at San Antonio, and therefore win the race. Concentrating on this strategy, we both fought for our breath at altitudes ranging from 15,000 to 17,500 feet for over three hours.

We breathed as deeply and as rapidly as possible to counteract the rarity of the air for that agonizing length of time, at the same time making the strategic run to the outside of the storm area which would put us in the winning position.

By 3:30 pm we were forced by our exhausted physical condition to come down, and Wollie and I debated whether we should open the valve and assume the risk of being forced out of the race due to the fold of the fabric adjacent to the valve. I finally determined the most logical way would be to open the valve as little as possible, allowing the gas to just *simmer* out and thus avoid subsequent gas leakage. Wollie listened as I pulled on the valve rope and we both offered a little prayer that the valve might seat again properly, and thus keep us in the running.

Our prayer certainly was answered, for after the valving the valve seated correctly and we started down. Within a half hour we dropped to within 1,500 feet of the ground and we checked our fall as well as our location near Redfield, Kansas.

We had made an excellent run to the outside of the storm area during this high altitude flight, but were really dismayed to discover on the 7:45 pm radio dispatch that three balloons had passed over Kansas City four hours ahead of us. We were consoled with the thought that they now were closer to the center of the storm area than we, and although behind the other balloons we were farther to the outside and still had victory in our hand providing we could run as far north as possible before we were deflected from our course due to the stagnation of the storm center.

Early that evening our speed picked up to fifty-five miles per hour at 2,000 feet and we were making excellent speed towards the north and east. The evening weather reports confirmed the deduction of the morning report that the storm area would stagnate over Minnesota due to an extensive fair weather area over the Great Lakes region.

Our speed continued to hold, our direction remained very satisfactory—in fact, everything was perfect until 4:00 am when Wollie, who was piloting the balloon while I took a few minutes sleep, awakened me with the information that there was a severe weather disturbance to the northeast of us. I observed the situation carefully and found that we could swing away from the rainstorm by going again for high altitude and by turning from a northerly course to a westerly course for a period of over an hour.

At 5:50 am we passed over West Union, Iowa. By this time we had covered sufficient distance to resume our northerly course with a safe margin from the thunder squall. I found that the winds, as anticipated, had shifted and would carry us more towards the northwest. At 9:30 am on the second morning we passed over New Albin, Iowa, and at 10:45 am over Caledonia, Minnesota.

The breezes were swinging more and more to the west and we found it increasingly difficult to conserve ballast, soon finding our reserve dwindled to five bags or 180 pounds. This ballast soon flew over the side, followed by considerable equipment.

At 1:40 pm the second day out from San Antonio, we commenced our final descent and tried a landing in a large hay field five miles to the north of Rochester, Minnesota. We were traveling at fifty miles per hour and swung down for a rip landing which is necessary under such high speed conditions. We ripped the balloon twenty feet above the ground —ample time to stop before reaching the end of the field.

But our craft did not deflate with the usual speed. We executed a hell of a bounce, at least seventy-five feet in the air, jumped the fence at the end of the field, and our basket finally came to rest on the edge of a railroad track. The ropes of the net and balloon were draped across a fence on the other side. We had jumped the tracks of one railroad and were now crawling out of the basket onto the tracks of the second.

In true motion picture fashion, we were just crawling from the basket at the edge of the train track when a train whistled. There was just time to run a hundred yards down the track to flag the train and prevent the destruction of our equipment. The conductor who descended from the train was most upset. He immediately ordered "the mess off his track!" I said, "Yes, sir, but if you'll put your crew to work, it'll help us get it off that much faster." He saw the light. The engineer, fireman, brakeman and conductor all helped untangle the balloon from the barbed wire fence.

In ten minutes' time we had cleared our craft from the scene and I had walked across the field to put in a long distance call to Edith in Akron to advise her of our landing. You can imagine my astonishment in hearing that the local newspapers already had advised *her*! It seemed conclusive proof that the speed of the press was greater than that of the telephone. It is still a mystery to me to this day how they reported the story so swiftly.

Wollie and I were taken into Rochester, to a quite unexpected reunion at the local hotel. Its manager turned out to be the man who had helped us race from Birmingham, Alabama, several years before. Then he was in the steel business but now was the proprietor of this Minnesota inn. The odds against our running into each other by our dropping out of the sky in a balloon were so infinitesimally small as to be quite impossible!

With no more than an hour's notice, this man immediately organized a luncheon in our honor. On the table was an improvised loving cup indicating our standing in the current contest. Only then were we informed that we had just captured first place in the 1924 National Balloon Race!

Ward Van Orman (right) and aide C. K. Wollam are shown where their balloon came down at Rochester, Minnesota. The Goodyear balloon, built to Van Orman's own specifications, had lifted off from San Antonio, Texas, site of the 1924 National Balloon Race.

# • 14 •

# *Rendezvous with the Zuider Zee*

With a congratulartory letter of President Calvin Coolidge in my hand, my aide C. K. Wollam and I felt an increased responsibility as representative of the United States in the International Race of 1924. In addition, if this race was won by Belgium, they would attain permanent possession of the Gordon Bennett trophy, DeMuyter having won it twice previously for Belgium.

Wollie and I sailed for Belgium on the steamer *Zeeland*. We had arranged with Captain Thomas to secure instructions in the methods of navigation used in marine work. Captain Thomas very kindly delegated his chief officer, Mr. Doughty, to instruct us. At first it seemed a rather complicated matter, studying precisely how the transatlantic liner found its way across the tractless expanse of the ocean. But before we were half way across we had made very satisfactory progress in celestial navigation. By the time we reached Plymouth, England, we were able to determine the position of the ship within two miles by observation on the sun or stars.

The navigation method seemed so desirable that on landing we wired the German Zeppelin Company for an aircraft sextant. We knew that in long flights above the clouds or over water it would be an invaluable tool.

I had arranged for the services of a meteorologist to assist in interpreting the European weather conditions which are somewhat different from those of America. I was extremely fortunate in securing the assistance of Dr. Limpertz, one of the foremost meteorologists of Europe.

In going over the weather conditions preliminary to the start it was evident that our course would be generally towards the southeast. A large fair weather area was stagnated over northern Germany. Being in the southwestern portion of this area, we were under the influence of northwesterly winds which would carry us toward the southeast.

Dr. Limpertz pointed out that upon reaching the northern foothills of the Alps, the winds would increase in velocity due to the narrow mountain valleys which funnelled the air and speeded the currents. Logically, therefore, we selected as our objective the city of Vienna or points further east or southeast.

The weather conditions at inflation time were perfect. We left the ground at 5:14 pm riding a gentle fourteen mile per hour wind towards the southeast. We rose to 2,000 feet, checked our speed again which now ran twelve miles per hour. Our ballast supply consisted of forty-two fifty pound bags of sand and 350 pounds of disposable equipment.

At eight o'clock we passed Tierelmont at an altitude of 3,500 feet, but soon found it necessary to drop back again to 2,000 feet to obtain the desired direction. About 9:00 pm the temperature had dropped to fifty degrees and we encountered a severe contraction of the envelope.

By 11:00 pm the temperature had slipped to forty degrees and the last traces of the sun were disappearing rapidly in the west. This was novel to us, being accustomed to the sun setting around 8:30 pm in latitudes of forty to forty-two degrees. We were so far north of those latitudes that the sun was still visible at this late hour.

We had used approximately 700 pounds of sand to counteract the contraction, which was a costly price to pay. Near 11:15 pm we passed over Malmedy having covered a distance of ninety miles in six hours.

Around 2:00 am we tried our radio set for American stations and attempted to receive WBZ in Springfield, Massachusetts, which was broadcasting a special program for our benefit. At 2:37 am we were rewarded by very faint sounds of music and felt absolutely certain it came from America for the wave length checked perfectly with that station.

At 3:45 am the first indications of dawn appeared on the eastern horizon and for some peculiar reason our balloon commenced to sink very slowly. About half a mile ahead of us we could see the outline of a thickly wooded hill which we would have to clear. We were reluctant to discharge any ballast to accomplish this, knowing that in a few minutes the sun would expand the gas and start us upward automatically. It was a delicate balance.

As we approached the top of the hill our craft seemed to lose some of its inclination to drop. Wollie and I waited with bated breath, gauging the height needed to clear the hill and estimating the seconds before the sun would begin to warm the gas. It was a tense few moments for our basket came down and actually missed the top of the highest tree by inches —just as we encountered the warming expanding effect of the morning sunshine.

Within a few minutes our altitude increased to 5,100 feet where we found a very weak current of about six miles per hour, carrying us onward in a southeasterly direction towards our goal. This current was extremely short-lived, and at sunrise the wind stopped and we found ourselves utterly becalmed over the village of Kaiserlauterne, Germany. With the increasing heat of the sun expanding the gas and increasing our altitude we now approached 9,200 feet in perfect equilibrium.

This dead calm was not entirely unexpected. It frequently happens in the vicinity of fair weather areas during the day. We fully expected that when the evening winds set in again we should be carried onward towards our destination of Vienna.

The equilibrium which we encountered at 9,000 feet was really remarkable. From 7:15 in the morning until 5:00 that afternoon, we did not have to throw away a single grain of sand or open a valve to keep this lovely steady position. The cold was pronounced, especially in the shade. About noon I felt the necessity of warming my feet by hanging them over the edge of the basket.

We spent the afternoon checking our weather maps and other data, trying various radio stations for weather reports but were unable to make contact. This was certainly in contrast to the forty radio stations which broadcast weather reports every few minutes in America during the National Races.

By 5:00 pm we were confronted with a serious decision. Lower winds had set in from the south and would carry us north towards Holland, possibly England or Norway. The winds which I had anticipated had failed us entirely and it was obviously impossible to proceed southeasterly toward Vienna.

In other words we had the choice of landing and getting credit for 225 miles which was only sufficient for second or third place in the race or retracing all of these miles in an effort to fly a still greater distance from Brussels in the opposite direction.

Rather than accept any place in the contest other than first place, we elected to try for England. With that decision, we knew it really *meant* first place or nothing.

A storm area moving in off the Atlantic which was then over the Bay of Biscay produced this erratic change of wind. With ever greater determination we started north at eight miles per hour, crossing the Moselle River on the second evening at sundown. Several picturesque castles were visible along the river. We identified the Moselle by the direction of its waters. In this particular location there were several rivers of similar appearance from the air but by studying the flow of the water over a dam towards the northeast, we had positive evidence that this was the Moselle.

At 9:45 pm we were flying at an altitude of 6,500 feet, finding it necessary for direction to stay at this altitude.

The cold and dampness was so intense that Wollie and I shivered under our leather flying suits, heavy woolen clothes and underwear. For some peculiar reason every time we rubbed our leather flying suits against a woolen blanket, heavy discharges of static electricity were heard. For that reason we were forced to abandon the blankets.

Throughout the night the coldness increased and the earth beneath us was covered with a heavy frost. About 4:00 am while I was studying the horizon, I noticed off to the north a very faint dividing line which appeared to mark the boundary between land and water. I felt reasonably sure it was the Zuider Zee, but wanted confirmation. For this reason I wakened Wollie and told him I was going to take a few minutes' sleep and to pilot the balloon, keeping the present altitude. True to my surmise, in about three minutes Wollie shouted, "Van, I see the Zuider Zee dead ahead!"

We immediately held conference as to the advisability of crossing the land-locked sea and the North Sea towards England or Norway. We checked our ballast and found we had nine sand bags remaining of the forty-two we started with. The attempt would have been foolhardy.

With the sad knowledge that we had made the poorest showing of any of our flights, we swung down out of the air and leveled off three hundred feet above the canals and dikes which crisscross Holland. It seemed impossible with our speed of thirty-five miles per hour to avoid landing in one of these canals. But again, by careful maneuvering, Wollie and I brought the craft to rest in a pea patch near Amsterdam.

As we landed the Dutch farmer with the typical wooden shoes came running up and I asked him if he spoke German, French or English. But with a shake of his head I knew some of his limitations.

You could see the worry in his face over the peas we had trampled down in landing and packing up our equipment. When we could corral an interpreter who could speak the language, I informed the farmer that we would be perfectly willing to pay for any damage done to his crops. This delighted him and he promptly routed out his farmhands to help us pack up. All of our equipment was carried a half-mile to the farm house on the backs of these husky Dutch farm boys. After a good breakfast prepared in the spotless kitchen by the man's wife, we were conveyed into Amsterdam where we cashed our checks and asked the farmer what he felt was a fair price for damages to his pea patch.

After some four hours of rather heated debate on the issue, involving intercession by the American ambassador and an agricultural expert, we settled on twenty-five dollars. We had been in the air over thirty-seven hours and had been practically without sleep for forty-eight hours, but instead of being sleepy now, we were indignant and felt we certainly were being imposed upon. Before he left the room, I told the farmer that the next time I landed on his farm, I would alight on a less expensive portion of it—the meadow, perhaps. His reply, in the only English he knew, is not fit for print.

The race results showed we had made a distance of 110 miles from Brussels after flying a V-shaped course of about 600 miles. Major Peck landed at Malmedy, making a distance of 90 miles, while Captain Honeywell landed near Rouen, winning fifth place in the race. Until this time I have never attempted to explain our poor showing in a race for we had the satisfaction in our hearts of knowing full well we had done the best we could.

In a race postmortem, it was interesting to note how DeMuyter won the race, his third consecutive victory plus permanent possession of the Gordon Bennett trophy for Belgium. During the first night, DeMuyter flew the same course we did, only slightly more to the south. At dawn he was in the vicinity of Chimay. He noticed the fickleness of the wind and maneuvered to swing toward the west, gradually arcing toward the northwest in the vicinity of Rouen. He proceeded to the northwest, crossing the channel at Malleville. He swung up toward England and pushed on to his final landing place at St. Abshead, Scotland, totalling over 650 miles and winning the contest for Belgium.

We were familiar with this maneuver which DeMuyter used for Upson had used it successfully in the 1913 race from Paris. But unfortunately I had no means of knowing that the storm area would move in over the Bay of Biscay and totally reverse the wind direction.

In checking over the weather maps after the flight, we felt entirely justified in not attempting to cross the North Sea towards England. That does not mean my aide and I were not terribly disappointed in not being able to win after the conscientious services of our meteorologist, Dr. Limpertz.

1925 ascent of the international balloons at the Gordon Bennett classic at Brussels, Belgium. The Goodyear entry is already in the air.

## . 15 .

# The Death Head Coffin
# Brings Us Luck

After having suffered defeat at the hands of the Belgian DeMuyter, victor of his third straight Gordon Bennett victory in 1924, I had to put steel in Akron's hopes for more international victories. Starting with the weather reports as the basis for improvement, I decided a still more efficient radio system would be necessary.

I interviewed Mr. David Sarnoff of the Radio Corporation of America about our problem, and with his cooperation I perfected not only a most efficient six tube super-heterodyne receiving set, but also combined with it the radio compass. Preliminary tests on these innovations proved most satisfactory.

My aide, C. K. Wollam, and I shipped our equipment to the 1925 national contest at St. Joseph, Missouri, and inflated our machine at the municipal airport there in the face of a very high wind. The ground swells were sufficiently awesome to delay our start and we did not leave the earth until almost seven in the evening.

The winds were carrying us due south. At 9:10 pm we were crossing the Missouri River in the vicinity of Kansas City, having just listened to a message from station WHO from Godfrey L. Cabot, president of the National Aeronautic Association. At 10:30 pm we received the desired weather reports from KYW, indicating definitely that we should continue south and southwest.

While flying over Missouri, we noticed our radio reception fading frequently. It appeared that some mineral deposits or other influences were acting upon our radio equipment. I also noted at the higher altitudes a marked increase in volume with a slight decrease in static. At 10:40 pm we were listening to our home station, WEAR Cleveland. And again I had the thrill of hearing my wife's voice coming through the stillness of the dark night while we were 4,000 feet in the air. It sounded so clear and natural she must surely be standing in the balloon basket wishing us, "Godspeed!"

All five of the army and civilian racing teams competing in this race carried radios. The program by station WEAR beamed to all of us in the air included the Goodyear Glee Club, the Wingfoot Harmony Four, the Friars Club, Smith's Metropolitan Orchestra and a variety of Akron vocalists and instrumentalists.

The silver gleam of the big bags was sighted over Kansas City and Liberty, Missouri a few hours after they made their ascent from St. Joseph. The P. W. Litchfield Trophy, named after the president of the Goodyear Tire & Rubber Company, would be awarded for the first time this year along with a $1,000 prize and the right to represent America at the International Race in June in Belgium.

One of the U. S. Army's entries was disabled before the race was started. The bag, the *S-16*, piloted by Captain Raymond E. O'Neill, swung about in the ground wind and the netting above the balloon gave way. The bag was ripped open and deflated. The Detroit entry also had a thrill for the thousands who observed the take-off. The balloonist W. C. Neylor, aide to pilot Herbert V. Thaden, was overcome by lifting gas a few moments before take-off. Though Neylor was revived, physicians insisted he should not make the flight, but the daring flier refused to give up and was loaded into the basket from the ambulance.

Doctors feared he would contact pneumonia because his lungs had been weakened by the gas. Nevertheless, the *Detroit* took to the air at 6:58 pm.

By midnight the first night, *Goodyear III* was making twenty miles per hour but was extremely handicapped by the cold, the temperature having dropped to fifteen degrees. By 5:00 am the next morning our location was twenty miles southwest of Springfield, Missouri. Beneath us we could see large patches of timber with very few roads. We noted also the absence of bridges. The roads crossed the creeks at fords and we concluded we had now passed over the boundary of Missouri into Arkansas.

At 9:46 am we flew over Lead Hill, Arkansas, and at mid morning we crossed over the White River. At this time we tuned in Station WHO at Des Moines and were assured we had chosen the correct course in flying southwesterly. The report stated that the North Dakota storm area had disappeared and we were now being carried along the eastern side of the fair weather area. By noon we were passing over Blue Mountain,

Arkansas, and a half hour later over Heber Springs.

It was a simple matter to identify these towns by checking the bends in the White River. But now both Wollie and I were beginning to feel the effects of flying continuously at 12,000 and 13,000 feet since early morning. But that is where speed and stability lay, and it cost us much of our oxygen supply. Also, the carbon monoxide in the gas which occasionally flowed out the opening in the appendix was nauseating us until it seemed impossible to stay in the air any longer.

But I also realized we were making an excellent sprint of it and would have to continue at all cost.

Late that afternoon after paralleling the White River across Arkansas, we crossed the Mississippi near Itta Bena. As the sun set into the west we at last descended to lower altitudes, finding the favorable currents closer to the ground.

By sunset hour we were flying over the desolate swamps of central Mississippi. The cypress trees standing in the bog beneath us were indeed depressing. However, at 6:30 pm we tuned in WTAM at Cleveland and found the weather reports most favorable, indicating the winds were going to swing more towards the east. Up until this time I had computed the distance to the Gulf of Mexico and found with our present direction we should reach the Gulf near Pensacola, Florida, about midnight. For that reason we really welcomed the shift which swung us eastward.

At 9:00 pm on the second night in the air we received the message from Station WTAM that all other contestants had landed except Honeywell. We were therefore implored by friends at the station to keep in the air to win, as Honeywell was still up. Although my aide and I were both physically exhausted by long stretches of little oxygen and too much nauseous gas in our system, this word of encouragement coming to us 800 miles through the air was sufficient to fix our determination for victory. We flew quite low the rest of the night, hoping to stay aloft until Georgia. Our morale was also sustained by another all night program from WTAM.

At 6:00 am the next morning we crossed the Mississippi-Alabama line near Pickinsville, Alabama. Only three bags of ballast remained of forty-two. At sunrise we were forced to ascend much higher to obtain air currents necessary to carry us eastward.

Too soon for our wishes we were compelled to swing down to choose a landing spot. Indeed, we came down several times and each time selected a long field to land in, but the wind was quite strong on the ground and in each case we would overshoot the field. Finally our drag rope caught in a little pine forest where, for a while, we bounced up and down in the tops of the trees for fully ten minutes.

After several maneuvers of pulling the balloon backwards along the drag rope to the trees in which it was caught and then releasing it, we succeeded in freeing ourselves and before our craft had a chance to pick up speed, landed in a corn field on a farm of Henry Vail, six miles south of Reform, Alabama at 9:00 am after 39 hours in the air.

We had difficulty finding the telegraph operator, being Sunday, but finally located him and sent out the landing report to the race committee.

On the veranda of the hotel that evening we set up our radio set and were delighted to receive the message from one of the broadcasting stations that we had won the race. After about a half hour, confirmation was obtained.

Some attributed our victory to the talisman which we carried. On a recent visit of Charles Nungesser, the late French ace of World War I, P. W. Litchfield, president of Goodyear, was given the famous Nungesser talisman as a token of good luck. Mr. Litchfield, in turn, generously loaned me the use of the talisman for racing purposes. The small bronze disk was perhaps a peculiar lucky piece at that, as it bore the image of a death head-inscribed coffin and two candles.

While the talisman may have had its effect, I felt that the success of this flight was largely due to the beautifully efficient radio equipment which we carried. Over fifty broadcasting stations brought us reports of the race based on press dispatches so that we were able to keep track of the location of other contestants practically on the hour. This in addition to the invaluable weather knowledge received and the marvelous influence of radio in maintaining one's morale aloft.

With this victory behind us and the satisfaction of knowing for a certainty that our methods of ballooning were correct, I again turned my attention toward Belgium with a determination to redeem myself for the defeat suffered in the previous year.

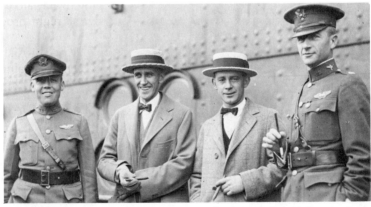

Balloon pilot Ward Van Orman (left center), his aide, C. K. Wollam (right center) are seen with military friends in the 1920s.

# · 16 ·

# Hundred-to-One Shot on
# a Tossing Ship Deck

Once more my aide Woolam and I shipped our balloon and crossed the sea on the S. S. *Leviathan* to Belgium. As on the previous crossing, the captain very kindly placed at our disposal the chief navigation officer of the ship and the trip was again occupied by studying the methods of marine navigation. The methods used on the *Leviathan* differed somewhat from the other systems and as we carried the German aircraft sextant with us, it provided a superb opportunity to compare the two.

Our experiments showed that an accuracy of position to within six miles could be obtained with the aircraft sextant compared with one-half mile with the marine instrument.

The marine sextant uses the natural horizon, but in flying and any appreciable elevation the natural horizon is somewhat uncertain and therefore the bubble sextant is more suitable. Nevertheless, upon landing at Cherbourg we felt well prepared in the art of marine navigation and believed it might be profitably employed in the coming race.

We inflated our balloons again at Solbush Field. During the inflation the weather was particularly propitious, and a careful study of weather maps indicated the most logical race target to be Spain. We had to consider both the meteorological and geographical aspects in picking this objective. It seemed that Spain would offer the greatest possible straight line distance from Brussels necessary for victory.

Our balloon was ready to start a half hour early and we watched the other contestants finish their preparations. When it came our turn to leave the field, both Wollie and I concentrated on the problem of getting our craft into the air with no frills or bows to the spectators.

We commenced at 6:20 pm Greenwich time with forty-three bags of sand ballast. We took off in a direction slightly south of west.

It soon became evident after checking the various currents available that we would have to shift our objective from Spain to Brest, France, due to a slight turning of the wind towards the westerly direction. At 7:45 pm we were flying at an altitude of 2,700 feet, making fourteen miles per hour. We had passed our most dangerous competitor, Lieutenant De-Muyter, a few minutes before, flying in a higher altitude. From 8:05 to 8:50 pm we were passing over Mons, Tournay and Douai.

In the early evening the evidence of the war-torn farms lay beneath us and one could make out the irregular lines of former trenches where the British had fought the Germans in western Belgium. Occasionally we could see shell holes but many were covered with sufficient vegetation to render positive identification difficult.

At 9:55 pm we tuned our radio to London 2 LO, and received news reports, correct time to check our chronometer, and weather reports which indicated that our change in objective to Brest was a sound one. It was particularly delightful to hear the Big Ben chimes in the background. At 10:30 pm we passed over Lens and Arras and at 10:40 pm were receiving a concert from the French radio station Radio Toule. At this time we measured the flashes of light from the lighthouse to the north of us, which gave us our location relative to the English Channel.

From 11:00 pm to 12:30 am we tried to interpret weather reports from the various French stations. At 1:00 am we were quite excited to receive the American station WBZ, confirming its identity by its wave length. At 1:50 am off to the north of us, we picked up a lighthouse flashing an interval of ten seconds with eight seconds eclipse, which we knew to be Touguet Point. Then at 3:00 am our hearts were lifted as we heard WEAR, our own station in Cleveland, very faintly.

The next lighthouses identified by their flash intervals were Cayoux and Treport on the West Jetty Light. By triangulation on these two lights it was a simple matter to fix our position, and by 7:30 am we had a magnificent view of the mouth of the Seine River passing directly over Havre out over the Bay of the Seine.

At the time our craft was over the English Channel flying at some 5,000 feet. Clouds had formed beneath us and we could hear a fog signal bellowing at Cape De LaHavre. Within a few moments, however, our speed picked up and we were zooming at twenty-six miles per hour floating out directly over the Jersey and Guernsey Isles.

As we looked down on those green and verdant spots, something seemed to whisper that I should check our direction more carefully. To my utter amazement I found that our present direction would carry us two miles north of Brest, France, missing land entirely and straight into the open Atlantic!

This was the thing we had particularly wanted to avoid and while we were not unduly alarmed at that point, we immediately took soundings of the currents above us and below us and actually tried the various altitudes from sea level up to 20,000 feet. Much to our surprise—and I suppose I should add concern—we found the currents to be absolutely single-tracked, and none of which would enable us to land at Brest. Even at *25,000 feet*, the desired current was non-existent.

A little later we passed two miles to the north of the Rock Dourds and then the North Sept Islands. From this point on our balloon continued to parallel the northern coast of Brest, five miles off shore, over the waters of the English Channel.

Using every device known to balloonists and meteorologists, we simply could not find the current which would swing us further south to land at Brest. At times we were so close to the shore that we could hear the carts rattle in the streets of the villages and the dogs barking in the alleys.

It was simply heartbreaking to be so near, yet so far.

To keep up our morale, Wollie offered to bet twenty-five dollars that we would swing north and land at Lands End, England. Knowing full well it was impossible, however, we then decided to face facts.

At 6:00 pm we had definitely missed Brest, but choosing to stay optimistic as long as we could, turned our aspirations towards landing at Quessant, a little island about twenty miles to the west.

About 7:00 pm we saw the island of Quessant six miles to the *south* of us and realized at that moment that we had missed the last bit of land between us and the United States 3,300 miles away.

We had sufficient ballast to fly 1,500 miles, but knowing winds towards the west do not continue any great length of time, we felt it would be suicide to continue to fly blindly on. As a matter of precaution, we decided to see exactly how far west we could fly before passing the steamer lanes. I drew a line on our map from Cape Torinana, Spain, to Land's End, England, and this line represented the danger line beyond which we dare not fly.

In reality the line represented the lanes of steamers from South America and Mediterranean ports steaming into the English Channel. Checking our time it was quite evident that we could fly until midnight. After determining this danger line we discussed the possibility of the winds reversing themselves in the next twenty-four or thirty-six hours, which might enable us to fly far out to sea and return on the reversal of the winds.

At 10:00 pm sharp we tuned in the London weather report.

The most discouraging bit of information we had ever received came in over our radio that night. The forecast indicated the winds were going to blow towards the *west* for three more days. Then to add a touch of irony to our dire straits, the London station then presented the Savoy Hotel dance orchestra. But we were in no mood for dance music nor did we feel like dancing at that particular moment.

For the next hour and a half, there was not much talk. I soon came to regret that I had become so preoccupied with mentally solving this bleak and foreboding riddle that I paid little attention to my aide. Seeing no other possible end to the matter than a horrible death in the ocean, Wollie had opened the cognac rations and had partaken liberally of their contents. Within some twenty minutes he had apparently lost all rational control, for without saying a word to me, he took out the rocket pistol and aimed in the direction of the balloon over our heads, hoping to end this terrible suspense once and for all.

He missed the 54-foot diameter bag by two feet. Of course had he struck the hydrogen-filled sphere with a fire rocket, it certainly would have exploded and dropped us to our deaths.

God surely was with us and I thanked Him personally for Wollie's awful aim.

But we were certainly disheartened. I would have sold our chances for about two bits at that point. My watch said 11:30 and I knew the magic hour was midnight when our balloon would turn into a pumpkin and leave us stranded in the middle of the sea. Now we had equipment to land in the water but did not desire to land in the water for we would be disqualified under the rules of the race. By "disqualified," I do not mean last place. You're kissed right out of the picture!

We had spent years in preparation and training for this contest, traveled 3,500 miles in the last week, and the thought of being disqualified seemed to overshadow any thoughts of personal hazard.

Quite suddenly an idea kept coming to mind which, at first, seemed so ridiculous that I discarded it. It was this: "If you don't want to be disqualified for descending into the sea, and have no land on which to a-light, there is only one choice left and that is to descend on a boat." As wild as the idea sounded we were forced in our dilemma to consider it.

I turned to broach the subject with my aide when Wollie's voice was the first to break the silence by almost shouting, "I am going to be first!"

I couldn't quite grasp his thought, so asked him, "What do you mean?" He said, "Well, Van, you have a family to take care of and if there is any choice between us, I am going to be the first to go to the unknown and leave you a fighting chance."

This spontaneous offer on Wollie's part to sacrifice his own life for my family stirred my emotions beyond description. The only reply I could make was simply, "If we have to go, we will both go together."

Just when things appeared blackest, I spotted a little light through the binoculars—a steamer rolling in 24-foot waves two miles to the southwest of us, heading for the English Channel. We didn't take our eyes from its bow and when it came within a quarter of a mile of us, I took out our five-cell flashlight—a powerful beam of about 1,500 feet—and pointed it in the general direction of the ship's bridge. Now I didn't *know* Morse Code, but I had a copy of it in a small book and I decided I had better learn sufficient of it in a hell of a hurry.

With the book as a guide, I signalled them the message, "We are going to land on board." I did not ask their permission to land, but simply flashed the statement that we would land on board their ship. To our surprise and delight, the boat responded by flashing every light on board.

Now I had no idea how this was going to be done. I simply knew it had to be done to save both our skins and the race. At the time we were making about forty-five miles per hour to the west and the ship was traveling approximately six knots to the north, and the thing that really made the whole stunt possible—was our sea anchor which we had carried for years and never used. Now a sea anchor is nothing but a big canvas cone about three feet in diameter tapering down to a six-inch hole with a bridle and a rope attached to it.

We swung down from 2,000 feet to thirty feet above the water and threw over the sea anchor which slowed our speed like the brakes of a truck from forty-five miles an hour down to four miles per hour. It seems to me to this day as if some unseen hand held our basket at just the right height so that as we struck the outside rail of the ship's forward deck, six sailors found it possible to grab on to the basket and hold it to the rail.

I quickly called to the captain to swing the boat around into the wind so our balloon envelope would be blown over the deck and not come in contact with the smokestack which could well have resulted in explosion and fire.

When the ship's maneuver was completed my aide and I jumped out of the basket, pulled the rope panel which slit the top quarter of the balloon which collapsed at our feet.

Those who are superstitious may be interested in the fact that we had crossed the Atlantic on the *Leviathan* which formerly was the S. S. *Vaterland*, a reparations ship of World War I. And when we sorely required a boat to land on, what should the name of it prove to be? Also the S. S. *Vaterland*, a 300-ton version of the big ship—but it's name was certainly symbolic under the circumstances. That ship looked awfully good to us!

So, sixty miles out to sea we had landed on the 25-foot deck of a tiny German freighter bound for Rotterdam, Holland from Cairo, Egypt. It had not been done before in the 150 years of ballooning history. The German sailors were highly delighted that the monotony of their long voyage had been broken up by such an event as the landing of a balloon in their midst at midnight. I must add that we were not at all displeased ourselves.

Ship's captain, Rudolph Nordman, spoke English excellently. He had been with the Hamburg-American line passenger service for many years and had been promoted to his own ship. At this point in the voyage he was down to salt pork and potatoes for himself and the crew. Talk about manna from heaven! On his table we put canned peaches, canned pears, canned apricots, canned blueberries, canned pineapple, peanuts, canned eggs, butterscotch! How the crew did welcome the change of diet.

We must have presented an unusual picture standing on the bridge of the S. S. *Vaterland* talking with Captain Nordman. In the excitement we had forgotten to take off our life preservers. We had placed our valuables and balloon log in a waterproof bag and tied it to the front of one of the life preservers. The bag dangled from the life preserver like the whisk broom on a Scotchman's kiltie. We left our balloon on the forward deck just as it lay and retired to the chief officer's cabin which he kindly vacated for us.

The next morning we rolled up our equipment on the forward deck and succeeded in packing it into the basket without so much as a little tear in the fabric. We were entering the English Channel about 9:00 am the next morning when Wollie sighted a peculiar looking sea gull which was rapidly approaching our boat from the southwest. When it landed on the aft deck, somewhat exhausted, it was apparent that this bird was a carrier pigeon. We felt some alarm knowing that the other balloonists carried pigeons, and possibly one had been swept out to sea beyond the point where we had landed on the steamer.

After resting on the aft deck half an hour and hastily eating a few bread crumbs which we offered, the bird flew off in an easterly direction as if to confirm our worst fears for other balloonists.

The *Vaterland* steamed slowly up the channel throughout the day at a speed of nine knots. The next morning while the ship was off Dover we released the two carrier pigeons which we had taken with us from Brussels. Now we sent them home.

That morning Captain Nordman confided in us that when he first sighted our balloon in the sky the night before he was not particularly anxious to put himself out to assist us assuming us to be French. When he saw our American flag swinging around about a hundred yards from the ship, he immediately gave orders to his crew to render every possible assistance. Throughout the entire trip to Rotterdam, Captain Nordman could not have been more courteous to us had he owned the steamer.

When we steamed into Rotterdam the following day I remember having a bit of a qualm. I knew that under maritime law he was entitled to half the value of our equipment for salvage. I said to myself, "Well, here we will see how the land lies." The crew was at lunch when the American Express truck pulled up to the side of the ship to take our balloon. I approached Captain Nordman who was going over some paperwork with some shippers. I said, "Captain, our balloon is ready to go ashore. Would you put it ashore?" He jumped up, called his crew into action, and in some few minutes the balloon was safely in the truck. I knew then he wasn't going to ask for salvage.

So in the next few moments I gathered all of the money together that Wollie and I had on our persons—about a thousand dollars—and again called Captain Nordman aside. I said, "Captain Nordman, you've been very fine to us. You saved both our balloon and our necks and here is a small offering we would like you to have." Now a thousand dollars was no small amount of money in 1925.

I can still remember his horror. He puffed himself up in all his teutonic dignity and said, "Well, Mr. Van Orman, I'll have you understand there are some things that money does not buy in this world." I answered, "Well, Captain Nordman, we're sorry, we only wished to show our appreciation. Perhaps a new sextant would be acceptable."

"No," he assured me, "I learned to navigate with my old battered sextant and it's close to my heart and I don't think I'll ever love another sextant as much."

I then answered, "Well, Captain Nordman, there appears nothing we can do at the moment, but I do want you to remember that we have appreciated what you have done for us and I hope that some day, somehow, we can return the favor."

When Wollam and I returned to Brussels, we made a bee-line for the American Embassy. The reaction of the American ambassador was exactly what I had hoped. "That's an incredible experience, gentlemen," he said, "but you certainly should do more than thank the man."

"Yes," I agreed, "but how am I going to do it?"

He said, "Well, we're supposed to be skilled in diplomatic relations and if you'd like, I'll have our Embassy handle the situation."

I found out later he wrote the following letter on the stationery of of the American Embassy commenting on Captain Nordman's skill in handling his ship, and thanking him on behalf of the American government for his cooperation:

> Mr. Van Orman, pilot, and Mr. Wollam, the aide, in the Goodyear balloon recently entered in the Gordon Bennett cup race, have informed me of your great kindness in lending them assistance in the matter of their landing on the *Vaterland* on Tuesday, the 9th of June. I desire to take this occasion to express to you my personal appreciation of your efforts on behalf of the American balloon and to congratulate you on the skill which you displayed in maneuvering your ship at full speed and at the same time lending aid and assistance to the pilot of the balloon in placing yourself directly under his line of descent.
>
> Mr. Van Orman was most enthusiastic in the manner in which you surmounted the difficulties attendant upon receiving him upon the deck of your ship, and desired me particularly to mention your capable navigation.
>
> I am taking the liberty of sending a copy of this letter to the general director of your company, in order that he may be acquainted with the appreciation felt by the American authorities of your great kindness in lending assistance to one of their entrants in the Gordon Bennett balloon race.
>
> With best wishes for your continued success in your career at sea, believe me,
>
> > Most sincerely yours,
> > WILLIAM PHILLIPS
> > American Ambassador

To this letter Ambassador Phillips attached the seals and ribbons of the Embassy and sent it to the American Ambassador in Berlin. The Ambassador there also had an opportunity of adding a second letter of endorsement with yet more seals and ribbons, saying the same thing in different words. From there the colorful parade of letters, seals and ribbons went to the German Foreign Office and eight or nine other stops, and by the time the directors of that shipping line saw that dazzling exhibit, they realized what a jewel they had in Captain Nordman.

He was immediately promoted to harbormaster at Danzig Free City.

In January, 1948, I received news from him that he and his wife had been forced to flee ahead of the Russians when the Communists took over Danzig. He took with him only what would fit in one handbag. He had forgotten my address in America in his hasty retreat, so he erroneously sent his letter to Goodyear in Cincinnati. Goodyear simply marked "No one here by that name," and sent it back to Germany.

A few months later Nordman tried the same approach again—sent the letter to Goodyear, Cincinnati, and it was returned again—"No such name here."

The Germans are a patient, persevering people so he tried it still a third time and some bright young girl down in Cincinnati simply crossed off Cincinnati, and wrote Akron and the letter came through perfectly. I have often wondered since just what we would do without bright young girls in the world who are willing to use their heads.

I realized that Nordman and his wife were experiencing extreme privation along with their neighbors. I immediately despatched CARE packages to him and pleaded to know what else I could do for him. Now this was opening the door pretty wide, but if you were to guess from here to next week, you would not guess what he asked me to send.

For the pleasure of his wife he asked for a cake of toilet soap. For himself he asked for a cake of shaving soap. Can you see the caliber of this man? I continued the CARE packages but the following May he was taken down with a kidney infection. Penicillin required considerable red tape to send out of the country at that time and before it could arrive, my good friend was dead.

Shortly after our return to Brussels that eventful day in 1925, we learned that we had been officially disqualified by the Belgium Aero Club under the rule which prohibits descending into the sea. Diametrically opposed to the reasoning and logic of that decision, the race was awarded to the Belgian Veenstra, who had not only descended into the sea, but nearly died after seven hours exposure in the sea near Punta Bruntra, Spain.

The affidavit of that landing was signed by two Spanish fishermen and read briefly as follows:

> On the 9th of June while we were fishing south of the Punta Bruntra, we have seen appear above this place a balloon from which hung a car, a balloon which was going to land towards Cune. As we had the intention to see what it was and to go on shore to pick it up and give help if possible, a sudden veering of the wind carried it off towards the sea before arriving at the said spot where we lost it out of sight, for it had then plunged in the fog. We were unable to find out to whom this balloon belonged, but we have seen an inscription like "Leopolde."

Of course we protested this decision under the rules of the contest which prohibited descending into the sea, but our protest was to no avail, being overruled. We left Brussels with bitter disappointment in our hearts and the memory of that unfair decision never has grown dim. We realized, however, that we had made our distance which was great enough to win the race by scientific methods. We knew we would be able to repeat that performance in the next International Race and demonstrate to the Belgian the rightness of our claims to the contest.

The day after the experience that nearly killed them, pilot Van Orman (center) and aide C. K. Wollam pose with Captain Rudolph Nordman, captain of the German steamer, the S.S. *Vaterland*. It was the first time in history that a balloon had landed on a moving steamer at night. The Goodyear team flew the longest distance in this 1925 Gordon Bennett struggle from Brussels, but was disqualified because landing on shipboard was not considered "landing on land."

## • 17 •

# We Spook Some Cotton Field Folks

With the demonstration of our claims in the Belgian race in mind, we entered the National Race held in Little Rock, Arkansas, the following spring. The weather conditions at the start seemed ideal. To the southeast of us over central Alabama was a large fair weather area. To the north of us over central Wisconsin was an elongated storm area. Obviously it would be a simple matter to work our way northward to the storm center and obtain the advantages of the high speed wind in the area.

Walter Morton, my aide on this flight, gave the impression of a high-strung racehorse tearing at the bridle, eager for the start.

After perfect conditions during the inflation, we left the ground fifth in line at 5:20 pm, starting northeast towards Missouri. At 6:20 pm we were two miles south of Jacksonville, Arkansas, making about fifteen miles per hour at 1,200 feet. At 7:06 pm we were over Ward, Arkansas, and at 7:45 pm tuned in our first radio station, WHO, at Des Moines for a weather report.

As the sun dropped in the west the desirable air currents were closer to the ground. We descended until our basket rode within fifty feet of the treetops. Of course this low altitude required constant vigilance. The vast expanses of pine forests over which we flew appeared to pass rapidly and our speed increased slowly, now averaging eighteen and a half miles per hour.

At 10:00 pm we tuned in WJZ, New York City, and listened to a message from David Sarnoff of the Radio Corporation of America, speaking on the history of ballooning and the value of the radio equipment to the flyer. It seemed absolutely incredible to me that there were no wires connecting us with New York City yet through the stillness of that night, Mr. Sarnoff's message reached us with perfect clarity.

Following the message we received a press report which claimed that we had dropped four bags of ballast on starting from Little Rock. The interpretation put on this move was that we planned to fly at particularly high altitudes. This scoop proved highly amusing to us at that moment because we were flying fifty feet above the trees.

At 11:00 pm as we passed near Hoxie, our speed increased to twenty miles per hour. A few moments later the radio station reported that one balloon had been sighted over Walnut Bridge. The reception quality of the radio seemed particularly fine outside of a slight bit of static. We were able to tune in three Los Angeles stations, several stations on the east coast near New York, also stations in Boston, Florida, Texas, Minnesota and Mexico City.

Shortly after 1:00 am we sighted an immense barn on fire. As we were going to pass directly over it, we threw over a half bag of sand which increased our altitude to 500 feet. As we passed over the fire we counted some fifty automobiles and could see the spectators watching the destruction of the barn. Making no sound whatever, our balloon glided unseen over this scene and into the darkness like a specter.

At 2:00 am we crossed the Mississippi River about ten miles south of Cairo, Illinois, and noted a rather sudden change in wind direction from northeast to east. Later that morning as we flew low over the hills of central Kentucky we noticed several black children playing in the yard around their cabin. Being quite low we shouted down to them, "Where are we?" but were greeted in return by their terrified screams. Some children scampered for the house and others to the nearest shed, obviously scared out of their wits.

As the heat from the morning sun increased, we gradually rose higher until we reached an altitude of 10,000 feet. There, our troubles seemed only to begin and instead of making any appreciable headway, we bounced up and down in the unstable air produced by cumulus clouds. For a period of three hours Mort and I fought this condition, using up our ballast like it was going out of style. Our gas supply likewise dwindled. When it seemed certain that this would force us to land early in the evening, we struck an exceedingly stable current at 7,000 feet which again started us rapidly towards the east at thirty-five miles per hour.

Somewhat to our surprise, we found the first range of the Appalachian Mountains exceedingly high—some 6,000 feet at various points.

Approaching the boundary of West Virginia and Virginia, we could see several forest fires burning vigorously on the mountain slopes beneath us. The little mining villages, nestled in the valleys of the mountain, seemed particularly depressing, consisting of fifteen or twenty cabins clustered around the blackened mine area.

We cheered up when we passed over the last range of mountains and dropped down to 2,000 feet altitude, flying straight down the Shenandoah Valley. At 5:20 pm the second evening we identified the town of Wytheville, reading the name on a garage about two miles away by means of our high-powered binoculars. The rest of that evening we continued to make satisfactory speed. Since we were approaching the coast, we shut off the radio set and manned a sharp look-out for the first signs of the Atlantic, particularly the lighthouses along Chesapeake Bay.

At 12:55 am I sighted our first lighthouse and wakened Mort. Knowing the swampy condition of the country ahead, we decided to play safe by not flying to the water's edge. Deliberately sacrificing a possible additional run of twenty miles, we swung down for a landing at 1:03 am coming to rest in a cotton field eight miles southeast of Petersburg, Virginia.

The ground wind was particularly quiet so we deflated our balloon by valving the gas through the valve in the top. As the balloon swayed gently in this cotton field, the door of a cabin about a hundred yards away opened and banged shut several times. One could almost see eyes peering out the opening of the door.

Finishing our work I stepped over to the door of the cabin in hopes of locating a telephone, and knocked vigorously. After ten minutes it was evident that either no one was at home or the occupants had no intention of answering my knocks. Returning to the craft, Morton and I curled up underneath the fabric of our balloon which now lay deflated on the cotton field and awaited the first rays of dawn.

At sun-up we were thoroughly chilled and had just started to build a fire when a white-haired Negro stepped out of the cabin and crossed the field towards us. He greeted us by asking, "Say, boss, did you all come down in that there machine last night?" I said, "We did," and explained to him that I had banged at the door of the cabin but received no response.

Sensing his probable fear, I said, "Say, weren't you a bit scared when you saw this balloon waving in your cotton field?" With obviously forced courage the old Negro replied, "No sir, boss, I wasn't scared—by my wife sure turned white!"

Our equipment was expressed back to Akron. We also learned that we had won the race making 848 miles against our nearest competitor's 635 miles. The satisfaction from this victory came largely from the knowledge that our method of scientific ballooning was again working perfectly and we would be in better shape than ever to compete in the approaching International Race from Belgium.

This was to be the opportunity of redeeming ourselves from the questionable disqualification of the previous year.

Belgian balloonist Ernest DeMuyter (with mustache in front of basket) is shown at the international race in 1925. DeMuyter was Van Orman's most formidable European opponent throughout his racing career.

## . 18 .

# Insulting a Messenger of Good Tidings

We again shipped our craft to Antwerp, the scene of the 1926 starting point. The S. S. *George Washington* was our ship and, as usual, we concentrated on the problem of astronomical navigation under Captain Cunningham. By the time we had reached Plymouth we were working again to the accuracy of six miles with our aircraft sextant and predicting its usefullness in the upcoming race.

The ship's navigation officer became most interested in aeronautics and went to the extent of getting up at 4:00 am to bid us goodbye at Cherbourg, where we disembarked. I recall very distinctly Captain Cunningham's parting advice, which was that Commander Byrd had demonstrated his ability in flying over the North Pole while we were at sea. Captain Cunningham, himself, had demonstrated the capabilities of the *George Washington* by breaking all records on the eastbound trip. He pointed out that it was now up to us to show what we could do with our balloon when we flew from Antwerp.

Just outside that city the balloons were inflated on the Wilryk Plain Military Training Ground as furious rain squalls whipped men and balloons alike. It seemed our craft would be dashed to pieces on the ground. Yet Morton and I felt absolutely confident of a blue-ribbon performance once we got in the air—*if* we got into the air.

We were twenty-seven minutes late in starting, but succeeded in making a most satisfactory beginning, ascending immediately to 800 feet and commencing in a northeast direction over Antwerp. Before leaving the ground we had seen five balloons wrecked during the squalls and

111

knew that only fourteen of the nineteen scheduled starters could possibly take the air.

Over Antwerp it became increasingly evident that in our northeasterly course we might have to skirt the Zuider Zee, the southern edge of the North Sea and possibly even the Baltic. We felt little concerned about these over-water flights for in our wicker basket we carried waterproof covers which really converted the basket into a boat. In addition to this, "L" shaped pontoons were basket-mounted. Nevertheless, as we well knew by this time, a water landing, in race terms, was paramount to disqualification and total failure. It was to be avoided short of death.

We ascended to 2,500 feet, swinging more to an easterly direction. This gave us positive assurance that we would not miss Norway. At 5:30 pm we crossed the frontier of Holland, and, as usual, it seemed when approaching Holland our troubles began. Two years previously we had encountered the trouble with the Dutch farmer over the peas we had destroyed. Just the year before we learned we had been disqualified for descending into the sea when the S. S. *Vaterland* had landed us at Rotterdam.

So as we now proceeded across this colorful land it was not totally unexpected that we should encounter more difficulty. Torrents of rain screamed about our ears. I mentioned earlier that to keep a balloon in equilibrium it is merely necessary to throw overboard a few handfuls of sand. But on this particular night, it required constant efforts of both of us to keep the machine up.

We were far from particular in attempting to maintain a set altitude. We were simply struggling very desperately to keep the craft from being driven down into the canals which criss-cross Holland. We threw over ballast by the thirty-pound bags as rapidly as humanly possible.

Usually when one wants to descend he simply pulls the valve allowing a certain amount of gas to escape. On this particular night, valving worked exactly opposite. The rain falling on top of the balloon produced a large depression around the valve which quickly filled with water. Upon opening the valve, the water fell fifty-three feet to the bottom of the bag with a terrific crash, running out the appendix and drenching us to the skin. Some of the water, of course, fell outside the basket and thus by valving the balloon, we actually caused it to *rise*!

The next few hours were simply a nightmare. The rain was costing us a terrific amount of ballast and at that rate it was quite evident we should only be able to last a few hours.

In addition, our balloon was gradually working to higher altitudes as the amount of rain which fell decreased. The temperature hovered around the freezing point and icicles hung like poised daggers from our rigging. At each slight rise or fall of the balloon, the expansion and contraction of the gas would cause the giant bag to crack and snap as if it were going to shatter like glass at any moment. Gradually, however, the rain ceased and by midnight we were 12,000 feet into the black night having made excellent speed towards the northeast.

And then there was something else. It was absolutely necessary to determine our location and yet the odds appeared great. Our detailed maps of Europe showing the railroads and the rivers were utterly useless when we couldn't see fifteen feet ahead or even the balloon over our heads. In addition, our splendid aircraft sextant was valueless, since it was impossible to pick out any of the stars or planets on such a night.

It seems in times of difficulty we have always turned to our radio set, and so in the inky darkness of this night at some 12,000 feet altitude I opened up the radio set and must confess my heart sank. It was drenched in water and the moisture had even condensed on the dials and rheostats on the front. I thought the set would be inoperable under the circumstances, but for thoroughness sake I turned the dials and to my surprise and delight, it worked—the first station we received was Berlin, Germany.

By maneuvering the loop of our radio carefully, we found Berlin which came in on a line east and west. The second station we received was Bremen, Germany. We found Bremen was particularly strong and on a line running southwest and northeast. Theoretically, of course, the intersection of these two lines would represent our location. However, too much was at stake to accept this position as final, so we tried a third station and found the only other station on the air at that time was Madrid, Spain. While some Spanish orchestra in Madrid played the true Spanish *Valencia*, we found our line from Madrid and laid it down on the map, delighted to note its intersection coincided with the intersection of the other two bearings. We were positive then that two miles southwest of us was Bremen, Germany.

A few minutes later a sudden contraction of the gas caused the balloon to descend rapidly and as we broke through the last layer of clouds at about an altitude of 500 feet, we gazed on a large and beautiful city beneath us. It required but a single glance at the river which ran to the northwest to identify this city as Bremen, proving the accuracy of our radio compass.

I felt the necessity for one of us to catch a little sleep and asked Morton to see if he couldn't get some shut-eye. He curled up in the little bed four feet long and two feet wide and soon dropped off. We were flying in an altitude of 600 feet and our maps showed the German territory over which we were flying to have an altitude of 180 feet, indicating we were clearing the ground by at least 480 feet.

Everything seemed to be going perfectly when the "wee small voice" whispered in my ear, "Look!" Immediately I flashed the flashlight over the edge of the basket and saw that we were within five seconds of crashing into the side of a hill at fifty miles per hour. Too late, of course, to throw ballast and clear it, so I grabbed Morton and shouted, "Hang on!"

Morton, roused from a sound sleep, did not attempt to rise from the bed, but grabbed the supporting ropes of the basket and braced himself for the shock. The pontoons absorbed a great portion of the violent blow and the basket staggered under the impact, bounding upward, clearing the top of the hill. Our jolted craft rose valiantly to 1,000 feet.

The radio compass location and resultant direction in which we were traveling showed we had two alternatives. One was to stay low and swing east of Germany; the other was to go fairly high and traverse the Baltic towards Finland. Both Morton and I felt positive it would be necessary to put the Baltic between us and Antwerp in order to win the race.

So we chose the Baltic.

Our ballast supply was hardly encouraging but we felt confident that we could reach land somewhere along the Baltic, even if we had to descend to bounce along the waves on our water equipment.

I did not want to *ask* Morton if he wanted to fly the Baltic with me for fear he might interpret that question as an indication of doubt in my mind. I also knew full well that if I wished to cross it, Morton was with me one hundred percent. For that reason we never even discussed the safety of doing the thing.

Indeed, one would have thought we were crossing the Mississippi River as we left the shore of the Baltic near Bolton Hagen, Germany. We could see little ferry boats bouncing up and down in the waves which lashed furiously at their hulls. Around the horizon in the light of early morning, we counted nineteen separate and distinct rain squalls, all of which seemed to connive to shed rain on our craft. But it appeared good fortune was with us for we succeeded in evading every one of these squalls.

In one case we plummeted from 12,000 feet to within 500 feet of the water and lost much of our precious sand to curb our fall. It was soon obvious that our ballast supply would only last for a short time and we would have to change our course to avoid running at least 400 miles further over the Baltic Sea to Finland, which was our present direction.

As we concentrated on our weather maps, it seemed evident that if we ascended to 22,000 feet, we should find a current which would swing us north and land us in Sweden. We did this and after a two-hour run we had crossed the shore line of Sweden near Ahus. Fifteen minutes later we were completely out of ballast.

We dropped downward rather rapidly and used part of the remaining equipment to check our fall but had little success in slowing our drop. We came to earth in a truck garden, rebounded up into a telephone pole, severing it from its wires, and dropping with it to the ground.

In a few minutes a large crowd of Swedish peasants gathered and tried to assist us in packing up our equipment. After securing an interpreter, we made excellent progress in packing, then loaded our gear into a typical Swedish farm wagon which was to take us into Solvesberg. As we left the field, looking towards the east, I was surprised at our proximity to the Baltic. Less than a half mile towards the coast was one of the Swedish lighthouses along the northwestern shore of the Baltic.

In other words one might say we had made Sweden by half a mile!

It was all most interesting. The experience of driving along the country roads to Solvesberg was so pleasantly curious because the country was so different from America. Two miles beyond where we landed we saw acres upon acres of fields covered with granite boulders fifteen to twenty feet high. Morton expressed himself in no uncertain terms on the hazards of landing in such a field. We passed also through endless miles of pine forests. At the farm houses the children stared at us—those peculiarly dressed foreigners riding on top of a strange basket on a wagon!

They evidently were so awestricken by this awkward sight that they forgot to make their little curtsy to the strangers passing their home. Passing the second farm house, Morton and I recognized this custom and made it a point to stare rather fixedly at each child, and in each case were rewarded by the forgotten curtsy.

Arriving at Solvesborg we found the official greeting of the Swedish government waiting for us. The chief of police was standing in the center of the road at the edge of the square with his right hand extended. However, instead of reaching forward for the traditional handshake, he had it extended upward—the international "stop sign."

He insisted that I get off the wagon and escorted me personally to the village jail. Here I found the manager of the power company, whose pole we had knocked down, awaiting me with a receipt for $25.00 already written out for the damage done to his telephone pole.

It was an *outrageous* price! Telephone poles probably sold for $5.00 and the labor of replacing the pole would likely be the same amount. I protested vigorously through an interpreter at such flagrant robbery, pointing out at the same time that we were perfectly willing to settle for damages incurred. The chief of police was very stubborn and he reinforced his authority with the threat that unless I paid the $25.00, we should have to work it out in jail. Through the efforts of Charles Heisler, American Consul, we settled the bill for $10.00.

Morton the next day was particularly blue and disheartened. By scaling the maps we could see we had made eight hundred and fifty kilometers or about 530 miles. To him it was a terrible run in the International Race. We had set our hearts on a win. I pointed out statistics of previous races, showing him that under the weather conditions in which we had flown, which were the most severe imaginable, races had been won with only four hundred kilometers. Morton simply couldn't believe we had made a good showing and his discouragement appeared irreversible.

About that time we received a phone call from our Goodyear manager in Stockholm and he said, "I'm sending over the nearest Goodyear dealer who can speak English." Indeed he did send over a fine Goodyear fellow, Tom Freuchen, who was trained in Sweden to be a diplomat. At dinner the splendid chap started with a considerable amount of soda and hardly a trace of scotch which quickly progressed to far less soda and more liberal amounts of scotch. With the fourth or fifth round of drinks, his diplomat's English deteriorated and with the conclusion of dinner, it had flown altogether out the window.

Morton and I excused ourselves so that we might wander about the picturesque village.

An unusual event happened when we were in a hardware store buying a can of oil to remove the rust from our instruments. A short, heavy-set man walked into the store. He approached us and started to talk to me rapidly in Swedish. He had on a dark blue serge suit, carried an umbrella over his arm and had a squatty derby hat on his head. For some reason or other he had singled me out and talked excitedly in Swedish. After he talked awhile he appeared to grow so excited that he jumped up and down!

Having no knowledge of the Swedish language, I gave him the courtesy of listening patiently for ten minutes, after which Morton and I turned our backs on him and walked out. He followed us into shops and out of shops. He would take off his hat and put his unbrella over his arm and stand wistfully in the corner looking at us much in the manner of a faithful dog.

The situation finally became boresome, however, and we decided to hunt up the interpreter of the previous day's session at the chief of police's office. Anticipating that the man with the derby hat was a representative of the chief of police and was about to bother us again over some detail or other, I requested our interpreter to tell him that we had *paid* for the telephone pole. To further inform him that our passports had been visaed and our balloon had been cleared through the customs and also was now in transit to Antwerp—and that we were not going to be bothered by the chief of police again!

Initiating his conversation with this statement, our interpreter asked the man with the derby hat what he wanted. His reaction was totally opposite from what I anticipated, for he smiled and looked extremely happy. Then he began talking very rapidly again, finally repeating that jumping up and down business. Our interpreter also became very excited and we had the suspense of watching these two apparently half-witted Swedes hop up and down in glee while they discussed some matter of great importance. Finally, after the most terrible suspense, the interpreter gave us the message.

Our branch manager in Stockholm had communicated with the man with the derby hat and had asked him to give us his congratulations and the message—

**YOU HAVE WON THE INTERNATIONAL BALLOON RACE, EVEN DOUBLING THE DISTANCE OF YOUR NEAREST FOREIGN COMPETITOR, LIEUTENANT DEMUYTER.**

The news was too much for Morton to believe. He insisted that he get the official telegram from the Aero Club of Belgium before he would leave the little village. Even with the gray telegram in his hands, signed by the Aero Club of Belgium, Morton could hardly realize it had actually happened.

We hurriedly returned to Belgium, hoping to fly from Copenhagen to Brussels by plane, but the weather reports indicated rain and as we had had ample experience with that to last us quite some time, we elected to take the train.

Upon arriving at Brussels, Ambassador Phillips advised us that King Albert had expressed his desire to have us presented to him at the Royal Palace. Of course we were delighted with this signal honor, and with the late Captain Gray of the United States Army and his assistant, Captain Johnson, Morton and I went towards the Palace with Ambassador Phillips.

The Ambassador expressed some anxiety as to whether the King would receive us in the cold Gold Room, which he reserved for the strictly formal occasions, and, I presume, the socially ambitious, or would he receive us in his little private office to which Ambassador Phillips had entrée. Ambassador Phillips was particularly delighted when we were ushered into His Majesty's presence in his little private room where one could observe the monarch's drafting instruments, slide rules and books on engineering, scattered comfortably over the desk and table as in any engineer's office.

Being an engineer myself, it was quite evident that King Albert had also been educated in that profession. He was vitally interested in aeronautics, owning his own private airplane. He was also keenly interested in possible transatlantic service by zeppelin. In addition he was cognizant of the splendid work of the United States Weather Bureau and commended them highly on their efficient organization. Altogether we spent some forty minutes discussing aeronautics and meteorology with King Albert.

During this time I noticed Morton was terribly uncomfortable. Beads of perspiration stood out on his brow. I felt sure that the presentation to King Albert could not, in itself, be the cause of such misery and it was not until we bade King Albert farewell that I learned the real source of Morton's trouble. The door had hardly closed upon us before Morton tore open the vest of his borrowed Prince Albert and with a sigh of relief exclaimed, "My vest is about four sizes too small for me and I simply couldn't breathe!"

Ambassador Phillips later expressed himself as being unusually delighted with our presentation. It seems King Albert was a rather poor conversationalist and it is usually the responsibility of the Ambassador to keep the conversation flowing smoothly. In addition a presentation usually lasted only five minutes and so we likewise shared the satisfaction of Ambassador Phillips. It was a fact, also, that due to the King's splendid training, personality and his courage shown during World War I, that he quickly became one of the best loved European monarchs.

Following the presentation, a series of banquets followed in Brussels, sponsored by the American Ambassador, the Aero Club and other organizations. More banquets in Paris, sponsored by the late Ambassador Myron T. Herrick and even on the steamship home. Later in New York and Akron the celebrations continued.

But once more the tremendous satisfaction which we had in winning the International Race was that our methods of ballooning were correct, and that the ambition of many years of effort and preparation had been achieved.

By virtue of winning the International Race we had brought the Gordon Bennett trophy back to America for the first time in thirteen years. Of course in doing so we had incurred the responsibility of defending the trophy in the coming International Race to be held in Detroit.

## · 19 ·

# Fearing Collision with a Mail Plane

By virtue of winning the 1926 Gordon Bennett race Morton and I were assured of a position on the American team the next year. We did feel the desirability of keeping in practice. However, in order to official-ly compete in the approaching National Race held in Akron in mid-sum-mer, we deliberately sacrificed a guaranteed position in the international contest to again earn our wings in the summer preliminaries.

The National Race balloons were inflated in the half-mile motor speedway three miles to the north of Akron. The inflation activity took place in the almost customary foul weather consisting of heavy rain squalls and thundershowers. During the early morning of the inflation the winds were from the southeast and would carry the balloons to the northwest.

From a racing standpoint, this would be quite unsatisfactory and un-certain, but as the time of starting drew near the winds shifted to the south, finally to the southwest, and as we left the ground at 5:20 pm we knew we would run towards the northeast. A storm area immediately to the north indicated the necessity for speed in order to curve north, and that direction was of secondary importance.

Our course during the first few hours was sixty degrees east of north at the painfully slow speed of eight miles per hour. We also chose a com-promise altitude of 1,000 feet, knowing that some of the contestants might endeavor to follow our maneuver and keep in sight of us. So we waited until after dark at which time we rose to a higher altitude and dis-covered a current of twenty-one miles per hour.

At this time we were about midway between two heavy thunderstorms, one about five miles to the south of us and the other eight miles to the north of us. It required careful maneuvering to keep our balloon in the space midway between these two squalls, knowing well the hazards of approaching too close.

At 10:00 pm we were just north of Youngstown, Ohio, and beneath us we could see the flashing of the airmail beacons which dotted the path of mail planes flying from Cleveland to New York. As we were crossing this path, Morton and I were startled to hear the terrifying roar of an airplane motor. Our hair seemed to stand on end. Immediately we grasped our two flashlights and waved them frantically—I might well say hysterically—in the direction from which we thought the sound was coming.

The suspense of those few seconds was horrible. For in our mind's eye we could easily visualize this huge plane tearing through the air at 100 miles per hour, crashing itself into our balloon. But as we scanned the horizon anxiously, hoping to locate the navigation lights of the plane in time, we were helpless to ascertain its position. Instead we were attracted by the headlights of an *automobile* below, rushing down the road at tremendous speed, and what to us had been a blood-chilling sound was, in reality, the noise of that auto engine. With a sigh of relief we lay down the flashlights, realizing our danger had been entirely imaginary.

Through the static of the thunderstorms on each side of us, we managed to hear the weather reports from Cleveland radio station WTAM. The static was so severe, however, that the receiving range of our set, which under normal conditions was 3,000 miles, had now been cut down to three hundred miles. We had hoped to pick up the message of David Sarnoff from station WJZ, but had to be satisfied with only fragments due to the heavy lightning.

Keeping our altitude at about 1,500 feet, we passed over Erie, Pennsylvania, and at 4:00 am found ourselves floating above Marysville, New York.

The clouds thickened and a little patter of rain on the top of our balloon warned us of impending showers. Fortunately the precipitation quickly ended but the cloud mass grew worse and we were entirely out of sight of the ground.

At 8:00 am we estimated we were leaving the shore of Lake Ontario just to the west of Rochester. It was not possible to see the lake at any time, but we could hear the mournful crashing of waves beneath us. Our speed was increasing quite steadily and by 10:00 am we had arrived at the eastern end of Lake Ontario and soon the Adirondacks were directly below our basket.

Our visibility continued to be poor. At no time since leaving Buffalo had we been able to view the ground or even Lake Ontario. Upon reaching the mountain country it was advisable to increase our altitude which we accomplished by throwing over two bags of sand.

Our craft was getting fairly close to a thunder squall and Morton and I endeavored to fly over it. On our upward maneuver we had reached 6,000 feet when we were caught in a terrific downpour. Obviously to force our craft upward against heavy torrents of rain would require an enormous expenditure of ballast, and also we were drawing desperately close to the thunderstorm immediately ahead of us. At each flash of lightning the concussion from the thunder was so great that our balloon quivered and shook.

The experience was quite like riding over a rough road in a motor car at high speed.

Choosing what we hoped proved the minimum of the dangers and to escape the storm, we reversed our tactics allowing the heavy downpour of rain to drive us down into the mountains. We dropped our drag rope which was 250 feet in length and allowed it to drag through the trees covering the mountains. This action slowed down our speed considerably which was just what we wanted to accomplish in order to allow the deluge to drift ahead of us.

Dragging a rope in this manner of course required careful use of ballast because tree branches could easily put us out of the race. If we got caught in any trees and stopped for over ten minutes we were disqualified for stopping. So after allowing sufficient time to allow the squall ahead of us to drift some fifteen miles, we once more climbed for altitude.

We reached 2,500 feet and saw a large lake beneath us running north and south and a close scrutiny of its shoreline identified the body of water as Lake Champlain. At the higher altitudes our speed increased to forty-five miles per hour. We soon were flying above clouds at least 5,000 feet in thickness and all we could see in all directions was the sea of cloud tops.

Navigation was now of primary importance. At forty-five miles an hour we would rapidly approach the Atlantic and that made it necessary to know our position constantly and accurately to guarantee a shore landing. We did not wish to sacrifice any mileage by playing unduly safe and landing forty or fifty miles inland; on the other hand we realized the penalty of disqualification for descent into the sea.

We worked continuously now with our radio compass, first with station WGY, Schenectady, while the radio orchestra played its morning selections. This gave us a line of position running from Schenectady, but since no other radio stations were on the air at that moment, we fell back on the aircraft sextant.

When the clouds above us permitted, we measured the angle of the sun and taking the time we secured the Sumner line of position, the intersection of which with the radio compass line fixed our position. To the best of my knowledge it was probably the first time the radio compass had been used in conjunction with the astronomical method of navigation.

All through that afternoon we made splendid speed of from forty-five to fifty miles an hour, flying over Vermont, New Hampshire and Maine, using the sextant and the radio compass. We were using WJZ at New York City, WEEI at Boston, WCHS at Portland, Maine. I was saddened only by the fact that we should fly over such inspiringly beautiful mountainous country only to have our view entirely blanketed by blinding cloud cover.

At 4:50 that afternoon our last position determined by the sextant and radio compass indicated that we should commence our descent at precisely 5:25 pm in order to land at Hancock, Maine, on the shore of the Atlantic. Promptly at that time I opened the valve and we descended slowly through the mist.

The first sound to greet our ears was that of a train whistle which was most reassuring, indicating that we were over land and that our navigation had been correct. While we were enjoying to the utmost this confirmation, we were suddenly distressed to hear the whistle of a boat. Quickly I checked back through my calculations which I found to be correct and could *not* ascertain why we should be hearing a boat whistle! It was alarming!

But in the next few moments we were reassured again by the noise of an *automobile horn!* Again our spirits rose and we visualized a perfectly satisfactory landing on the shore of the Atlantic.

The balloon continued to drop quite slowly through the wet air when our doubts again rose to the surface at the putt-putt sound of a motor launch. It was not only nerve-racking, it was disheartening.

Just before we broke through the clouds, the most welcome sound which had yet reached my ears was that of a flock of song birds. I knew then positively that we were over land, that our navigation had been correct.

We broke through fog 150 feet above the ground and landed in a pasture.

Howard Young, on whose land we landed, was the first to greet us. We asked him if we had landed near Hancock, Maine. He seemed quite surprised as he looked up into the fog from which we came, and asked us how in the world we had known we were near Hancock. We explained to him our method of navigation with the radio compass and sextant.

It was then our turn to be surprised, for as we turned and looked towards the southeast of us, the direction in which we were headed, we saw the shore of the Atlantic Ocean *fifty yards away!* We had saved Mt. Desert Island to the south and east of us in which direction we would have gone, as a safeguard against possible errors in navigation.

In other words we had allowed ourselves an error of about seven miles which we felt ample. Actually we had landed within fifty yards of the calculated landing position. Such accuracy might have been accidental, of course, but I did feel that with a little care and skill, navigation above the clouds by means of the sextant could be carried out to within an accuracy of three miles.

The results of the race showed that we had covered 718 miles against the 650 miles of our nearest competitor, E. J. Hill, and 595 miles for the United States Army balloon piloted by Captain Kepner. In addition to winning the National Race for the third consecutive time we gained the permanent possession of the Litchfied Trophy. The real source of our satisfaction came from the knowledge that our method of ballooning had again stood the acid test, enabling us to navigate safely and accurately over the clouds to land on the shore of the Atlantic. That was the real test of flying blind.

The weather conditions of this race, in retrospect, were particularly interesting. The progress of the storm area which appeared slightly to the northwest of us at the start necessitated keeping abreast of it. In running too far ahead of it swung some contestants too far to the north, or dropping behind the storm as it progressed easterly caused others to swing too far to the south. The weather reports we received by radio proved of the utmost value in keeping constant tab of our position relative to the storm squalls.

In addition, the geographical features added further complications. That is, to make the greatest air distance from Akron, one had to swing well towards the northeast. Indeed, the storm area devoured those contestants who wanted to make too great a distance. The storm winds swung them too far to the north and out of the race.

By keeping abreast of the storm cells as the radio had enabled us to do, we were able to strike the happy compromise of taking the middle course through the path of the race pilots who swung too far to the south or too far the opposite direction.

Morton and I were two happy men.

Ward Van Orman (left) and Walter Morton inspect the sextant they will be using when their Goodyear balloon competes in the 1928 National Balloon Race out of Pittsburgh, Pennsylvania. The race would prove a tragedy when lightning struck the envelope, dropping the fliers to earth, killing Morton. Van Orman was to survive with a broken ankle and enter upon the study of feasible ways of curbing lightning dangers.

# Trying for Florida
# the Hard Way

With the approach of the International Gordon Bennett classic in Detroit on September 10, 1927, there arose the necessity for developing more adequate equipment, particularly a supersensitive vertical speedometer, or "vertimeter," as we named it, and also an alarm altimeter.

Before undertaking the development of the vertimeter ourselves, we endeavored to borrow this type of instrument from the Army. Due to considerable delay in the transaction, we lost patience and dug into the instrument's development on our own. The result of building our own was extremely satisfactory and our vertimeter was so sensitive that by lifting it just four feet off the ground, it would indicate the speed of ascent and descent.

To duplicate actual flight conditions, we selected one of the highest buildings in New York City to test the new instrument. Again, successful. In fact the elevator man became so interested in our instrument that he neglected to watch the floors as we passed them at express speed. The only thing that saved us from going through the roof was the fact that the car was equipped with an automatic stop.

The other much-needed instrument mentioned above was an alarm altimeter. The purpose of this appliance is easily recognized when one considers that in the past we had been forced to glue our eyes upon this control for thirty-six to forty-eight hours continuously, simply to keep our craft at a certain predetermined altitude.

The strain, of course, from this constant vigilance was pretty severe and for that reason we felt the necessity of developing the alarm altimeter, which would automatically signal when a required altitude had been reached. We took our problem to the aircraft instrument manufacturers and were surprised to learn the extremely high cost which would be involved in the manufacture.

By taking our neighborhood jeweler, who always calibrated my instruments, into our confidence, the alarm altimeter was developed as it now stands—and at very low cost, indeed. There is a moral there, I am sure, but is too sad to pursue.

The apparatus was particularly valuable, as I say, since one simply set it at a desired altitude and when that altitude was reached, the alarm indicator automatically operated a small electrical buzzer.

As an added touch of refinement, we added a small red light in case absolute silence was required while endeavoring to communicate with someone on the ground. While we never flight-tested the instrument before the International Race, we nevertheless duplicated flight conditions under vacuum representing altitudes up to 25,000 feet, normally the maximum reached in racing.

Our balloon was shipped to Detroit and prepared for inflation at the Ford Airport. A preliminary study of the weather conditions on the day of the race indicated we had an excellent opportunity for making a run northeasterly up the St. Lawrence River valley, possibly landing somewhere near Lake St. John or the Straits of Belle Isle. The winds were motivated by a storm area located over Chicago and Lake Michigan.

Morton and I were in particularly high spirits because our favorite direction was a northeast run. About three o'clock that afternoon we were disconcerted to note that the winds had shifted suddenly from the southwest into the northwest. We were slightly handicapped during the afternoon by showers and gusty wind conditions but succeeded in keeping all of our equipment perfectly dry.

By the time we were ready for the starter's gun (or cannon in this instance) our balloon was in perfect condition and Morton and I stepped into the basket confident of making an excellent run in the race and defending American ballooning honors in proper fashion.

The first balloon to take off was the Spanish *Hispania* piloted by Major Maldenade. He was assisted by the late Major Molas, who later lost his life in an altitude flight in Spain. Five minutes later the Italian balloon took off, followed by the English balloon and in turn by the German balloon.

Morton and I started fifth, leaving the ground to the second at 4:20 pm ascending to an altitude of 5,000 feet and beginning in an east-south-east direction.

Upon ascending, we looked down on the airport to see the thousands of cars that were congested on the roadway. We felt that ballooning was the most satisfactory method of transportation from the airport that particular afternoon. In a very short time all of the balloons were airborne—four ahead of us and ten stretched behind us in an almost straight line.

Fifteen minutes after we were in the air, it was evident that the possibility of getting up into Canada had passed. The storm area had traveled so rapidly that we were now to the rear of it and our course would be either south or southeast. Looking over the geographical situation at the same time, it was obvious that to make the maximun direction from Detroit we should select as our objective some point on the peninsula of Florida.

It was likewise just as evident that if one were carried too far towards the east, his flight would be terminated by the Atlantic Ocean in the states of Virginia, North or South Carolina. For that reason we were particularly careful to select those currents which would carry us south and south only.

We noticed the Belgian balloon, piloted by our old nemesis, Lieutenant DeMuyter, passing us at a higher altitude, but neither Morton nor I were much alarmed at this stage of the race, knowing full well that he probably would be carried too far to the east in his effort to secure maximum speed rather than the most favorable direction.

At about 6:10 pm the yellow German balloon which had been trailing us a few hundred yards had evidently located a slightly faster current and passed directly underneath us. At that particular moment Morton said, with a twinkle in his eye, "Let's drop a sandbag on them!" indicating it would be a simple and effective way of putting one contestant out of the race.

It turned out later that the pilot of this balloon became excited over a thunder squall in the distance and landed on Sugar Island near the mouth of the Detroit River.

Shortly before dusk we started out over the waters of Lake Erie and by a peculiar coincidence, Cleveland station WTAM was playing "Muddy Waters." We were now flying at an altitude of 800 feet in stable air. Beneath us, eight large boats loaded with iron ore were visible on the glistening waters. As we passed directly over them we were greeted with the deep bass whistles and the mad waving of their crews.

Our direction now swung more and more to the south. On the southern horizon we carefully watched a thunderstorm flashing away and illuminating huge banks of clouds about twenty miles away.

Fascinating, indeed!

Beneath us we could pick out the little islands which dotted Lake Erie at that particular point. Our balloon passed directly midway over the Middle and Double Sister Island and over Middle Bass and Pelee Island. At nine o'clock we could discern in the southwest the flashing of a lighthouse and by the timing of these flashes by stop watches and referring to our list of lighthouses, we readily identified it as Marblehead, Ohio.

Shortly after crossing the shore line, lights of a large number of motor cars flashed in a brilliant nocturnal scene. Quite obviously it was the main highway between Cleveland, Toledo and Detroit.

We tuned our radio set into WJW at Detroit and listened to the weather reports given by C. G. Andruss, who was again the special representative of the weather bureau. These reports confirmed our decision to fly towards Florida.

We listened to several other radio stations, getting reports and checking our chronometers to have the exact time for use in making stellar observations.

About midnight we passed over a very large city in central Ohio but were unable to identify it at the moment, for none of the electric signs indicated its name. Finally we did, however, see a familiar windmill sign which is used by one of the chain restaurants in the midwest.

From that we were able to identify the city of Columbus, Ohio. The rest of the night the thunderstorm boomed and flashed some twenty miles ahead of us so we were rather careful not to make sufficient speed as to overtake it.

Dawn found us crossing the Ohio River at Vanceburg, Kentucky. It was a simple matter to check this town by the "U" shaped bend which was located in the river at that point. About eight o'clock that morning we were greeted with the usual Kentucky welcome consisting of several rifle shots, evidently from some mountaineer who decided to see if he couldn't bring down that small balloon which he saw in the air. Fortunately we were flying at 5,000 feet, somewhat out of range for squirrel guns.

Being Sunday morning, Morton and I had the pleasure of tuning our radio to the Cincinnati station WLF and thoroughly enjoyed one of the church services from that station at an altitude of 8,000 feet. At noon we received the latest weather information from the morning observations.

Florida still looked good.

We were getting into rugged country and required sextant observations on the sun. Our 12:30 pm observation indicated we were at a latitude of 37 degrees - 30' north and at a longitude of 83 degrees - 25' west, which would put us somewhere near the little village of Netty, Kentucky.

As the afternoon progressed, the topography became still more pronounced and for some peculiar reason our radio seemed to lose its efficiency. We had always depended upon it for our radio compass work, but it was quite evident that if it continued to decrease in efficiency at the rate it had then between 12:30 and 2:30 pm, it would soon become useless.

At 2:30 pm we started over the range of the Big Black Mountains near the border of Kentucky and Virginia. At 4:30 pm we again located our position, near Pilot Hill, Tennessee, in the eastern portion of that state at the junction of the Great Smoky Mountains and the Bald Mountains.

Those peaks loomed up ahead of us, some of which extended to 4,700 feet above sea level. At five o'clock we had reached the plateau on which Asheville, North Carolina is located. To the west we could see the Pisgah River in the distance, but our progress was slowing. We had been running fifteen to twenty miles per hour. Now we had dropped to twelve.

As the evening progressed our direction had swung still further into the south and at nine o'clock we were crossing the Blue Ridge Mountains on the border of North and South Carolina. At ten o'clock we ran into a most unusual condition. The wind had dropped down to eight miles per hour and there was some difficulty in making progress consistently toward our Florida objective.

On one occasion while skimming the top of a mountain peak, a downward current swept us into the valley. We succeeded in running up the opposite slope only to be caught in a vertical current at the top and carried upward where we collided with an opposing current. Our balloon was then actually carried backward and hurled down again, nearly touching the original peak over which we had just flown.

For a period of three hours Morton and I used every strategy known to balloonists to stop this loop-the-loop business. We had attempted the higher altitudes, ascending as high as 10,000 feet, and also the lower altitudes, but it seemed impossible to force our craft out of that peculiar swirl of air. We continued to go around and around in a vertical loop. In effect, we were making absolutely no progress and it seemed ages in the clutches of that damnable current—looping-the-loop all this time, taking at least fifteen minutes to complete each loop.

Finally at 1:00 am by some unknown maneuver, we managed to get out of this local condition and continued flying—making five and six miles per hour toward the south. The stars that night were particularly bright and there was little difficulty in checking our position by using Jupiter for longitude and Polaris for latitude.

At dawn we looked down on western South Carolina and our sextant observations enabled us to identify our location as Basley, South

Carolina at 7:15 am. All night long our radio set was absolutely useless. For some unknown reason, practically all stations were blocked out.

Considering our slow speed, Morton and I concluded that the race would be exceedingly close for all contestants and if we simply flew the usual forty-eight hours which is the normal endurance of this type racing craft, we would have no outstanding chance of winning the race.

We had specifically designed our balloon for endurance and felt that by staying in the air through the third night, we could win the race. Two nights in the air had already elapsed and we were now rapidly approaching Georgia. If, with the very light winds which were now carrying us along, we could stay in the air the third night, we would not only win the race, but also break the American endurance record.

Admiring this plan, we had worked to save our ballast as carefully as possible. Our Goodyear balloon crossed the Savannah River near McCormick, Georgia, at 11:00 am.

At noon we were within twenty miles of Augusta and a check on our ballast supply indicated that we undoubtedly would be able to fly through the third night. At 1:00 pm the balloon ascended to 13,000 feet and by 3:00 pm we were flying over Wadley, Georgia.

Somewhere beneath us, the roar of an airplane motor was heard. Looking down we sighted the aircraft flying several thousand feet beneath us. Later we learned that this plane had taken off at Wadley to ascertain the name of the balloon flying over the city, but inasmuch as the plane had a ceiling of only 7,000 feet while we were floating at 13,000 feet, it failed in its objective.

It was particularly trying that afternoon flying at the high altitude with the Georgia sun beating down upon us. It burned severely, while in the shade it was acutally cold due to the thirty degree temperature encountered at this altitude. Then, too, even with the use of oxygen, breathing was difficult and it was simply a question of human endurance as to how long we could last at this altitude. The only consolation we had was that we were conserving ballast and would definitely survive the third night.

Eventually the sun disappeared in the west and sufficient ballast to fly fifteen more hours was in the basket.

Although weary of body from the fifty-one hours already spent in the air, Morton and I were enthusiastic and overjoyed at the prospects of breaking the American endurance record and attaining victory by landing in Florida. We both were sure that almost within reach we had another victory in this International Race.

But it seemed fate would have it otherwise. At 7:45 pm of the third night we were startled to notice that a tremendous heat thunderstorm had developed ahead of us. By timing the intervals between the lightning flashes and the concussion reaching our ears, we estimated the storm to be one and a half miles away. The situation was simply heartbreaking. Morton looked at me and I looked at Morton with the realization that either we would be forced to land immediately or take a tremendous risk in passing through the heart of the squall. The decision was quite simple. We had victory in our grasp if we wished to pay the price, but the price possibly would be our lives.

It was out of reason.

We immediately prepared to land and swung down to within 500 feet of the ground, bringing the balloon to rest in a corn field a mile and a half north of Adrian, Georgia. In a very few minutes large crowds of spectators clustered around the machine. Since the field was too rough for deflation, the crowd carried our balloon half a mile down the road to a meadow where we proceeded to vent the gas from the big sphere.

The ground wind was so gentle that there was no difficulty in doing so. When the envelope no longer supported the basket, Morton and I stepped around to pull the bag over on its side in order to remove the valve and accelerate the deflation process.

While thus occupied, the crowd, seeing it was our intention to pack up the balloon, thought they would assist and so disconnected the foot ropes of the net from the load ring. This, of course, opens up the bottom of the net. The first indication of what had happened was given by the sliding of the envelope out of the net and we shouted to the crowd, "Hands off!" feeling that someone might possibly become entangled in the net and be carried into the sky. The envelope then slipped free from the net, starting rapidly upward, disappearing in the southwest and into the thunderstorm which had forced us down within sight of victory.

It was rather disappointing to lose our balloon under such conditions but I felt that since the valve had been removed from it, it would land within a few miles. With heavy hearts we packed the remaining equipment and carried it into the town of Adrian where we spent the night.

Acting entirely upon a hunch early the next morning, I visited the telephone exchange and asked permission to use their office to make out our reports, landing certificates, etc. In the back of my mind I felt in a very short time we should have word of our lost balloon. True to the inspiration, the telephone rang at 10:15 and a farmer living ten miles to the southeast at Gilly Springs advised the operator that a balloon had been found on his farm. It was a simple matter to motor over to the spot, pack up our lost equipment and prepare it for shipment.

Morton and I knew we had made a good run in the race but not sufficiently outstanding to give us a decisive victory. The official results confirmed our opinion. E. J. Hill of Detroit, one of the American contestants, landed fifty-seven miles to the south of us at Baxley, Georgia, entirely out of ballast at the time. Mr. Hugo Kaulen of Germany came in second, landing three miles ahead of us at Fort Valley, Georgia, and we came in third.

While it was disappointing not to have won the race, it was pleasing to learn that the contest was retained in America by virtue of Hill's victory. Our greatest satisfaction arose from the fact that our method of ballooning had made it possible to have gained the victory had we been willing to pay the price, which we were not.

One of the foreign contestants was particularly disgruntled with the race in general. Although the inflation only took twelve hours as contrasted with thirty-six and forty-eight required abroad, he still maintained that the gas supply pipes were too small. Likewise, he resented the curiosity of the newspapermen who were naturally anxious to extend the foreigner every courtesy.

To quote just one of his comments which appeared in the foreign press following the International Race, this pilot said, "Though there were long articles in the newspaper about my aide and myself with our pictures, we were hardly allowed time to put our balloon in shape and for this the arrangements were miserable. I am compelled to say this in spite of acknowledgement of our hearty reception in the press. We got all of our information second or even third hand."

"We first received the official program with all of the other spectators on the starting field. There was no meeting place for the pilots to discuss the weather conditions. We had to sign papers until we got cramps in our fingers. I do not know whether I was always pleased but too much is too much. What really surprised me, however, in this land of unlimited possibility, was that in spite of the deficient preparations the starting of fifteen balloons went off so well."

These criticisms, of course, were written after this pilot had returned to Europe, so we naturally did not have opportunity to make an official reply. However, we learned that in the next year's contest this same contestant was taken in hand by the foreign ambassador at Detroit and evidently reformed.

And things are eventually equalized. It seems that in that second contest which followed, his balloon landed in a tree near Lynchburg, Virginia, about midnight. This contestant, thinking he was on the ground, and with the possible obstruction of his view by his large beard, looked over the edge of the basket, saw everything apparently clear and stepped into thin air. He landed several feet below in a heap, spraining his ankle.

# • 21 •

# Friend Morton is
# Struck Dead

This is certainly the saddest chapter to write, even after forty-eight long years have come and gone since the terrible event happened.

I think the best way to begin the story is through the eyes of someone else; through the eyes of a shrewd and experienced competitor in balloon racing—Captain William E. Kepner. The following adventure story of that awesome race in its entirety, and what happened to the Goodyear balloon, later appeared in the Sunday Magazine of the *Omaha World Herald* on January 11, 1931.

Bill Kepner won not only the National Race of 1928 which he here describes, he also went to on represent America in the Gordon Bennett Race held once again in Detroit the same year—and again emerged victorious.

The following is how Captain Kepner remembers the terrible ballooning tragedy of 1928:

> The day broke cloudy, then overcast, with an occasional spit of rain to dampen the ardor of the fourteen pilots and equal number of aides. The great day of the national elimination balloon race had dawned—none too fair! As each contestant earnestly scanned the sky, he no doubt wondered what the day would hold for him. Fourteen giant gas bags were being spread out on their respective starting places with all the care that could be given them.
>
> Preparation is equally as important as the race—it is indirectly responsible for all the success. While the balloon is being inflated, the pilots and aides are also busy gathering supplies and studying maps. The weather on this day, May 31, 1928, promised a trip to the northeast. This was ideal as to

direction and distance. From Pittsburgh, any direction north of east would give more than 400 miles with the possibility of the Maine coast offering 600 miles.

We all congratulated ourselves. The sky was clearing, too. That meant an ideal race. But by noon conditions were less encouraging, though certainly there was scant warning of the terrible experience we were to undergo. The sun was even shining through occasionally. Our balloon, the *Army No. One*, was starting ninth. Lieutenant Erickson, my aide, and I were ready early and watched two civilian balloons and then Lieutenant Paul Evert, with Lieutenant U. G. Ent as his aide, take off in five minute intervals.

As we watched Evert ascend in a perfect sail-off, little did we dream that he was to lie a couple hours later dead from lightning, his balloon on fire—the hydrogen in imminent danger of exploding before the courageous Ent could land himself and Evert's body!

Van Orman took off No. 5. Within two hours, Van's beautiful balloon was to go up in smoke at an altitude of 2,000 feet, leaving the basket with Van unconscious and Morton dead to hurtle downward to the ground. Finally our turn came. We were next. We hoped to win but there were thirteen other balloons and they were all manned by good pilots. The team that won this race would certainly be entitled to the victory. Five forty-five! At last the starter's signal. And we were off. In a perfect get-away, the sky for a path to travel, we were the masters of our journey.

But we were not long to dominate the journey—the wind was taking us east northeast, the leading balloons had disappeared. Some in the clouds farther ahead, others in newly formed clouds overhead. As we gazed around taking stock of our position one hour after take-off, we observed Captain Hill's balloon following us. He had gone higher, while we, staying low, had passed him on our way northeastward.

Then the vicious-looking cloud appeared in the northwest. We were being rapidly sucked into it; in fact we were already under its very edge. It was no use to go up—any movement must take us into it. There was nothing to do but ride unless we decided to land. We had gone through storms before which had looked as bad so we determined to ride it. Things now began to happen. We were rapidly sucked north into the blackest part of the cloud. At a little over 1,000 feet altitude we were enveloped in it. Up we went, the hydrogen expanding and pouring out of the appendix due to the decreasing atmosphere pressure as we went higher. This meant that we were also getting heavier and the balloon must sooner or later begin its rapid fall.

I looked up at the bag scarcely fifteen feet above my head. Its huge silver shape had practically disappeared in the inky blackness that had completely enveloped us. Only the merest portion directly above was at all distinguishable. The impression was ghastly. The air had become icy cold. It dawned on me that this was no ordinary storm. It was eerie and unnatural. I felt like a child with goblins about—and would gladly have been anywhere else than there—I heard Eric remark laconically, "Well, guess I might as well get into my parachute."

He put on his parachute, tied the release ring to the rigging and sat on the edge of the basket. I hastily did the same. Lightning had commenced and fearing that if the balloon was struck we might not be sufficiently conscious to get out of the basket, we reasoned that by sitting on the edge of the basket we would fall into space and the rope attached to the release ring would automatically open the chutes.

The lightning was now crashing all about us. The inky darkness had changed to a greenish yellow color. The giant bag over our head was whirling and being thrown to right and left. Of course the basket acted as a 1,500 pound pendulum attached to the bag, following it all over the sky. There were times it seemed as if our equipment would surely fall out of the basket. The violence of the air currents lasted only a few minutes but those minutes were hours to the two occupants of the stray balloon adrift 4,300 feet above the earth. We were utterly helpless and entirely at the mercy of whatever power it is that controls all.

There is no way adequately to describe it but the impression is burned upon my memory. This turbulent condition existed for us but a few minutes; then down we came faster and faster. Where formerly we would have required a couple bags of sand thrown out to stop our descent, we now threw twelve bags as fast as we could open them and pour the sand out. By pouring out sand, it could hurt no one, but to throw a whole bag from such an altitude might easily kill some person below.

We came falling out of the cloud only a few hundred feet above the ground. Thank goodness we were over a woods and not a town! It was pouring rain, seemingly bucketsful, right into our basket and all over us. We were soaked. Our basket had a rubber cover on the outside and this was catching and holding the water like a huge bucket. However, we were concerned more with stopping the fall of the balloon, yet we must continue down—or go back into that infernal thunder and lightning.

After what seemed an age, our balloon at least appeared to be checking its precipitant fall. The sand we were throwing overboard was making it light. We hesitated about 100 feet off the ground and being light started to rise again. We had had enough of altitude over that spot! We weren't going back into that storm center directly above no matter what happened! There was one chance that we might, by flying low in the valley, let the storm go by. That was only one chance in a thousand but we were desperate and took that one chance. Later events proved it to be a worthwhile choice but we were not yet free from trouble.

We started to maneuver by valving hydrogen and alternately throwing sand. We didn't have to valve very much because the basket was catching lots of water and getting heavier all the time. But a hundred yards off to our left another balloon came dropping out of the cloud and still another followed almost immediately. The first one was Lieutenant Evert's balloon; the second a civilian balloon. They both apparently intended staying down and we laughingly agreed they must have had about the same experience we had. The wind caught them and both balloons appeared to be chasing each other as they careened madly over the ground, up a small ravine to disappear in a rainy distance up north of us.

About this time Erik remarked, "Here comes another and it looks almost as if it might hit us!" We were then about 500 feet above the ground and going rapidly east by north in this small valley. The balloon was Van Orman's. He went by on his drop, the loose edges of the bag flapping and crackling in the fog. He must have been pretty high for he seemed to have lost about a fourth of his gas. That meant probably 9,000 feet by density ratio of atmosphere. What had he been through at such a height? Only Van can tell you but I venture it was plenty. Comrades in misery, we waved and shouted to them as they passed but I don't suppose either one heard.

If they did they paid no attention. Both were busy throwing sand. I saw out of the corner of my eye a farmhouse below. It looked as though Van Orman would hit it. We held our breath and waited. He missed the house by only a few feet, appeared barely to touch the ground, then rose rapidly. They must have thrown a lot of ballast or had not valved any at all when near the ground. They rose rapidly and passing us again went back into the clouds. Well, they could go up as far as they wanted; as for us, we were staying low. Our temporary peace was short-lived. We were caught in a down-gust and down we came. However, we were still in our valley and it didn't matter.

The lightning continued. Seemingly with renewed vigor—if that were possible—it was terrific and it appeared to cross the sky just over our heads. Would it never end? Now our drag rope was dragging on the ground, Erik received a couple light shocks of electricity from somewhere though it was not serious. Now things began to happen again. The valley was a regular wind tunnel and we were traveling at a very high speed—just clear of the ground and following the valley.

The leaves on the trees flowed by like a green liquid. We couldn't land now if we wanted to. We must keep on. Our drag rope caught momentarily —then freed. It leaped up just so the lower end was higher than our basket. The end dropped again. This time it wrapped around the treetop. To the top of the tree it broke with a report like a shotgun. Why the jolt didn't break our necks, I don't know.

The valley turned; we smashed against the ground in front and burst both air pontoons on the basket while both Erik and I scrambled about in an effort to stay in the basket. Again we bumped and the sextant fell on Erik's back, almost putting him out. Everything was a mess in the basket— food, water, sand, clothing and instruments—all were mixed together.

The balloon by now was positively heavy. I somehow managed to get a bag of sand and throw it over just as two high-tension lines suddenly appeared in front of us. The basket cleared them, thank God, but the drag rope didn't. As it crossed the wire, a bluish flame about two feet long shot up the wet rope. Our speed saved us for the rope was off the wires in a second. It was a close thing to being electrocuted, but we were saved.

Hardly had we caught our breath when another electric line assembly appeared. This time there were six lines. Our basket went just below the lines, the huge gas bag above, and there we performed a perfect jackknife around the wires as helpless as we possibly could be. There seemed absolutely no chance to get out alive. I was certain that death was a matter of seconds away at best. However, Providence had ordained otherwise and for some mysterious reason there was no fire. The speed with which we hit forced us out of the mess somehow.

In far less time than it takes to tell of it, we were once again careening across the country vainly endeavoring to get up a little higher. Our next experience was to hit a railroad telegraph pole. We broke it off and it hung from our basket while we dragged several feet. We swung outside the basket by our hands while pushing with our feet and were finally able, with difficulty, to dislodge the pole. It seemed the weather had now decided to let us alone. While we were pushing the pole off, the storm passed overhead and an absolute lull occurred within five minutes.

Erik hung outside the basket and cut a hole in one corner of our platform to let out a little water and we managed to rise to an altitude of some 800 feet. There was a gentle wind blowing us to the south. We had practically reversed our course. It was 7:50 pm. All that I have written here had occurred in little over a half hour from the start of the storm.

The storm was still active to the southeast of us but we were going south and it was a comfort to know we were not going into it. We WERE thankful to be alive though we were drenched and it was exceedingly cold. We were groaning. Our teeth chattered. No one ever saw two more miserable creatures! Our flying suits were wet but the fur looked inviting and I just stumbled into mine, wondering from just what type of pneumonia I would die. Erik looked at me dully for a moment, then freeing himself from his silk parachute, he got into his suit, too. The suits, wet as they were, kept some of our body heat in and we got along somehow.

About midnight we accidentally spilled some water and rose to 5,300 feet. It was certainly cold. The rigging froze so that a rope would crackle when it was bent. The wind was taking us farther south up there so we stood it for awhile. But there is a limit to human endurance. Finally we had to come down. We valved and descended to just off the surface. It was much warmer there and a wind was blowing us to the southeast at the rate of twenty-five miles per hour.

This would take us to the coast much quicker, but we could do no better. A little later we again ascended to an altitude of 7,000 feet. About 5,400 feet it was snowing. We did not linger long at this altitude. Once again we valved down to the treetops. Here we remained until daylight, not knowing our exact location except that we were over forested mountains. At daybreak we flew above the Potomac River near where it empties into Chesapeake Bay. We found a thin stratum of air 400 feet thick that was flowing south and we managed to stay in this stream until it disappeared near the mouth of the Rappahannock River. There the wind was carrying us directly toward the mouth of the bay and out over the Atlantic.

The sun was shining from a cloudless day. We had gone as far as we could in this machine, and so we landed in the last field of dry land near Weems, Virginia. We were sure that someone else had won the race but we felt we had done our best so had no regrets. The kindly people who helped roll and pack our balloon weren't interested in any race. They were only concerned with this huge bag that had dropped out of the sky.

We headed for home. As I stepped up to the ticket window at Richmond, Virginia, a tired and weary traveler, I gave my name to the agent. He looked startled, then asked, "Are you the fellows who won the balloon race?" I could scarcely believe it. But there in his hand was a newspaper with my picture on the front page.

We had won the National Balloon Trophy!

In truth, Bill Kepner very much deserved the victory, but the event was more than an adventure for us. It was disaster.

We inflated our balloon at Bettis Field near McKeesport, Pennsylvania, using bottled hydrogen in cylinders containing some 200 cubic feet each. As usual, I spent most of the morning at the Weather Bureau and was in hopes of a northeast run up into New England towards Maine or possibly Nova Scotia. Outside of the remote possibility of a thunderstorm, it was pretty promising that we could make this course.

Having completed the inflation on schedule, we were ready to start on time—5:20 pm. Promptly on the second our balloon rose from Bettis Field and started on its flight. At first we had difficulty in balancing our balloon off. We ascended to 300 feet, then dropped again to within ten feet of the ground, showing that we had started up just a little too heavy. In as many seconds three bags of sand were emptied. Our craft steadied and rose to 1,000 feet. Ahead of us four balloons were visible and behind us several more trailed in the distance.

Being particularly interested at this time in our direction, we checked our course with the compass and found it to be forty degrees east of north. After noting the direction we tried our radio equipment for possible evidence of thunderstorms and were much pleased to find the air remarkably free from static. At 5:40 pm we crossed the Allegheny River at an altitude of 1,800 feet and started out over more rugged country to the east of Pittsburgh.

In studying the sky about 6:00 pm I noticed the cloud mass to the west of us darkening a bit. The lower edges of these clouds, at an altitude of about two thousand feet, were being tossed about by some vertical current.

As a matter of instinct I ordered Morton to put on his parachute and I did the same so we would be prepared in case of any serious development of this storm. On clear days when there is absolutely no storm about, parachutes were never worn as they were quite cumbersome. Purely as a matter of safety first in this instance, we strapped them on.

About five minutes later it seemed to us that some unseen hand grasped the top of the balloon and started to draw it rapidly upward. Our speed accelerated and our vertimeter, designed to register vertical currents up to thirty miles per hour, had reached its limit. The hydrogen gas was pouring out the bottom of the appendix at a furious rate. The balloon started to spin, caused by the diamond shape mesh of the net. Due to this spinning action, the basket started to wind in crazy cirlces produced by the centrifugal force.

Neither Morton in his twenty-five years experience in flying, nor I in my twelve years, had ever encountered anything so severe as this. We were being whipped rapidly upward and after passing the 8,000 foot mark, there began a tremendous downpour of rain which ordinarily would have started our craft plummeting. But due to the terrible vertical current which literally held us prisoner we continued upward to 12,000 feet where we met with a blast of hail.

The noise of the hail on the top of the balloon was terrifying and we feared it would puncture the fabric on the top. This hail marked the turning point of our memorable ascent, and we started downward at equal velocity and with no less degree of panic.

Morton, whose duty it was to keep the balloon in equilibrium, was pouring sand over as rapidly as possible while I watched the effects of his efforts on our instruments. After the release of some five bags or one hundred and fifty pounds, with no appreciable results, I decided it was time for drastic action. We now had reached an altitude of 8,000 feet and it was necessary to check our balloon before crashing into the side of a mountain. To speed up this work I took my knife and cut off bags of ballast as rapidly as possible and inside of two minutes I had cut away eighteen bags of sand. Ordinarily the release of this amount of ballast would have been sufficient to check almost any descent, but in this case it seemed no more effective than casting overboard so much tissue paper!

It was evident, considering the intensity of the storm, that it would be desireable to land, but our downward speed was so great that I realized it would be simply impossible to accomplish this feat. We bent our knees to absorb the terrible shock of the basket striking the ground. We were dismayed to observe that our instruments were smashed when the crash came. Up again we started and were soon caught in another vertical current, rising at a speed over thirty-five miles per hour! At 10,000 feet we commenced dropping downward at an equal velocity.

We once more desperately endeavored to check the descent, but to no better avail. We struck the ground a second time so hard it knocked our hats off. Our balloon bounded again into the air. We had hoped to land on the second bounce but our decline was too fast and were now at an altitude of 2,000 feet. Morton was sitting in the basket and I was standing upright watching the thick clouds around us, when a hundred yards away from us we sighted the Army balloon piloted by Captain Kepner and Lieutenant Erickson, who were dropping at a terrifying rate of speed.

Erickson looked over at us, shouted, "Alley-oop!" and disappeared in the clouds beneath us. At the same moment I turned and faced the east, when out of the darkness appeared death itself—a flash of lightning two feet in front of my face. Instinctively, I turned to ascertain if our balloon was ignited by the exploding flash. I recall seeing the appendix clearly and the bottom of the envelope, when everything went absolutely black.

Five hours later I regained consciousness to the sensation of flies buzzing about my eyes and nose. I swished my hand but to no avail. Then it struck me that it was not flies at all, but drops of rain bouncing off my face. As I ever so slowly collected my senses, I realized that I was lying with my head on the ground and my feet and body in the capsized basket which now rested on its side on the ground.

Truly, this seemed the resurrection itself. It was particularly difficult at the moment to comprehend exactly what had happened. It was evident that we had made a landing but I could not fathom how we had done it when my last recollection was my resigning myself to my fate while attempting to check the flash ignition of the balloon. My next thought for Morton's safety. I called for him but received no response. I assumed he had gone to a farmhouse to summon help to pack up but thought it peculiar he should do so without saying anything.

My feet were wedged in the basket underneath some equipment. With difficulty, I succeeded in removing the gear which imprisoned my feet. Then, terrified, I discovered Morton sprawled on the bottom of the basket, terribly tangled in the clothing, food, and equipment. I thought first that he had probably been knocked unconscious. I took his pulse and couldn't find any! I was unwilling to believe that anything had happened to Morton that could not be remedied by prompt medical attention. I acted accordingly.

I looked about to get my bearings and saw in one direction the light of a farmhouse. Spurred by the urgent need of medical aid for Morton, I started out at a dead run across a muddy field towards that farmhouse. My ankle had been paining me considerably by this time but I simply believed it was severely sprained. It would have to work as far as the farmhouse. But after two steps it was evident I had no control at all over my left foot. It had been broken.

I crawled back to the basket where I attempted to shape a make-do crutch from some of our equipment. This proved impractical and in desperation I started to crawl backwards across the fields, dragging my useless foot. I had gone only fifty feet when I realized the severe shock had now rendered the muscles in my right foot useless. It would be absolutely impossible to reach the house.

I tried to clear my mind as to the next logical step and the only thought which would come was that of shouting at the top of my voice. Conserving my energy by concentrating it all in shouts at half minute intervals, I prayed someone would hear. All the while the thoughts of the other airmen lying injured in the Pennsylvania hills raced through my mind.

It seemed that Providence was with me again. Inside of five minutes I heard someone shout in the distance. With renewed strength I shouted another time and pointed the flashlight in the general direction of the response. Soon a farmer came hurrying across the muddy fields, through the inky blackness of that night. Immediately I sent him running back with instructions to get doctor for Morton as quickly as possible. When the physician returned I received the most severe news of my flying career.

Old Mort was taken home, far beyond the realm of aircraft. The bolt of lightning had struck him full force, penetrating the shoulder and exiting at his knee. With his passing I had lost one of my closest friends. Through fair weather and foul we had for years shared the joys and sorrows of riding the winds aloft. Now we parted forever.

It was heartbreaking to be carried off that field alone, leaving Morton in the hands of strangers.

Later, at the farmhouse, the doctor realizing that I was in need of a stimulant asked if there was any liquor around. As prohibition was in effect, the cautious farmer answered that he never had such things there, but another man, who had arrived with the doctor, said, "John, you know very well you have a jug of moonshine out in the barn!" After drinking a large glassful of the pure white liquid, I forgot about my pain for a little while. I even forgot Morton for a little while. In truth I forgot everything and resigned myself to a sweet and drowsy peace.

I was taken to a hospital in Greensburg, Pennsylvania and x-rayed. After a 3000-foot fall, and after having the balloon almost completely burned up, all that was wrong with me was a broken ankle. I called my wife from the hospital bed and was startled to hear her say, "Van, you old fool, you know you can't win a balloon race by coming down this early!" After she was through I mentioned that we had had a somewhat uncomfortable landing and that I had strained an ankle a little. Had I said any more, she would have wanted to come to Greensburg and see how I was.

It was only a matter of weeks until my ankle knit together in good shape and I found myself back in normal condition. As the months passed it was still difficult to reconcile myself to the loss of Morton. There was some consolation in the knowledge that he had died doing the work he loved so well.

Reconstructing the accident from the evidence on hand and an examination of the equipment, I found that the lightning had struck the side of the balloon at about the equator, passing along the envelope downward in front of my eyes, and had struck Morton. In the few instants which elapsed I had time to look upward, at which moment the balloon exploded with sufficient force to render me unconscious. The lower three-fourths of the balloon burned completely.

A tattered piece of fabric about twenty-five feet in diameter remained in the top of the netting. Then our craft, in flames, started to drop rapidly. A thousand feet away from us an Army balloon, piloted by Lieutenant Everett and assisted by Lieutenant Ent, saw us fall. To quote Ent's words verbatim:

" 'My God! Look there, Everett!' I cried. Lieutenant Everett looked in time to see a balloon falling out of the clouds at rocket speed. It was strung out in the form of a collosal necktie. I saw it disappear behind a hill. 'I'll bet those poor fellows are done for!' Everett remarked."

It was pathetic to realize that Lieutenant Everett's words of sympathy for us were his last, for a moment later his balloon was struck by lightning and he, too, was killed instantly by a bolt.

Evidently my own position in the falling basket was such that my head had rested on the edge of the basket and my feet were wedged on the bottom. The balloon struck the ground with such awful impact that my left foot was broken and I was pushed further into oblivion by an impact to my head. The radio set was splattered as if dropped on a concrete pavement from several hundred feet of altitude. Our pontoons had been ripped their full length. Canned goods carried in our basket were flattened by the landing shock.

The four factors which Providence provided for me were:

First: that the lightning, for some unknown reason, did not strike me.

Second: that just sufficient fabric remained in the top of the net after the explosion to act as a very small parachute.

Third: that my head rested on my wrist on the edge of the basket, and

Fourth: The wonderful shock absorbing qualities of the pontoons had spelled the difference between life and death.

Shortly after Everett's balloon was struck, a third balloon, within half a mile of where we landed, was similarly struck by a bolt. Fortunately the flight assistant, J. F. Cooper, who was hit, was not fatally injured. He received severe surface burns from which he managed to recover quite satisfactorily.

I knew the obvious question would be asked—Was the value of ballooning consistent with the risk involved? To that question, I felt there was but one answer—that free ballooning was the world's laboratory of the air. Men used it to develop their instruments, their methods of navigation, and most particularly, a most thorough study of meteorology. Yet if we wished to continue to use the free balloon as the laboratory of the air, some protection had to be designed to protect occupants during storms. With severe electrical discharges playing about the balloon, pilots were an excellent target—a human body is a better conductor of electricity than the rigging or the air, itself.

While convalescing in the Pennsylvania hospital, I began to plan an electrical research project. With Arthur Austin, inventor of the suspension insulator, as my partner we were offered full use of the Ohio Insulator Company laboratories in Barberton, Ohio. Our object was to find solutions to the effects of lightning on balloons, airships and airplanes. As a result of our probes, we also introduced for the first time a serious formal examination of hazardous vertical currents, a deadly factor of flight even in the late 1970's.

At the time the rigid airship *Shenandoah* was built, German engineering advisors insisted that the design need not concern itself with a vertical current factor exceeding *eight miles per hour.* Yet in the storm that claimed Morton's life, we had proven conclusively that the destructive vertical current that slammed our balloon about traveled in excess of thirty-eight miles per hour.

After the *Shenandoah* was wrenched to bits in a thunderstorm over Cadiz, Ohio, the world suddenly learned that vertical currents can reach a metal-twisting destructive force of 100 miles per hour in a thunderstorm and up to 400 miles per hour or more in tornado winds. A transport plane flying at 300 miles per hour hitting one of these currents is like an automobile hitting a four-foot chuck-hole—something has got to break. Even today, too many heavier-than-air pilots ignore these warnings. The intensity of a thunderstorm should be recognized by *everyone* concerned with flying, for such storms can tear the wings off of any airplane envisioned by the mind of man—now or in the year 2000. For nothing in our existence is as predictable as the thoroughly destructive forces of nature.

Austin and I began our work with the theory that lightning was dangerous and hazardous. Our first step was to set up on a laboratory scale the paraphernalia which would accurately duplicate the force of lightning, a balloon, an airship and an airplane. We built an outdoor laboratory consisting of a counterpoise ten feet in diameter, fifty feet long and suspended twenty feet in the air. It was this machine, charged by a 27 million volt transformer, which produced our version of lightning bolts.

Beneath the counterpoise we slung a balloon basket with a metallic dummy taking the place of the balloonist. Surely if a man's body served to conduct high voltage electricity, a metal dummy would provide more than a fair test of this device!

During our research we caused electrical discharges to pass from the counterpoise to the basket while photographing these blasts with an electrically timed camera. We suspended miniature balloons wet and dry in the path of these discharges and photographed the effects. We sought straight answers to the problem of dangerous lightning during flight.

We pursued this work for more than a year. As a result of these experiments I discovered that sixteen wires, four on a side, hung in a square about the basket protected the balloonist from electrical discharges aimed at the basket. By means of miniature balloons we definitely proved that lightning does actually leave its course to avoid striking a dry balloon. But in a thunderstorm it's the other way around. You're always wet from rain which accompanies a thunderstorm. So lightning deviates from any other path to hit this *better* path which is a wet balloon.

Expanding our experiments to airships, we found that airships had enough metal framework in their content to be literally immune to lightning. In the case of airplanes, there was also enough metal frame work to pass safely through an electrical storm. Should a bolt strike a plane, the only evidence would be a tiny spot about the size of a pea where the lightning struck and came out the other side. However, the aircraft ignition system is vulnerable and does require beefing up for protection against lightning.

Again this certainly is not to suggest flying through storms! That is foolhardy and will always remain foolhardy, even if the aircraft is the size of a super bomber or the DC-10!

A full report of our experiments on the effects of lightning on balloons and aircraft—the only such study ever undertaken to the best of my knowledge—appeared in the *Monthly Weather Review* of August, 1931, and is obtainable today in all major libraries.

Dr. Austin and I spent a year of hard effort applying theory to reality. The acid test was to be the upcoming 1929 Gordon Bennett balloon race in St. Louis.

Allan McCracken, my new aide, and I would serve as flying guinea pigs.

Coveted Gordon Bennett trophy was awarded three times (a fourth win was disputed) to Akron, Ohio's Ward Van Orman who represented the Goodyear Tire & Rubber Company over the span of his near-storybook international balloon racing career in Europe, America and over scattered areas of the Atlantic Ocean.

## · 22 ·

# Our Basket is Encrusted in Ice

Eleven of the balloonists who had braved the electrical storm which claimed two of their comrades in the previous year's elimination races were ready to take off on another quest for national flying honors at Pittsburgh on May 4, 1929.

Our prayers were for clear skies and favorable winds but two or three among our number were pessimistic enough, cautious enough or smart enough to arm ourselves against a repetition of the 1928 disaster.

As indicated in the previous chapter, Austin and I had devised a cage-like affair to protect balloon pilots against the kind of terrifying experience that took Morton's life. Our invention was an adaptation of a *faraday cage* which attracts electrical bolts to itself instead of the balloon occupants. We had experimented with the device for months, lashing it with over a million lightning-like volts of electricity.

The cage was installed around the *Goodyear VIII*'s basket and we predicted that within a year, all or most of the participating racing balloonists of the world would request such a device for their own craft.

I noted with some interest that Captain William Flood and Lieutenant U. G. Ent of the Army Air Corps had scrapped their radio for the 1929 race because they believed it a contributing factor in the disastrous crash of the Army bag the preceding year.

Nevertheless, I could not help but question the logic and good sense of scrapping their primary means of communication. For me, I would sooner dispense with the balloon basket, itself—and rations, firearms and clothing—than give up the life-saving radio during a race!

Some four days after the start of the race from Pittsburgh, a dispatch to the *Albany Evening News* from Essex County, New York reported the landing of the *Detroit Times* balloon entry piloted by Edward J. Hill and his aide, A. G. Schlosser, in the wilds the preceding afternoon. After being without food for thirty-six hurs, Hill and Schlosser reached the settlement. Their flight distance was recorded at 350 miles.

McCracken and I voyaged 405 miles, but our distance was exceeded by my friend Tex Settle, pilot of the Navy balloon *No. 1*, who negotiated 900 miles! This left Tex and I, together with Bill Kepner, winnner of last year's National and International Race, as official U. S. representatives in the Gordon Bennett race to be held in September in St. Louis.

In recording the 900 miles, Settle set a new record for 35,000 cubic foot balloons using hydrogen gas. The previous mark had been 848 miles which I had set in 1926. The distance run by Tex was not a record for national races. Before 1926, bags of 80,000 cubic foot capacity were used in the national marathons. The record of 1,073 miles flown by Alan R. Hawley from St. Louis in 1910 was approached by Wollam and I with a 44-hour 1,072 mile flight in 1924, but Hawley's record was never broken in this country. The longest flight in competitive racing on record was made by the Frenchman, Maurice Bienaime, in the Gordon Bennett International Race from Stuttgart, Germany in 1912. His distance: 1,334 miles.

In the Pittsburgh contest, I must say that it was again an emphasis on meteorological knowledge, out of which grows an acute undefinable instinct, that saved our skins. Flying near Lake Champlain, New York, with low gas supply and ballast nearly exhausted, McCracken and I observed cloud formations below us. The phenomenon instantly indicated to us that a violent atmospheric disturbance would be brewing in our line of flight within moments.

Feeling that we had made the most of our flight under existing conditions, we decided to go with what we had already accomplished and landed near Plattsburg, New York. After packing our balloon and going into town, we learned that just one hour and fifteen minutes after we landed, a tornado had struck Berlin, New Hampshire and did damage estimated at a quarter of a million dollars. Berlin was in our direct line of flight!

The *Goodyear VIII* undoubtedly would have been near the vortex of the tornado had we continued in the air.

Before leaving the subject of the 1929 Litchfield Trophy race, I would like to point out "Cap" Clarence A. Palmer as an example of one to whom honesty and true sportsmanship was the only name of the game.

With dawn breaking that Sunday morning of the race over the

village of Donegal, Pennsylvania, Cap Palmer pulled the ripcord of his balloon. Cap had sailed away in splendid confident fashion less than nine hours earlier from Pitt Stadium in Pittsburgh but had come to rest on the ground scarcely fifty miles from the starting point!

The ripcord was pulled by Palmer after he managed to extricate the balloon from a tree. The big bag was clear at the time and its crew could easily have continued on its way, but Cap Palmer had been forced to leave the basket in order to cut away entangling branches.

"I must report that being unable to extricate my basket from a tree, I was forced to leave the basket to cut the balloon loose from the entanglement," he cabled, "and in so doing I automatically disqualified the entry. I am reporting the flight as ended at this point."

The things Palmer did not explain, however, deserved more consideration. Association officials in Pittsburgh were alert to the sportsmanship shown by the Akron balloonist and immediately made public the entire story.

Collapse of the hopes of the Akron Business Club balloon followed an interval in which expectation was high that Cap Palmer's getaway from the stadium and demonstration of his keen judgment would result in triumph for the silver balloon. He had managed a perfect ascent barely clearing the walls of the stadium with a maximum load of ballast. The other bags had chosen an east by northeast course by various currents and it appeared probable that all would float over New York state and either be halted by the coast or manage a precarious flight over the wilds of Maine.

In either event the distance traversed would be definitely limited by the stretch of land between Pittsburgh and the Atlantic seaboard. "I decided to try for a southerly course, perhaps gaining distance by taking advantage of favorable winds toward Florida," said Palmer. His strategy was promptly approved by both Army and Navy officials who had been close observers of weather conditions and take-off.

"In order," reported Palmer, "to bear in a southerly direction, it was necessary, because of prevailing winds, to hedge-hop—that is, to fly close to the ground, allowing the drag rope to trail the surface."

He proceeded throughout the night in that fashion—the end of the rope skimming over the land, occasionally touching a roof or brushing the side of a building. Such a process, when the weight of the rope is taken from the balloon's lifting power, is the same as releasing ballast and the bag will hop into the air. Then the rope dangles clear for a time, but once its weight asserts itself again, the balloon drops and the rope touches the ground.

The method is aptly termed "hedge-hopping." All went well during the night for the Akron Business Club balloon except that the steady downpour of rain seemed to increase as the balloon was borne southward.

"As dawn came," said Cap Palmer, "we were standing in two inches of water in the basket but we seemed to be making fair time and were steadily edging southward. Suddenly, however, the balloon veered toward the earth. We discovered that the drag rope had caught in a tree. There seemed to be some prospect that it could be jerked loose, however, and there was no immediate anxiety. But before we could extricate ourselves or cut the rope, we were blown against a tree and the ropes and network of the balloon became hopelessly entangled in its branches.

"We struggled for nearly three hours," Cap's aide Walter Griffen reported, "endeavoring to get loose without leaving the basket, but when dawn came, it was apparent the job was hopeless and Palmer climbed out of the basket. Working both from the ground and in the tree he managed to cut us free."

It was a deserted countryside with the dim light of early dawn—scarcely sufficient to enable the nearest household to recognize the balloon even if he knew one to be in the neighborhood. The two men were alone with their problem. The bag itself was undamaged, its ballast undiminished. The rain had almost ceased and the favorable breeze stirred the leaves of the tree—a breeze that might bear them southward to victory.

"But you see, gentlemen, I had to get out of the basket—and that disqualifies the entry," Cap Palmer said.

★ ★ ★

Beginning their ascent at four o'clock, September 28, 1929, nine pilots carried the flags of six nations into the air in the eighteenth competition of the James Gordon Bennett International Classic. It was the third to be held from St. Louis and was attended by over 50,000 spectators.

After the start of the race at 4:00 pm our *Goodyear VIII* floated at an altitude of fifty feet for a good three hours, the length of time it took to reach Alton, Illinois at nightfall. Riding a ten mile-per-hour current that bore us far to the northeast, we were in constant danger of colliding with the treetops which we were clearing only by a few feet. It kept both of us tense and watchful until dawn.

About midnight we were struck by a line squall that some pilots complained of as the worst ever seen in a race. Indeed, bounced by the winds like a bit of driftwood on the sea, the Akron bag was maneuvered to an altitude of 8,000 feet. There, our lightning shield was adjusted and parachutes strapped on by us both. Lightning slashed on all sides and rain and hail whipped our faces.

As we ascended to 10,000 feet over Elliot City, Indiana, a severe snowstorm developed! Our little basket swayed and bumped about and became encased in ice. At this time our observations showed an air current was developing below that would have carried us back to St. Louis. We decided to ascend still higher. During the climb the temperature dropped from ninety degrees to zero!

The bag valve was constantly filling with water which had to be drained to prevent freezing. Then over Lebanon, Indiana, the storm forced our bag down. Down we came, jumping from current to current, until, within 500 feet of the ground by throwing out more ballast we managed somehow to steady the ship. Our balloon again commenced to climb—past 10,000 feet, past 20,000 feet, up to 30,000 feet we soared, due to the heat of the sun.

The ballast we had discarded to attain this altitude was a potpourri of items. Our thermometer was the first to go overboard. Over the side went our oxygen tanks, thermos bottles and parachutes. Then came the blessed radio and spare clothing. Had there been time, we probably would have stripped ourselves of the clothes we were wearing to lighten the craft.

Ultimately, of course, we descended from the heights and when no favorable currents were found enroute, our bag gently alighted in a pasture three miles southeast of Troy, Ohio.

It was without a doubt one of the most difficult races I had ever flown. From midnight Saturday until we landed near Troy at 5:45 pm Sunday, we were constantly fighting storms. We did our best to direct the balloon between them. As disappointing a run as it was, more importantly it was the most severe test of meteorological knowledge we could have been put through. The fickle weather and positively weird combinations of currents I never again encountered in my career. The results of our experiments on that trip were incorporated in the training of pilots at the Goodyear School.

I have said many things up to now about radio. But I cannot say too much. In this race as in others, it was our radio that decided the outcome of the contest in our favor. Because of it we always knew the direction the winds were expected to carry us. Then, too, we learned on the second day that two of the other balloonists had been forced to earth. This report, together with the concerts by stations scattered throughout the United States, bolstered our team's morale and caused us to continue the race long enough to win.

It is difficult to accurately describe our feelings our second night aloft—worn with lack of sleep, our energies at low ebb from constant exertion, heads light from the lack of oxygen and high altitudes, we whirled our radio dial and listened for several hours to a program of good music from Cleveland station WTAM. I knew that radio had much to do with our success in that race. And I knew, too, that I would never enter another race without a complete radio receiving set. It had proved its worth and it was with considerable regret that I finally had to chuck it over the side to gain a final sprint of distance.

Our winning flight distance from St. Louis was a mere 354 miles, only eleven miles ahead of our nearest competitor. The Army entry, with Captain Bill Kepner and J. E. Powell, his aide landed near Salina, Ohio, 343 miles from the starting point. Third in the race was the Navy balloon piloted by Tex Settle, well known in Akron through his affiliation with the Goodyear-Zeppelin Corporation.

Settle and his aide, Lieutenant Winfield Bushnell, brought their craft to earth in Dixon Township, Ohio, after traveling a distance of 315 miles.

One accident marred this race. D. Eduardo Bradley, pilot of the Argentine balloon, suffered a crushed knee when his balloon slammed into a tree near Fairbanks, Indiana. He was taken to a Terre Haute, Indiana hospital for treatment as was his aide, Lieutenant Francisco J. Cadaval, who was shocked and bruised.

I would like to say a word at this point about the barograph instrument which all contestants carried in the race. The barograph, of course, provided the official record of a balloon's flight performance. The first night of the 1929 Bennett race, McCracken and I rode what is called a temperature inversion all night long—a steady straight line of flight just over the tree tops. Indeed the unusual phenomena likewise reflected as a perfectly straight line on the barograph—just as you'd draw with a ruler —and this was the question in Orville Wright's mind when he asked us to come to Washington to explain our log.

Orville was chairman of the contest committee of the National Aeronautic Association. We had sent our balloon landing certificates and barograph to him for his approval.

"I have your barograph record here," Orville said. "Is there any way you can adjust the thing from the outside?"

I answered, "Yes, you just put the key in the bottom of the barograph and you can adjust the altitude for anything you want."

Wright asked, "Did you adjust this barograph before or after you left the ground?"

"No," I answered, "the only adjustment I made was to bring it to zero at the time we left the field, and as you will see, we flew on a line all night long."

He noted, "I didn't know that was possible."

"Well, that's the result of a temperature inversion," I replied. "The upper air is warmer than the lower air and it is a balloonist's dream. The balloon automatically flies itself."

He said, "Well, I'm glad to have your explanation because I never realized there was that possibility."

Now here was an extremely brilliant man; the man who *invented* the airplane, yet he did not know of this characteristic of the weather. It was simply because in an airplane you fly through weather so fast, you don't appreciate what's going on. You therefore foster far too little respect and appreciation for stormy, violent weather.

It is why for years and years I have urged that a course in ballooning be incorporated in the requirements for every commercial and private pilot's license.

The International James Gordon Bennett Cup races took off from *Cleveland Airport* (above) in 1930. A loyal Buckeye, Ward Van Orman, with aide Allen MacCracken, won the sprint by ballooning to Boston in 27 hours, 56 minutes, their second consecutive international victory. The year before, when Ward and Allen ballooned from St. Louis to Troy, Ohio, in 24 hours, Orville Wright called Van Orman to Washington to congratulate him for adapting a sophisticated use of celestial navigation to the science of ballooning.

## . 23 .

# Busy Scoops and the Eight Thousand Foot Bounce

Dropping 8,000 feet to earth when caught in a vertical air current and bouncing up again into the clouds, sleeping for the first time while racing, needing to draw upon our oxygen supply when forced into rarified atmosphere, averting being carried out over the Atlantic Ocean. . . these were just a part of the experience McCracken and I discussed with newsmen the morning after the nineteenth annual Gordon Bennett International Balloon Race became history when we were compelled to land the gas bag *Goodyear VIII* at 9:30 pm in Canton Junction, Massachusetts.

Upon returning to Cleveland we were escorted to our room atop the University Club by state commander of the American Legion, Richard Paul of Canton.

We had just ordered a huge steak for breakfast when reporters and photographers knocked on our door at 10:00 in the morning. They made themselves at home and it occurred to us that the quicker we could tell them our story, the quicker we could get to those steaks.

"Yes, we had sufficient gas and ballast to carry us approximately 100 miles further than we flew," I conceded, "but there is little use sailing over the Atlantic Ocean, is there?"

When asked, "How it was that we were able to bring our balloon over the backyard of Daniel Toomey of Canton, Massachusetts, who, with a son and neighbor, pulled the bag to earth?" I had to declare that we knew *exactly* where we were. "How?" some reported asked. Simply by the reckoning I had previously made by shooting the stars with my sextant. Also, we had maneuvered the balloon over the lights of Toomey's Gas Station. All that was left to do then was to call down and ask for help to get us down.

"Toomey must have been startled to hear voices coming out of the night from nowhere," observed a reporter.

"It's funny," McCracken and I confessed, "we get a kick out of that —sailing through the night and watching people scurry from their homes when our 82-pound hemp dragline pulls across a tin roof. It makes a peculiar rasping sound and I can imagine how the people feel. Sometimes they turn on every light in the house and come running out to look everywhere but into the sky—where we are."

"Did you know you were going to land in Boston?"

"Yes. When we started, it seemed like we would finish up in the St. Lawrence Valley in Canada, but in passing over Lake Erie, it became evident where we would land. Weather predictions given us before the start were surprisingly accurate as were reports of the variable currents. Earlier we had prepared for landing in the Canadian woods and had equipment consisting of gun shells, hunting clothes, food and many other things. All this we had to throw overboard near Springfield, Massachusetts in the middle of a huge storm that surrounded us on the east, north and south. We also encountered some bad weather over Lake Erie. The storm came in from two directions, from the northwest and southeast. West of the Hudson River we again hit the bad weather, running into a heavy rainstorm. But a remarkable thing was that on the eastern side of the river the sky was bright and clear."

By this time our steaks had arrived and it was indeed a hearty breakfast. No cereals for us. We each had ordered steak and potatoes, some orange juice, coffee and rolls. Neither of us had taken the time to dress as yet and the photographers looked a bit worried. McCracken was clad in nothing more than the skin in which he was born and I in my shorts.

The room in which we sat eating was littered with kit bags, instrument cases, clothes, maps, charts and official reports. On one of the beds laid the most valuable article in the whole room—the sealed barograph.

"Just as we were nearing Norwich, New York," I told the news seekers, "we were about 8,000 feet up when suddenly we were caught in a vertical air current. We began to drop rapidly to earth. That little ballast scoop was worked overtime by Mac. Somehow we misjudged our distance and we struck the ground, bounced back into the air, cut loose the big drag line and shot up again to 8,000 feet or more, and passed on from that place."

The 1930 race enjoyed unusually good news reportage. I particularly fancied one writer's comment about the balloons:

"They may land on a wilderness or on a lake or on a mountainside. Some of them may not be heard from for a week. The end may not be so colorful. That is what makes a balloon race unusual. It starts in a fanfare of trumpets—and it ends somewhere, anywhere."

I recalled that the balloons had been a half hour late in getting off, but were started in particularly rapid succession once the super speechmaking, the presentation of flowers, the broadcast announcers, the photographers and dignitaries were out of the way. The *City of Detroit*, having drawn first postition was off first at 5:02 pm after being walked slowly to a spot in front of the grandstand from its "filling station." The others followed at five-minute intervals.

Bands blared *The Star-Spangled Banner* while the American entries got away and the national anthems of the others as they, in turn, were loosed to the winds.

The *City of Detroit* rose very slowly drifting south. The *Belgica* next off, soared south, then east. The *Barmen*, from Germany, went slowly east. The wind was shifting at the takeoff so that at first no one could make any sense of the different courses the crafts were taking. The *City of Cleveland* received a real cheer as it drifted eastward. The next balloon, *Goodyear VIII* and the French entry, *Pierre Fishbach*, went out southeast, but in a few minutes turned northeast.

As the gas bags drifted away, airplanes wheeled overhead carrying officials, photographers and a radio broadcast set. The Goodyear blimp, *Defender*, buzzed merrily around. First reports of the course of the balloons came from Euclid Beach Park where five of the racers were seen by holiday crowds. They were 1,000 feet in the air and making fair speed up the shoreline toward Lake Erie.

The foreign balloons presented a sharp contrast with the American entries. Patched in many places with their nets and ropes spliced, the German, Belgian and French bags, all of which had flown in many races looked the part of battle-scarred veterans. Captain DeMuyter's *Belgica* was especially tattered with more than 100 patches in its fabric.

Trim *Goodyear VIII* and the *City of Cleveland*, also a Goodyear balloon, were almost new and were in superb condition for the contest.

Always a lively commentator of the news, Cleveland *Plain Dealer's* Julien Griffin wrote a colorful wrap-up of the race as of noon of the second day:

> Dodging through fierce thunder squalls, lashed by driving rains and floating under low-hanging clouds, six silver and brown balloons carrying pilots seeking the Gordon Bennett international balloon trophy were believed to be nearing Buffalo early today.
>
> The giant fabric bags that rose from Cleveland Airport late yesterday

afternoon encountered weather conditions worse than any the pilots ever went through in their flights for fame and honors. Starting at midnight the entire lake region was lashed with thunderstorms. Sharp flashes of lightning added to the pilots' dangers. The cold rain and cool wind prevented the balloons from rising more than 300 feet. Precious ballast was saved in the hope that the sun would enable the spheres to rise automatically today.

The latest report from any of the balloons was from a Buffalo airmail pilot who said he saw an unidentified balloon fighting a storm over Dunkirk, New York. The pilot's vision was impaired by the driving rain and he nearly collided with the floating balloon, he reported. The balloon pilots waved frantically with flashlights and a crash was averted.

The other five balloons are believed to be somewhere in the same vicinity. Weather forecasters expressed the opinion that air currents carried the bags along the shoreline of Lake Erie but that they were not blown over the water. It was predicted early today that the ultimate destination of the balloons will be somewhere in the wilds of the St. Lawrence river valley or the wooded hills of Vermont or Maine. There is the possibility that some of the crafts may be carried as far north as Labrador.

Reports that a balloon sank in Lake Erie off Avon, Ohio were discounted today. Three coastguard pick-up boats spent hours cruising in the choppy waters and were unable to locate the balloon reported down last evening.

The race contestants were traced as far as Erie, Pennsylvania last night where it was reported that three passed over the center of the city shortly before midnight. The storm broke at about that hour. Thunder squalls will continue to prevail in the lake regions the greater part of today, the weather bureau at Cleveland says, and the pilots are expected to use every trick known to balloon science to find currents that will carry them northeastward away from the storm."

Griffin had been right on the forecast. The storm area over Hudson Bay and the high pressure area over the east Atlantic coast states would produce southwest winds which would possibly carry us down the St. Lawrence valley.

Near the starting times, the huge balloons tugged at the guy ropes as if anxious to jump the gun and get away before the storm. Food enough for eight days was carried against the possibility of landing in an isolated spot. So were axes, knives, pistols and shotguns. Ground crews finally taxied the bags to a large circle formed by Gordon Bennett "personality girls" who were chosen by the press. The Goodyear blimp hovered in the skies. Airplanes darted about like Junebugs. Farewells were said before the microphone and the balloons rose slowly.

We cast off at 5:20 pm on Labor Day with thirty-eight 30-pound bags of sand as ballast and slowly ascended to 800 feet. There we caught a northeasterly current which took us southwest over the little college town of Berea and directly away from our objective to avoid disclosing our true plans to the other contestants.

Over Berea we increased our altitude from 800 to 1,000 feet and from there we caught a southwesterly current which carried us back toward Cleveland at a rate of 17.5 miles per hour. We passed over Cleveland at two miles south of the Terminal Tower. I recalled memories of bygone days when we passed directly over the Case campus at Wade Park and University Circle. I wondered if the "civils" were still surveying and re-surveying Doan Brook and the campus as we students had done back in 1915. In those days the Cleveland Museum of Art was just under con-struction and the whole lovely development of today was little dreamt of then.

With two exceptions at this point, all of the other balloons were far ahead of us. We increased our altitude to 1,300 feet, bettering our speed to twenty-one miles per hour, passing over the city of Willoughby. *Goodyear VIII* reached 1,900 feet as we crossed the shoreline of Lake Erie just west of Madison. Our tentative course up the middle of Lake Erie in a northeasterly direction was due to cross the eastern end of the lake near Buffalo. By now we had 29 bags of ballast left out of the original thirty-eight. The evening contraction had cost us only 270 pounds. Not unusu-ally severe.

By timing the flash intervals of a lighthouse, we identified our posi-tion as being five miles north of Ashtabula out over choppy Lake Erie, making twenty miles per hour. By 11:00 pm we found ourselves off Erie, Pennsylvania with thunderstorms to the northwest and east of us and we encountered a windshift from southwest to west-southwest which fur-ther indicated a shift of the meteorological situation. This was later con-firmed by radio weather reports of Station WTAM and the airway station WWO of the Cleveland Airport.

The news necessitated shifting our objective from the St. Lawrence Valley to the northeastern states. We were afloat in the vast sea of air that extends from the ground to five miles in the sky. Somewhere in this air sea were favorable winds. Our job was to find them, to get into them and to stay in them despite varying conditions and topography throughout the day and night. To win, this would have to be done with the most economical expenditure of gas and sand possible.

Our first brush with civilians occurred in the New England area, the story of which first appeared in a local newspaper as follows:

> The first report that the balloon had been sighted in this vicinity came to the *Observer* office at Woodstock just before 8:00 pm. Freeman Nelson of Pomfret Center who was in South Woodstock at the time had sent in a re-port stating that the balloon was flying at a low altitude. The pilot kept flashing a light on the balloon's name—*Goodyear VIII*—which was plainly discernible even at times when the light was not focussed on it.

According to Mr. Nelson, the pilot shouted to him requesting that he notify the nearest newspaper of the balloon's presence in the vicinity. Mr. Nelson stated that a cable hanging from the basket of the balloon was trailing almost on the ground, and that he had been informed by residents of West Woodstock that the cable had come in contact with buildings and trees on his property. To Mr. Nelson, the gas bag of the balloon appeared somewhat deflated and he was skeptical as to whether the aircraft would even clear the ridge of East Thompson.

The Thompson residents reported the balloon had a higher altitude over the eastern sections of that town but residents of Thompson Hill reported an experience similar to that of the West Woodstock man. Miss Florence Wiley said this morning that the trailing rope had hit the Wiley residence and that the pilot shouted a warning to onlookers, cautioning them to keep away from the rope.

When we crossed the shoreline of the lake at 1:05 am we were five miles east of Dunkirk, New York. From this time until dawn our course was east-northeast over the western part of New York state. During this period, my aide and I had more sleep than in any balloon race I ever flew in—two hours of it!

We crossed in succession Penn Yan, New York, Interlaken and Locke. At 8:15 we were two miles south of Cortland at 8,000 feet making 28 miles per hour. It was at this point that one of the rarest courtesies was extended to us.

Our balloon approached the city from the southwest, quickly disappearing in the gathering clouds hovering above the town. Below us, summoned by a resident in the vicinity of the Cortland Airport, Lieutenant Harold R. Maull hastened to the hangar accompanied by his wife and was soon in the air in a small plane, searching the clouds for our aircraft. Mrs. Maull was first to sight our huge balloon after they had spent a full half hour flying through the high clouds, taking great care to avoid accidentally hitting the *Goodyear VIII.*

I had watched the man's slow circling climb towards us and admired his persistence in his supposed task of bringing a photographer up to take a picture. As the plane came free of the clouds, the sun expanded the balloon's gasses, causing it to ascend even further. Lieutenant Maull climbed after it but was not able to reach us until we were 7,000 feet in the air. Climbing high above our balloon the pilot went into a dive and stalled his motor when he was directly under the balloon.

With the motor silenced, Maull called up to me, "Just wanted to let you know you are over Cortland, New York!"

It was a kind, unselfish gesture.

It was later in the morning when we were crossing the city of Norwich that we dropped from 8,000 feet to the ground. From the sky above the clouds our big white racing balloon was caught in a freak descending draft of air. We were pressed almost straight downward at a frightening rate of speed. The craft fell like a plummeting high speed elevator and we found ourselves powerless to check its dive. We frantically shoveled sand to lighten the burden of freight which the gas bag carried, urgently attempting to provide more buoyancy and lift. Eight thousand feet—more than a mile and a half—our aerial craft dropped! As we saw the earth apparently rising up to meet us, we both wished we'd jumped with our parachutes before getting so low.

But it was too late to make a safe parachute jump and we certainly feared that a bad crash—one that might prove fatal—was inevitable. When the balloon was within a few hundred feet of the earth, however, it evidently reached the bottom of the downward draft of air, striking a horizontal current, for it suddenly commenced to sink less rapidly.

Still it kept dropping until the basket hit the earth with a thump that threw the two of us off our feet but left us whole, if banged about a bit. Then our bag bounced like a rubber ball and was caught in an equally strange ascending current of air that returned us in quick order to our 8,000 foot altitude.

We reached our maximum speed of 33 miles per hour over Schenevus, New York, at an altitude of 10,800 feet. At noon we sighted another balloon ten miles to the north, evidently at 16,000 feet while we were flying at 13,000. We assumed it was either Blair or the Cleveland balloon or Hill in the Detroit craft.

Crossing the Hudson River in early afternoon there was fine weather over Stockport but toward Albany the sky was covered by heavy thundershowers and to the south and east were other storms. The storm to the east was so close that the reverberations from the lightning and thunder shook our craft like an automobile on a bumpy road.

An hour later we crossed Great Barrington, Massachusetts at an altitude of 14,400 feet. The entire area of clouds and thunderstorms had evaporated. Now, everything east of the Hudson was clear. At 4:15 pm we crossed Springfield, Massachusetts, and our speed had slowed to ten miles per hour. Our ballast was getting low and so we threw overboard 200 pounds of equipment—oxygen bottles, spare clothing, rations, two-thirds of our water supply and maps we would not be using the remainder of the race.

Perhaps the most extraordinary coincidence of the whole flight occurred at 4:30 pm when we sighted a peculiar airplane to the east, just crossing the east central portion between Connecticut and Massachusetts, flying in a southwesterly direction.

But it was not a plane of the Boston to New York airways. In checking we found it was no known American make of plane. Then it occurred to us that that scarlet plane was that of Coste and Bellonte, passing us just before finishing their transatlantic flight an hour and a half later in New York.

This was a remarkable coincidence for those early aviation years to think that we, starting in a free balloon race from Cleveland and they in an airplane from Paris should sight each other in our line of flight!

At evening we crossed Eastport, Connecticut at 200 feet and our course shifted to east northeast and we headed directly for Boston. In explanation of our varying speeds, let me say that the clue to ballooning lies in the fact that the air is always in motion. Generally speaking, warm air is pushed upward by heavy cold air, which, growing warmer, is thrust aside and tossed upward by still more cold air. The rotation of the earth leaves the atmosphere lagging a bit behind the movement of the earth itself. And so from any given point on the earth, the entire massive atmosphere is moving around the globe in an opposite direction to the earth's own movement and moving air and winds may and often do move at different velocities at different elevations.

When we passed over Woonsocket, Rhode Island, we had two and a half bags of ballast and 100 pounds of equipment; sufficient for our flight for the rest of the night. By now we knew we would have to stop in the suburbs of Boston at about 9:30 pm. We crossed Franklin, Massachusetts at 8:30 and Walpole, Massachusetts at 8:50 pm. Here we initiated a sharp lookout for lighthouses for the Atlantic and light from the suburbs of Boston.

At 9:05 we sighted our first lighthouse and heard the first boat whistles from the Atlantic. We prepared for a landing because we didn't care to come down in the sea as we had in 1925. Valving our balloon down at 9:16 pm, we landed in a lot 60 feet wide by 100 feet in length, the smallest target I have ever landed on during all of my races, not counting the bobbing deck of the S. S. *Vaterland*.

The *Belgica*, captained by Captain Ernst DeMuyter, himself a four-time victor of the Gordon Bennett trophy, appeared to have covered the second longest distance, 435 miles, but was faced with the possibility of being disqualified because of a report that a farmer loosened his drag rope from a tree at Esperance, New York.

DeMuyter denied that the rope had been cleared from an obstruction, explaining that what actually had happened was that he had lowered his radio set to a farmer to lighten his load.

Captain DeMuyter turned the trick for Belgium in racing triumphs in 1923, '24 and '25, retiring the original cup, then began the succession of American victories and two U. S. Gordon Bennett trophies.

It must be said that the most colorful event of the 1930 race was the landing of the *Belgica* at Adams, Massachusetts. Leon Cockelbergh, De-Muyter's aide, jumped from the basket of the balloon as it passed over over Mt. Greylock to lessen the ballast and permit the bag to stay in the air a little longer. His effort was to no avail, however, for the *Belgica*'s gas was soon exhausted. The aide was unhurt and wandered into a farmyard some four hours afterwards.

But the Cockelbergh action held out an additional possibility for disqualification. Rules required both pilot and aide to remain in the basket to the conclusion of the flight.

After *Goodyear VIII*'s win with a 550-mile distance came DeMuyter with 456 miles (challenged on technicalities). Landing places of the other balloonists with the distances scaled by the Goodyear-Zeppelin Corporation experts were the *Barmen* of Germany with Dr. Hugo Kaulen and Karl Goetze, pilots, landing in Pittsfield, Massachusetts, 425 miles; *City of Detroit*, piloted by Edward J. Hill and A. C. Slosser, landing at Coeymans, New York, 428 miles; the *City of Cleveland*, piloted by Roland J. Blair and Frank Trotter of Akron, landing at Copenhagen, New York, 355 miles; and the *Pierre Fishbach*, France, piloted by Albert Boltaird and Jean Herbe, landing at Beamexville, Ontario, Canada, 174 miles.

I might say that while the flight of *Goodyear VIII* had been flown on the most modern scientific basis, the jaunt of Blair and Trotter, both former students, was far more exciting. They, too, battled squalls during the night and in the morning found themselves flying at an altitude of 11,000 feet over northern New York state, east of Lake Ontario.

The novice pilots, who had surprised the ballooning world by taking first place in the Houston National Race the previous July 4, were in perhaps the best position of any team in the contest, expecting northeast winds to drive them toward Newfoundland, the farthest point from Cleveland in an eastern direction. Their hopes were dashed when they struck a cold air current and were sent hurtling earthward as the gas in the bag of the *City of Cleveland* contracted.

Instead of throwing out valuable ballast as they approached the ground, the youthful pilots figured their ship would strike and bounce back into the air, precisely as ours had done. Their strategy would have worked, too, had it not been for a clump of trees which tore and gouged the envelope, disqualifying the pilots. It was unfortunate luck and I cannot give them low marks on their strategy or their thinking in any respect.

There was an extra-special celebration following the race inasmuch as the banquet at downtown Cleveland's Pick-Carter Hotel was held jointly for the Gordon Bennett balloonists and also the celebrated aviators of the National Air Races. One of my favorite pilots over the years was Roscoe Turner who was known for his swashbuckling ways as much as for Bendix and Thompson Trophy victories.

Edith and I had the privilege of sitting with Roscoe at the head table, which meant that Roscoe's pet lion, Gilmore, who dined at the Waldorf with Roscoe, slept in his private suite with him in New York, and had a racing plane named for him, frolicked *under* the head table. My wife turned to me and said rather calmly, "The Colonel's lion has its paw a-bout my leg." I said, "Well, I'll do something about that," so I said, "Roscoe, I want to compliment your lion on his exceedingly good taste, but would you please put him on the other side of you away from Mrs. Van Orman's leg. She is appreciative but is not fond of a lion making love to her limbs."

Also about that time Edith and I were at a race gathering at the Lake Shore Hotel in neighboring Lakewood, Ohio. I took two bottles of King George IV scotch with me which was given to me by Ted DeWitte, the most talented National Air Races promoter. One was for the race, he said; the other for the celebration.

I met Jimmy Doolittle at the hotel and instantly liked and admired him and it was a mutual comraderie that is just as strong today. And it all began that night in 1930 when he joined our party and fell in love with King George IV and he stayed with us, re-telling all of the great stories, until he had loved the bottle to death.

Stanley Morash, member of the Class of '38, Case School of Applied Science, presents the Case Alumni Gold Medal Award for scientific achievement to Ward Van Orman, Class of '17, at the Case Alumni Sheraton-Cleveland Hotel banquet on May 13, 1977.

## . 24 .

# *Crazy Johnston's Legacy*

With six big bags ready to cast off on a wind-whipped afternoon of July 18, 1931, preceding the 21st national lighter-than-air contest, old-timers were reminded that fifty-eight years earlier Akronites also had been thrilled with a balloon ascension out at the old Hall Fairgrounds.

John Johnston, a farmer living in Northhampton Township arrived at the fairgrounds with his homemade balloon. The big bag had been filled with gas downtown and was towed up to the fair by one hundred men and boys. Johnston was a pioneer and balloonist and was so far ahead of his time, many called him "Crazy Johnston."

But Johnston had faith and so had his devoted wife. His wife helped him make the balloon in the cellar of their farm home. Mrs. Johnston did most of the sewing, using thousands of spools of thread and she went to the fair to watch him do his great stunt.

Twenty thousand people were there that day coming from far and near. Johnston, the farmer pilot, was dressed in working clothes. There were no badges pinned to his breast; there was no one to sing praises to his daring adventure into the clouds. People had not yet become air-minded. Johnston alone was able to envision the coming of aircraft that were to fill the skies and fly around the world in eight days.

Johnston the farmer had been a great reader. He had a scientific mind and he had devoured many scientific works.

"The people call me crazy," he would say, "but the time will come when the greatest roads of transportation will be through the skies."

The hour arrived for Johnston to make his flight in his homemade

balloon, *The Summit*. Bands were playing. Many inclined to think Johnston crazy, couldn't help but cheer. Johnston climbed into the basket.
All other attractions at the old fair were halted. The suspense and excitement caused many women to faint.

"Cast off!" shouted the pioneer balloonist.

Slowly at first the balloon started to climb, but tragedy was just
around the corner. A sudden gust of wind blew the big bag against the
tallest tree. More people fainted. No one was cheering now for all could
see the big gaping hole, down near the bottom of the bag. Johnston,
quick to grasp the dangerous situation, threw out all the sand ballast.
Then, like a rocket, the balloon shot heavenward.

Johnston saluted the crowd below. How the people did cheer. Fate
decreed Johnston should be carried off in the direction of his farm
home. The balloon was noticed to suddenly drop. A crowd awaited to
hear the news. Johnston landed alive but brokenhearted and wrecked
financially.

His balloon was salvaged and sold as a covering for haystacks. Johnston lost his home. He died poor. His tombstone in Northhampton Cem-
etery tells you where he is buried. This windy summer day in 1931, not
many living remembered Johnston and how he died for something he
thought someday would become a reality.

Two winners of the '31 Akron race would get places on the American
team in the Gordon Bennett. As winner of the previous year's international contest, I was automatically entited to U. S. leadership in the
Bennett in the fall. So for once I accepted the responsibility of referee
and okayed Trotter and Blair to pilot *Goodyear VIII*. It was a decision I
regretted almost immediately. It was a terrible feeling not going up with
the bag.

It was a pretty wild show even before the race got started. There was
a race for airplanes powered with OX-5 motors and another race between the Goodyear blimps. The Thomastown Schoolhouse, the airport
administration building and the Goodyear-Zeppelin dock served as
pylons. The Akron glider club also provided exhibitions of auto-towed,
shock-cord launched glider flight. Mrs. Babe Smith jumped from a
balloon harnessed in a parachute and there were airplane acrobatics
by Harry Harter.

The national race, over twelve hours after weigh-off, was won by
Tex Settle and Wilfred Bushnell for the Navy. They battled storms for 215
miles to Marilla, New York, were finally forced down because of exhausted ballast and severe thunder showers. Trotter and Blair took second position by landing at Stephensville, Ontario, 190 miles from Akron.
Edward Hill and Arthur Schlosser, flying the Detroit WJR entry, took third

place in a run to Erie, Pennsylvania, 110 miles away.

Captain Karl Axtater and Lieutenant H. H. Couch landed at Custards, Pennsylvania, for an 80 mile run. Some idea of the storm conditions the fliers encountered can be imagined by the fact that L. P. Furcolow and John Rieker of the *Del-Mar-Va* traveled only 20 miles to a point four miles north of Ravenna and Army's *Balloon No. 2* piloted by Lieutenant Edgar Fogelsonger and John Tarro was forced to earth at Brimfield, Ohio, only 16 miles away!

Witnesses said the occupants of the Navy balloon who with the aid of a farmer loaded the bag on a truck and drove away toward East Aurora, New York, almost immediately after landing. Mrs. Charles Grosendahl, on whose farm the craft landed, said the balloon had swept over them almost at ground level and was being tossed about unmercifully by the windstorm that had lashed the area. Near the farmhouse the balloon dipped suddenly to the ground and was hurled against a fence.

Also a dozen farmers somewhere east of Akron were likely to be looking askance at their wives and daughters that night as a result of the Akron celebration. They perhaps found it hard to believe that the bouquets the ladies clutched so prettily in their arms had come hurtling down from the skies. But such was the fate of the flowers which sponsors handed the balloonists immediately prior to ascent.

Former Case classmate and noted Cleveland builder Ab Higley presents Van with floral horseshoe for luck, a gift from school friends, just prior to Van's lift-off at the Cleveland Gordon Bennett International Balloon Race in 1930. Van Orman won the contest with a flight of 542 miles.

A sea of perfect quietness is a joy known only to a handful on earth. Something close to it is encountered by glider pilots, but the free balloonist is unbridled of any sort of vehicle about him. For many, free-ballooning in the blackness of night, broken only by the silver of stars, is akin to a spiritual experience.

# · 25 ·

# All for War, Glory, Fungus and Cosmic Rays

**News Report**
**by**
**W. G. Quisenberry**
United Press Staff Correspondent

*London, August 13, 1932:*

Six world powers have begun a race for supremacy in the stratosphere—that freezing region ten miles above the earth where airplanes
can attain the speed of bullets. The next war, it has been said, will be fought
in the air. The latest scientific discoveries about the stratosphere which
only one man so far has pierced, now make that prediction almost doubly
certain.

Germany, France, Britain, the United States, Russia and Belgium are
the nations bent on being the first to conquer this rarified upper region.
Some seek to wrest its secrets with powerful rockets.

Others such as France, Britain and the United States are secretly assembling stratospheric planes designed to streak through the aerial no
man's land at 500 to 1,000 miles an hour. Leading scientists of the world now
agree almost unanimously that the stratosphere opens up the most amazing possibilities ever known for bullet-like transportation. Experiments
in Germany and Russia have shown that rocket planes controlled by radio
and carrying deadly explosives can be hurled across the Atlantic in five
minutes and directed into the hearts of great cities.

Planes carrying passengers over the same route in one hour is an
almost immediate possibility, say the men who have carried out stratospheric experiments backed by secret subsidies by their governments.
France already has finished two planes capable of piercing the stratosphere
constructed with hermetically-sealed cabins to keep their pilots from
freezing or dying from lack of oxygen.

They are now being tested under the eye of the air ministry. Britain

167

has now drawn up plans for a stratospheric plane which will carry thirty men, propelled by a 2,000 hp engine. The United States and Russia have concentrated on rockets and have made several sensational experiments in that line.

Germany is a leader in both rocket and stratospheric plane experiment. But only Professor Auguste Piccard of Belgium has made a successful flight into the stratosphere. His first balloon flight carried him 50,000 feet above the earth. Piccard now awaits better air conditions before starting on his next ascent.

To be sure, my friend Piccard needed only slightly better weather to go again. He seemed satisfied that as a result of his first adventure, the world already knew something more about cosmic rays which some scientists believe hold the clue as to whether the universe is running down or is destined to live forever. Measurement of these rays was one of the most important scientific objectives of the journey. The cosmic rays striking the earth from somewhere in the upper regions constituted then, as now, one of the great puzzles of science.

When Piccard's second ascent did take place, roughly a year after the first, the first radio messages from the stratosphere kept the world informed of progress in the Belgian's flight of twelve hours.

The sudden rise of temperatures from sub-zero ten miles in the air into the heat of an Italian summer day caused Piccard and his aide, Max Cosyns, to be overcome temporarily. The exterior of the gondola was painted all white, an improvement suggested by the near roasting the occupants suffered on the previous year's flight when one side was painted white and the other black.

The black was intended to absorb the sun's rays and warm the gondola from what the professor expected would be freezing temperatures. Instead, the sun shone so warmly on the middle globe that the heat was terrific.

Piccard was particularly concerned in checking conclusions he had made regarding cosmic rays his first trip out. The new gondola weighed about 1,750 pounds and was fastened to the balloon by eight cables attached on the outside. It had nine windows, three of them on top permitting a view of the balloon itself and three others a view of the sky. Through three lower windows, the occupants could look down at the earth through the tops of the intervening clouds.

Serious trouble on the first flight which nearly cost the lives of Piccard and his companion was chiefly caused by their inability to open a manhole or to operate the safety valve and release the gas which was holding them becalmed at an altitude midway between the stratosphere and the earth.

By March 8th of the following year, the now world-famous scientist had arrived in Akron, Ohio, accompanied by his twin brother Jean who lived in Marshaltown, Delaware. The Goodyear scuttlebutt was a projected American stratosphere flight, again by Piccard. He talked to Goodyear officials about a balloon for such a flight. Auguste, rarely one for cordialities, would reveal no details of his plans but his brother admitted there had been conversations with Chicagoans regarding a possible flight from there in the summer, connected in some manner with the Century of Progress fair.

They were in a great hurry.

"We've come for business," said Auguste. "Yes, of course we're considering a flight. It happens that rubber companies make balloons. Yes, that is why we are here."

The ascension Piccard would make would be of about the same altitude. About ten miles, he said.

"We need not go higher. That is high enough for the study of the cosmic rays," Piccard replied to a question.

Asked if these rays could be put to use, Piccard indicated that these investigations were purely scientific in their nature.

Practical applications "were a matter of the distant future." Piccard was interested in getting a new slant on the cosmic rays—to study them over America—so that he could compare his records of previous flights with new data. Variations in the flight records might provide important clues as to their nature of the cosmic material.

Though Piccard wouldn't give details about the balloon he had ordered in Akron, it was easily assumed that one suitable for his purpose would have to have about 500,000 cubic feet capacity and would carry a sealed car beneath it.

A straight-laced fellow to the extreme, he was, nevertheless, an individual of the highest personal courage. He was a veteran of several balloon races, including the Gordon Bennett. It was simply that his personal discipline outshone any obvious desire to impress either peers or the public generally. He hated small talk.

On April 13, 1933, Max Cosyns, the young Belgian physicist who had accompanied Professor Piccard to the stratosphere the previous summer, announced he was in training for a return trip of his own in June. Cosyns hoped to set a new altitude record and added "a wrinkle of his own" to techniques for the flight.

He hoped to take a helper balloon along to act as a sort of "brake." The main balloon would be the *F. R. N. S.*, the bag Professor Piccard used on his previous flight, and his helper balloon would be the *Belgica*, which Captain Ernest DeMuyter had used in several Gordon Bennett races. Captain DeMuyter was to pilot the *Belgica* while Cosyns would have with him as assistant, Jacques de Bruyn, another young physicist.

The *Belgica* was expected to hold the stratosphere craft at certain predetermined altitudes, facilitating the study of cosmic rays during the flight. There would be telephonic communication between Cosyns and de Bruyn in the gondola of the *F. R. N. S.* and DeMuyter in the "brake" craft.

By valving gas or throwing out ballast according to directions from the scientists, DeMuyter would be able, it was thought, to decrease or add to the lifting power of the combination aerial laboratory.

At 30,000 feet the brake balloon would cut loose and Cosyns' craft would rise to its ceiling. It was hoped this would be above 54,776 feet recorded by Piccard when Cosyns was along as an assistant. While there would be much scientific observation on the flight, the main object of the attempt would be to bring to Belgium the world's altitude record, then held officially by Switzerland, since Professor Piccard, although a teacher at the University of Brussels, was a Swiss citizen.

Like the other two super ascents, the June attempt would be financed by the Belgian National Fund for Scientific Research. The big double ascent would start from southern Belgium. Piccard's second flight had begun in Zurich, Switzerland and ended when he brought his balloon down on a lake shore in Italy. In his first trip into the stratosphere in 1931, Piccard reached 51,793 feet and bumped to a landing on an Alpine glacier.

As to the Piccard brothers and their planned ascent from Chicago, it was not long after their meeting with Goodyear officials that Jean Piccard asked me to pilot their stratospheric venture! It is at this point that I must confess to the reader my prejudice in regard to the Belgian duo, based, I suppose, on trifles. Nevertheless, when two are seated nearly in each other's laps for many hours ten miles above the earth, nothing is trifling. Therefore I have always had an eye for detail when it came to picking partners for races or matters involving scientific endeavor which, by their nature, would lock us in the air as partners for a long period of time.

I would make it clear at once that my feelings toward the Piccards was entirely social and not the least scientific. That is very important. My own personal dislike for Jean Piccard started when it came to my attention that he wore inverted chicken baskets as helmets. The day he visited the Goodyear plant he bounced around all over the lot and insisted on drinking from the laboratory spigots instead of the drinking fountains in the hall.

I thanked Jean for asking me to pilot the largest balloon in the world for him. It was, after all, a hell of an honor. But refuse him I did. I suggested that he contact Tex Settle, my arch competitor in the Bennett and

Litchfield races. Tex was the naval aircraft inpector at the Goodyear-Zeppelin Corporation. The catch was that Jean wanted to go along as aide on the expedition.

Well, I warned Tex ahead of time and he soon got the same feeling about Piccard that I had. That was when Tex decided to go alone to the stratosphere. I objected strenuously to that notion and told him so. He was as mulish as I was so I went over his head to the board of trustees.

Now Settle and I were as close as two men could be. No one had I ever trusted or admired more. When my beloved wife Edith passed away in 1932, Tex sat with me through the night in our living room in front of the casket. That's what I mean by friend. But now he misinterpreted my motives entirely. He assumed I wanted the glory for myself and offered to withdraw from the flight in my place. I backed off rather quickly at that point, determined not to pursue the matter further, and Tex Settle readied himself to go ten miles into the sky alone.

"I'm damned enthusiastic about it!" "No, I don't consider the flight in the least dangerous," Settle told the press. It was the only incredibly stupid remark I ever can recall him making to anybody, for Settle was an uncommonly brilliant fellow.

At the time I was asked quite often if I considered the adventure of questionable scientific significance. I didn't like the word questionable. It always was a matter of balancing benefits to be received against the risk involved. I never questioned the benefit gained from stratosphere flights. It was entirely a question of value in terms of knowledge gained versus human life risked. Inasmuch as it was Tex Settle's life at risk, I considered the price too high.

Under the auspices of Chicago's Century of Progress exposition, Settle would step into a metal gondola slung beneath a 600,000 cubic foot balloon some day between July 1st and July 20th depending on the weather. Asked how high he expected to go, Settle pointed out that with a balloon 100,000 cubic feet larger than that used by Piccard to obtain 54,177 feet the preceding summer and with conditions as favorable for flying as existed during the Piccard ascent, he could hope to go higher.

The spherical airtight gondola in which Settle would ride had been built by the Dow Chemical Company of Midland, Michigan under Settle's general supervision.

The bottom of the gondola would be equipped with a large donut-shaped landing pontoon to be inflated on the way down. It would take the shock out of landing or float the car if it landed on water. Heavy flying clothes would be the chief protection for the fliers against cold. Special intruments for meteorological and cosmic ray study were provided by the University of Chicago.

A slow ascent into the stratosphere with frequent stops for scientific observations was planned by Tex after take-off. Instead of reaching the peak altitude in three or four hours as Auguste Piccard had done, Settle hoped to give himself at least twelve hours to reach the eerie upper air regions. The flight was scheduled to start at midnight.

The car, built of magnesium alloy, one-fourth lighter than dura-lumin was just large enough for one or two fliers, ballast and instruments.

"It's possible we will find ways of utilizing our surplus oxygen to inflate our landing pontoon on the way down," Tex told reporters. "It would be impossible to inflate it before starting because the expanding air would probably burst it."

The car was shipped to Akron for final inspection with the bag before going to Chicago. Commander Settle was unable to say how much ballast would be carried or whether small lead shot similar to that used by Piccard would be used through a double valve in the upper air. Lead shot *could* be used up to 14 or 15,000 feet where the gondola would be sealed for the trip into the stratosphere. An extremely careful weather watch would be maintained prior to the flight. It was common knowledge, however, that 200 mile-per-hour winds sometimes sweep the stratosphere.

Up to that point the highest altitude Tex Settle had ever experienced was 26,000 feet in the 1929 International Balloon Race.

I am very happy to say after the fact that Jean Piccard accepted Settle's decision to fly without him in the spirit of a real sportsman. Not only that, he made himself tremendously useful in the days leading up to the ascent, helping the rest of us in every possible capacity. During this time, he invited me to meet his family—perfectly lovely people. I came in time to like the fellow immensely but never his chicken basket hats in which he appeared just as erratic as hell.

One of Jean's contributions was to keep the press off our backs so that others of us directly responsible for getting the balloon in shape could get things done. Jean was far more interested in cosmic rays than I was. What's more, his chicken hats made him a reporter's dream. Newsmen figured all scientists were nuts anyway. Jean Piccard looked the part. He seemed to know what he was talking about, and he kept the reporters busy for hours.

"What cosmic rays are," Jean told reporters, "are what nobody knows and what we hope to shed a little light on. We know something of their properties but we don't know where they come from or anything much about their nature. We know a cosmic ray is very much stronger than the strongest ray of light. We think it is not continuous like a thread but consists of a succession of separate particles traveling at immense speed."

"The arrival of rays," he said, "results in sound which can be heard by means of amplifiers. They are very much weaker near the earth because the pressure is greater and the rays are absorbed in the air.

"Dr. Arthur H. Compton, professor of physics, University of Chicago thinks they are reflected from the earth's magnetic field and are emissions of electrically-loaded corpuscles. Dr. Robert A. Millikan, chairman of the administrative council of the California Institute of Technology, believes they are ultra rays of exceptionally high frequency and short wave length."

Piccard added, "These learned gentlmen periodically debate the question before the American Association for the Advancement of Science, whose body believes either may be right. Both Dr. Compton and Dr. Millikan are going to provide instruments to be housed in the gondola.

"What practical application might be gained with such knowledge? The question does not go away. My brother Auguste has said, 'It may be possible some day to liberate energy for the rays as a substitution for the power we now obtain from coal and oil deposits. These latter inevitably will be exhausted,' he pointed out."

\* \* \*

While Tex did not believe he was taking a particularly long chance, flights into the stratosphere before that of Piccard almost invariably ended in unconsciousness if not death for the aeronauts. In 1862, Henry Tracy Coxwell and Glames Glaisher made one of the first recorded flights through the highest of the icy cirrus clouds of the stratosphere. A rather ordinary balloon of some 60,000 cubic feet lifted the two aeronauts from the ground at Wolverhampton, England. They rode in an ordinary wicker basket filled with meteorological instruments.

It was a bright September day and the bag rose rapidly. They released a carrier pigeon at the three-mile point and it dropped like a stone. Another was released at four miles and it flew vigorously away. And the third, loosed a little later, dropped. By the time the third bird was released, both men were gasping for breath.

Glaisher lost his sight and the power of speech. His head rolled over on his shoulder and he found himself unable to life his arms to set it straight. Coxwell, who also felt the effects of the rare air, was then unable to see as he weakly beat the frost from the neck of the balloon. He froze his hands so badly that he could not pull the valve cord to release gas and permit the balloon to drop. The two semi-conscious men sprawled in the basket, their life slowly ebbing from their bodies.

They were unable to read their instruments. They wanted to go to sleep. How long they were in that condition is not known, but Coxwell finally succeeded in throwing off some of the deadly drowsiness, took the valve rope in his teeth and pulled. Then he lost consciousness. Both men regained consciousness as the bag dropped into the heavier air at about the five-mile point.

When they regained strength they released another pigeon at about four miles altitude. It flopped about and perched on top of the bag. Upon reaching the ground, the aeronauts found they had no record of the exact altitude they had reached. They claimed, however, that they must have reached 37,000 feet—over seven miles. But their record has been disputed ever since because both were semi-conscious at the highest point of their ascent.

But even if their flight took them no higher than the 29,000 feet their critics conceded, it was no mean attempt when it is considered that no aviator in the early 30's would venture half that high without electrically-heated clothing and life-supporting oxygen.

The next successful attempt to reach the very high altitudes was made by a German doctor named Surig in 1901 in a balloon called *Berson*. He and his aide adopted oxygen masks for their anticipated flight and gained practice with them while climbing mountains.

"It is known generally to mountaineers," he later wrote, "that in climbing up to great heights, their strength vanishes and they begin to feel sick. Quite the same happens in a balloon, but in greater altitudes, therefore, the effort of climbing is only a secondary cause for the mountain sickness. Now we are able to take oxygen with us in the form of compressed gas and by inhaling it, we can protect ourselves against height sickness."

He soon would discover that oxygen was only partial protection at the high altitudes, however. Dr. Surig wrote of their record-breaking flight in the 30,000 cubic foot balloon. "The balloon was filled with hydrogen by the military aeronautical troop in less than five hours and it rose with an enormous quantity of ballast consisting of sand and iron filings."

"Within an hour a height of 16,000 feet, which is higher than Mt. Blanc, was obtained. We then made about 3,500 feet an hour until at half past three o'clock the maximum, namely six and one half miles, was reached.

"The wind was extremely slow and irregular up to 30,000 feet but here in the region of cirrus clouds, a strong western gale blew. By abstaining from exertion as much as possible, the use of compressed oxygen did not become necessary below 18,000 feet, and as soon as we took it in greater altitudes, fresh strength and vigor returned at once. Thus we arrived in good condition at the height of 30,000 feet, feeling sometimes a weariness which, however, has as its reason a short night's rest before we started."

"This fatigue soon turned into a considerable apathy and occasional falling asleep, from which state, however, we easily recovered by shouting and shaking one another. No sort of heavy unconsciousness overtook either of us until the last set of observations were made at an altitude of 33,500 feet. Contrary to many former descriptions, the perception of the senses had not diminished. We could read our instruments quite accurately and the notes we made are quite distinct."

The events that took place at an altitude above 34,000 feet are a little confused to both of us. It seems that finally we became too weak to breathe regularly and deeply and therefore we did not get enough oxygen. The falling asleep became more frequent and therefore more dangerous. When my aide found me asleep at that point, he resolved quickly to pull the valve."

"He succeeded but the effort was too great. He collapsed altogether and lost consciousness. Before or after this act, I, too, remember several clear moments when I tried to impart more oxygen to my sleeping partner—but apparently in vain. Apparently both of us had lost our breathing pipes and then sank into a heavy swoon from which we recovered almost at the same time, finding ourselves at 20,000 feet. We are very sorry that we cannot state exactly the altitude to which we really ascended."

"But the ink of the barograph was frozen so that registration above 30,000 feet became so imperfect that the weak link at 36,000 feet may be objected to, or at least discussed..."

Since the Dr. Surig flight, precautions were taken against the ink freezing in barographs. Later models contained a smoked cylinder on which the fine point of the needle traced its record. After the famous 1901 flight, many men dared the asphyxia of the stratosphere.

Tex Settle would be one more.

Professor Auguste Piccard was by no means out of the picture just because Settle was going to pilot the balloon. Both he and Jean Piccard popped up in Akron on July 5th that eventful year of 1933 to assist in a final inspection of the stratosphere balloon.

The gondola was a seven foot metal sphere constructed to be sealed airtight. In one test, air was pumped into the gondola to create an interior pressure of 20 pounds above atmosphere pressure. Soapy water was used at all joints to determine any presence of leakage. Testers also listened for the hiss of escaping air. Later, Settle moved into the gondola and lived there for twelve hours to determine that it was possible to sustain life in the interior during flight.

National Broadcasting Company engineers went aloft in the Goodyear blimp *Defender* testing the radio equipment Settle would carry in the gondola. During the flight test, messages were sent to several NBC stations, principally those in New York and Chicago.

Even if something should go drastically wrong with the balloon and gondola in the stratosphere, the jig would not necessarily be up. Settle was to take along an artificial lung designed by Frank Hobson, civilian engineer for the Navy. The lung originally was conceived to sustain life while a man is escaping from a disabled and submerged submarine. In the same manner, Settle would count on the lung to keep him alive if he parachuted through the rarified atmosphere of the upper reaches of the stratosphere to levels at which air contained enough oxygen to sustain life on its own. Considering the thorough and careful manner in which Settle conducted tests of the gondola and its fittings, this seemed like a remote possibility, but there was no sense in missing a bet.

One of the chief factors effecting the altitude that Settle could gain was the purity of the gas with which his 105-foot diameter balloon was inflated. Because of this, the hydrogen used at Chicago was the purest that could be commercially produced.

"Each tenth of one percent of impurity in the hydrogen," Glen Carter, consulting engineer assured, "would offset its lifting power to such an extent that several hundred feet of altitude would be lost."

The walls of Settle's gondola were only an eight of an inch thick. Spread over the seven-foot diameter frame, it was relatively as thin and light as an eggshell—but airtight and tested by air pressure, dry ice, heat and water. The windows were three or four inches in diameter. Two were of fused quartz to permit spectroscopic examination of solar light, particularly of ultra violet rays. Some of the other windows were optical glass for screening red rays and for high altitude photography.

Inside the sphere was a camera, a shortwave wireless for receiving weather reports and communicating. Below were storage batteries, bags of lead dust for ballast, liquid oxygen, chemicals to absorb carbon dioxide and give off heat, instruments for measuring cosmic rays, navigating instrument, sandwiches, thermos bottles, emergency rations and a small hammock which served as a seat.

On top of the ball formed by the lodge ring ropes was what Settle had dubbed the poop deck. Here he might have chosen to lounge in the open air during the early hours of the ascent until time to crawl inside and bolt the hatches.

Although the balloon could be inflated with 600,000 cubic feet of gas, it was to receive only 125,000 cubic feet of hydrogen at the start of Settle's midnight ascent. The envelope soon would be expanded to full size under the sun's warm rays and the lighter atmosphere above. Then at full expansion the gas would be escaping through an open appendix at the bottom. At approximately ten miles up, the gas would expand ten times or to 1,250,000 cubic feet. It was expected only 60,000 cubic feet would be left when the sphere landed.

This trip, the bottom of the ball was painted black to absorb the sun's rays for warmth in early morning. In the afternoon while the chilly stratosphere was some 60 or 70 degrees below zero, the top of the car was painted white to reflect the rays when the sun was high and hot.

Tex Settle's strategy was to idle his huge craft a few thousand feet above the earth and allow it to drift westward perhaps as far as Omaha. Then as the warmth of the rising sun made conditions more favorable, he would begin the dash into the upper regions. He hoped to go higher than any man had ever gone before and from where the curve of the earth, which few men had ever seen, was visible.

A drift to the eastward into the stratosphere was expected by Settle to carry him toward the Atlantic. He hoped the craft would settle to earth between Chicago and Cleveland but admitted the landing place could not be estimated more closely than 500 miles.

With the skies above Chicago bluer than they had been in weeks, Settle retired for a few hours sleep. A heavy guard stood over the balloon and gondola at Soldiers Field, the huge amphitheater from which thousands were expected to watch the start of the epic trip.

If all went well during the flight, Tex hoped to be able to let the world listen in on the bombardment of cosmic rays. He had the transmitter of his radio connected with the cosmic ray equipment that would permit the transmission of electrical impulses caused by the rays.

Two antenna would trail from the balloon gondola during the flight, a receiving antenna 20 meters long and a zeppelin-type antenna and transmission line. At the end of the receiving antenna would be a drift ring indicator which would be useful in determining the speed and drift of the craft.

Precisely at 3:00 am on August 5, 1933, the largest balloon ever built made a spectacular take-off from Soldiers Field for a flight into the stratosphere, but the daring enterprise ended before it was well begun when the big gas bag crashed into a welter of ropes and rubber fabric in the midst of a railroad yard.

A faulty hydrogen valve brought the projected voyage into the blue void of the stratosphere to a sudden end. Only the expert maneuvering of Tex Settle saved the craft and himself from destruction. When he became certain he must land, Settle peered beneath him and saw stretching away to the south the Chicago River. On the one side were the dark outlines of buildings that offered every hazard, but on the opposite bank was a comparatively open space—a junction of the Chicago, Burlington and Quincy Railroad yards.

Settle had glided over the rim of the stadium on his ascent, his craft climbing rapidly to 5,000 feet. The pilot, who intended to await the sun, drifting at low altitude, decided he was too high too soon. He pulled the hydrogen release cord, planning to descend to about 2,000 feet. The valve which had caused some consternation before the take-off, stuck. Gas escaped rapidly from the bag and the craft sank.

Settle quickly released ballast overboard but the bag deflated so rapidly he was unable to check his plunge. I believe that with the help of an aide in the gondola, he could have done so. Searchlights from the stadium which had followed the balloon upward, plied on it as it lost altitude. A stream of lead dust which Tex carried as ballast poured from the bottom of the gondola. The pilot guided the ship skillfully down through a maze of wires extending over the warehouse district.

The gondola bumped on the rails, rose several feet in the air and settled again between sets of railroad tracks. He quickly managed to release the highly inflammable hydrogen in the envelope without injuring himself or causing excessive damage to the balloon.

The bag, although nearly deflated, remained upright and Settle leaned from the hatch atop the gondola and called to witnesses, "I'm all right. Notify Soldiers Field at once." He then released the remainder of the hydrogen and the bag came to rest a second time seventy feet away. Flares were posted along the tracks to halt trains. Orders were given to re-route main passenger services. Thousands rushed to the scene. Police and fire squads added to the confusion. Settle's wife, one of the last to say goodbye to him before he sealed himself in the aluminum globe at the take-off was one of the first to his side. She raced from the stadium in an ambulance to the landing scene.

Earlier, at 2:15 am, Dr. Allen D. Albert announced that Commander Settle wished to test the gas valve and requested quiet. The crowd's response was perfect. The stadium was suddenly still. Settle pulled the valve and listened for the escaping gas. I listened with him. So did Sam Townsend, Settle's personal aide. And Mrs. Settle. We all heard the escaping gas but there was uncertainty whether the closing of the valve was audible. Tex tried to test again and consulted with Townsend and myself.

Our somewhat hesitant decision was that the valve had closed and that its inaudibility was due to its considerable height. All of us waited and listened. No more gas was heard escaping so we agreed that the valve must have closed. During the wait however, those familiar with ballooning suspected that the valve was not functioning properly and sensed the threat of trouble that was to follow. Settle promptly proceeded with the business of weighing off.

At 3:00 am, I helped him give the command "Up ship!" The huge pear-shaped balloon floated off gracefully and made a beautiful sight under the illumination of eight million candle-power searchlights. It seemed no more than seconds to the waiting crowd before he was seen to be heaving ballast from his falling ship. It actually was twenty minutes.

After we all had time to sleep on the idea, however, we unanimously came to the conclusion that there was *nothing* wrong with the valve on the balloon—except, of necessity, the 600,000 cubic foot bag was only inflated about a sixth of its capacity. This left many yards of loose fabric at the bottom. The lift of the hydrogen naturally carried it all to the top as the heavier outside atmosphere pressed upon the fabric at the bottom, creating an airtight condition in the vacuum inside.

Apparently the valve cord got caught in a fold of the loose fabric. Even in tests, Settle had to use most of his strength to pull it free and open the valve and during one of the tests, the valve failed to return to its place as it should have. Once Settle obtained the 5,000 foot altitude, he was able to pull the valve cord and open the valve—but the springs weren't strong enough to close it again.

This was the theory that seemed most reasonable. In any case special attention was devoted to avoiding the possibility of such a difficulty on the next attempt. Most of the organizations which had aided the ill-fated attempt soom declared their desire to help the naval officer in a second try. The *Daily News* informed Settle of its willingness to cooperate again. The Dow Chemical Company agreed to recondition the gondola. Union Carbide and Carbon Company okayed another supply of hydrogen.

There was to be no advanced build-up the next time. Tex Settle and sponsors alike took the position that the next attempt was only a completion of the first which ended unfortunately in the middle of Chicago. What was to be said about the next flight would be said during it and after it. For the same reason, arrangements for the site and time were made with a view of what was best for the balloonist, not the spectator.

Once aloft after a daybreak take-off, Tex would proceed almost immediately to the stratosphere this time. The waiting period would be eliminated. A shift to the Akron airport as a departure site also was thought to provide more clearly ideal conditions due in considerable measure to the bowl shape of the stadium that had hampered inflation at Soldiers Field and necessitated a delay of several hours in getting the flight underway.

On September 24th of that same year, the Russians tried an ascent of their own. It was even less successful than Tex Settle's aborted effort.

After trying seven times to get the craft into the air, Russian scientists in Moscow gave it up. It was believed the engineers miscalculated the amount of hydrogen needed to raise this sphere.

On October 10th it was announced that Settle would definitely take an aide, Major Chester L. Fordney, a Marine Corps officer, into the stratosphere this time.

Of interest was a newspaper story on October 12th to the effect that the Russians finally made it more than twenty feet off the ground. At least they said they had. In fact they claimed credit for a trio of Russians rising an unheard of 63,000 feet off Russian soil. They also claimed a world parachute jump record made by V. N. Evseev of the Red Army who reportedly leaped from an altitude of 23,616 feet, equipped with an oxygen mask and a barograph. The Russians said Evseev allowed himself to fall 23,124 feet before opening his parachute.

Settle stated he did not think he and Fordney could reasonably expect to reach an altitude of more than 58,000 feet, nearly a mile less than the altitude claimed by the Russians. The claim of a new altitude record had not yet been recognized by the Federation Aeronautique Internationale. The matter was chiefly one of size of the balloons used. The balloon Settle and Fordney would use was 600,000 cubic feet capacity while the Russians were said to have had a 25,000 cubic meter or nearly 875,000 cubic foot sphere—almost half again as large as the Settle-Fordney bag.

Settle was sure that taking Fordney along would not materially affect the altitude he hoped for. He explained that the Marine could be used as emergency ballast on the way down and be sent overboard via parachute. This possibility lessened the necessity for saving ballast at the top of the flight to the extent of concentrating on Fordney's weight.

By Novenber, weather conditions still were not perfect for the adventure. The incredible delay was rough on the pilots, but even rougher on scads of special fruit flies on the ground. Harry H. Harriman came up with the *Beacon Journal* story:

> 50 million fruit flies can't be wrong. Well, maybe they can . . . if the big, bad cosmic ray gets after them. The fruit fly is a great nuisance around overripe bananas and leaking-bung wine kegs, but despite her unlovely characteristics, this little pest has gained a place in the sun, or perhaps more properly, in the field of science. Without benefit to biology, the fruit fly may be described as a rather low form of life which multiplies with great rapidity and has an enormous progeny, a short life cycle and rapid development from babyhood and maturity to old age. This makes her an ideal subject for certain types of scientific experiments. It has been determined also that the violet ray, when applied to the female fly, produces mutations or changes physical characteristics in the offspring.

As an experiment in the power and character of cosmic rays, a Chicago university professor decided to subject the fruit flies to the rays' influence at high altitude. Dr. Arther Compton, world reknown investigator, recently discovered that forests exercise a similar power of the mama fruit fly. Thus it was that Lieutenant Settle had listed a jar of virgin female fruit flies as part of the balloon cargo for he and Major Chester L. Fordney to take into the far away stratosphere, the realm of the cosmic ray.

Every newspaper reader knows how long unfavorable weather has delayed this ascension. But distressed reporters trying to find new and interesting ways to describe that prolonged wait, had nothing on an unsung hero in a Chicago University biological laboratory. In order for the test to be valid, this patient individual had to provide a fresh culture of virgin female fruit flies every 24 hours, to be in constant readiness. So while Settle and his aide have waited for the flight—as the days became weeks and the weeks grew into months—it may roughly be said that a lot of fruit flies have gone over the dam.

Now with the flight preparations transferred to Akron, there is some question as to whether all this labor may have been in vain. According to R. J. Stephenson, who is Dr. Compton's assistant in charge of experiments, if the Chicago laboratory has word of the actual start of the flight 20 hours in advance, a jar of suitable flies will be rushed here either by plane, auto or mail. But you know by now how unsure these stratosphere flights are. A lot of people in addition to the desperate fly raiser in the windy city would like to see the affair all through and done.

Major Chester L. Fordney had long since readied himself for the busiest twelve hours of his unusually active life. His was the responsibility of superintending the six or seven scientific experiments which were the chief reasons for the flight. Although appearing the typical devil dog in his striking Marine uniform, Major Fordney had a leaning toward textbooks. He was a Michigan University graduate in engineering and had been attached to naval air forces though he was not a pilot. Special cameras, delicate instruments which scientists had devised to study matters beyond the laymen's ken—far beyond the laymen's ken—and a scientific log of the flight all were his responsibility.

Two types of measurements would be used to register the conductivity of gas for cosmic rays. There was the cosmic ray telescope and instruments by which it was hoped to determine the direction from which the rays were most intense. Major Fordney would have a polariscope to carefully study the polarization of light. At extremely high altitudes, light diffusion is different from that of the earth.

Another duty would be to take samples of rarified air for Dr. Hopkins, noted scientist from the University of Illinois. And the U. S. Department of Agriculture requested that Major Fordney take aloft some spores, single cell organisms, for their own special study. There also would be additional duties; of photographing with the infra-red camera using special plates, and taking barometric readings. Of course another was the now famous fruit fly test.

Also Fordney was to conduct a study of the ozone layer, which would be made with the help of the Gaertner-quartz spectrogrpah. This study was to be an attempt to measure the ultra-violet limit of the solar spectrum.

To give Major Fordney the jitters, you merely had to ask him the *practical* advantage of such experiments. To the student, laboratory worker and scientist, they were of intense interest and value in extending theories and developing new lines of investigation. But few if anyone would predict how newly discovered facts might be turned to practical value.

Nevertheless, on the day of the ascent, radio history was made when the pioneer stratosphere explorers placidly carried on conversations with mere earth inhabitants. Miles above the earth, Settle and Fordney contacted the NBC station at the municipal airport to the amazement of Akron radio listeners and persons tuning in over the entire Red Network. Cleveland's Tom Manning, WTAM announcer, asked the men in the gondola what they planned to have for lunch and Fordney's voice came back, "Well, we're going to have a banana, maybe an apple and some hot chocolate."

Settle and Fordney landed in a New Jersey marsh after reaching an altitude of 61,237 feet which was recognized as a new world's record. The Federation Aeronautique Internationale made it official on study of the aeronauts' completed records. They did not receive such records from the Russian flight.

The Dow Chemical Company planned to use the gondola for exhibition purposes. The stratosphere balloon was to be kept at the Rosenwald Museum of Science and Industry at Chicago.

The first scientific result of the stratosphere flight showed that life in the form of fungus spores or molds can survive eleven miles above the earth where humans would die if unprotected. This was announced by Dr. F. C. Meier, plant pathologist of the Department of Agriculture and was interesting news to Commander Settle and Major Fordney.

The spores of seven kinds of fungi or tiny plants which the balloonists carried aloft attached to the rigging of their balloon lived through the sub-zero temperatures, low atmosphere pressure and increased ultra-violet light to which they were subjected, geminating readily after their return, Dr. Meier reported. It was the first time in the history of science that living spores had been sent to such a height above the earth and brought back for scientific analysis.

Among the spores sent aloft were those of common bread mold

known to every housewife, the bread mold that causes "bloody bread" by germinating a blood-like area after the bread is baked, and strawberry rot that causes the "whiskers" sometimes seen on berries at marketing time.

They were carried inside and outside cotton balls tied to the gondola of the balloon. Meier sought to learn how high in the air they might travel and live to show that these spores, too small to be seen without a microscope, are among the heartiest forms of life in existence!

It was announced that though the spores survived the atmosphere flight, the conditions they underwent may have caused changes not yet apparent but which might conceivably show up as the fungi developed. Tests that would cover many months would be made to learn whether development of the fungi was stimulated, their vigor altered or their heredity qualities changed.

Meanwhile, scientists at Pasadena, California, added their assurance to that of Dr. Arthur M. Compton of Chicago that data of great importance to an understanding of the nature of the cosmic ray was obtained by the Settle-Fordney adventure. The Californians completed the development of movie film picturing the action of the cosmic rays and were enthusiastic in declaring it the best ever obtained.

Dr. H. Victor Neher at the California Institute likewise assured that cosmic ray studies would be greatly advanced by the pictures obtained by the balloonists. "For the first time," he said, "a continuous record of the activities of the cosmic ray at so great a height has been available to science. On each of the pictures these rays have left an unmistakable imprint of three lines. That pattern fitted together should produce facts regarding these rays which should go far in clarifying many doubtful points of their study."

"However," Dr. Neher added, "the studies cannot be completed until the companion records taken on the flight reach the institute so that the time at which each picture was taken and the height of the balloon at that particular moment can be precisely ascertained."

Dr. Neher said other photographs and records at even greater heights had been obtained by Dr. Robert A. Millikan by the use of free balloons, but that instruments carried by these free bags were necessarily of the lightest and most delicate types. Consequently, the results obtained had been imperfect.

Van Orman (left) is shown with friends Jean Piccard, a Belgian scientist, and T. G. W. Settle of the U. S. Navy, both of whom conducted useful experiments with cosmic rays after ascending high altitudes in sealed spheres.

# · 26 ·

# *Indigo Noses Over the Mountains and Bedbugs in the Cowshed*

I was painting the fenders of my car that stifling August day in 1932, but my thoughts were across the sea at an airfield in Basle, Switzerland. In about a month I would be there as pilot of the Gordon Bennett race and I knew too damn little both about the city and its people.

Nothing short of a miracle could have been responsible for the doorbell buzzing just at that moment. Edith came into the backyard talking about a man named Schmidt to see me—from a transportation company in New York!

I hastily doffed my overalls and washed off some of the paint. The visitor, it turned out, had brought some papers which his best friend, the son of a German sea captain, had found among the effects of his father who had died recently. Among the papers were two small photographs of myself. The papers, it seemed, told the story of my landing out at sea on the deck of the *Vaterland* in 1925 from Brussels.

"It was the great event of the old captain's life," said Herr Schmidt, "when you landed on his rolling ship at midnight off the coast of Brest. These papers, telling the story, were his most treasured possessions. His son wanted you to have them."

The visitor and I reminisced for quite a while before it occurred to me that I had been rude in not asking his own origin.

"And where do you come from yourself, Mr. Schmidt? Are you a native of Germany?"

"My home is Basle, Switzerland," he replied, and that is the point of the story, after all. Schmidt gave me all the information about the city I could have desired. Not only that, he wrote letters of introduction to prominent citizens and informed me of the inns of the town, where the best cheeses were sold and the location of the town swimming hole.

Then I went back to painting those car fenders, surer that the world wasn't such a big place after all.

As I went to the air in 1932, I was alert for the buzzes and red lights from my instruments like a locomotive engineer watches for block signals. Just as an engineer might get his signals from the block ahead, I could set my instruments to flash a whole string of warnings when a predetermined altitude was reached.

I believe even before 1932 I had the most complete instrument kit of any balloonist, but that year I took still newer gadgets aloft. One of the most interesting was a new type of vertimeter which performed four functions by the mere turn of a handle. With a valve set in one position, the instrument served as a statometer, recording on its scale a total change of altitude of only 50 feet. In three other positions the instrument would register changes as high as 533, 800 and 1,333 feet per minute.

This instrument was a departure from the statoscope used in normal free balloon flights which registered changes in altitude by showing expansion or contraction of air in a container upon a colored liquid in a U-shaped tube.

A bubble breaking on one side or the other of the U-shaped tube of a statoscope which I had used many times indicated that my balloon had ascended or descended fifteen feet according to the side upon which the bubble went. But my new instrument, the incremeter, would indicate an even smaller change of altitude. This had its value because initial changes of altitude usually were very slow and could be easily counteracted at the time with minimum waste of ballast or gas. As the ascent or descent continued, the change was, of course, accelerated. More gas or ballast was required to correct the condition and consequently the flight was shortened.

The incremeter showed a change of as little as ten feet. It consisted of an air container with a top of goldbeaters skin which responded to expansion or contraction of the air and made a series of electrical contacts, also activating a buzzer or red light. An automatic device relieved excessive pressure on the membrane when increments of altitude of more than 175 feet had been reached.

Other improvements aboard the Goodyear balloon in 1932 included a speedier system of celestial navigation which required only four to five minutes to compute necessary observations as against thirty to forty minutes using marine navigation. In another area we had come up with a quite incredible chemical compound that gave long life to the balloon fabric and lightened the entire fabric so that changes of temperature had less effect on the gas.

One of my first errands in Europe before the race was to pay my respects to Frank Lahm in Paris who offered complete data on radio broadcasting schedules for all European weather bureaus. I also purchased maps covering all of Europe east to the Urals and south to the Mediterranean and north of Africa.

Bearing the colors of eight nations, seventeen balloons were to ride the winds September 25th, from Basle, Switzerland, in quest of aviation's senior honor, the James Gordon Bennett trophy. Duels and counter-duels would mark the twentieth running of the classic. Three American teams would attempt to retire the award permanently and to keep in tact a string of victories that began in '26.

From the American point of view, of course, permanent ownership of the trophy, which was the third to be at stake since young Frank P. Lahm bore the Stars and Stripes to victory in 1906, was the *major* goal.

The sportswriters wrote of an air duel between Ernst DeMuyter of Belgium and myself. DeMuyter, black haired, mustached and lean of limb, scored his first success in 1920, skipped a year and then swept to world supremacy by triumphing in three successive contests. As the youngest competitor in the 1913 race, he had taken defeat seriously and began an intense study of meteorology during the war. He gathered the first fruits of his knowledge in 1920 when, though first to land (except for one balloon forced down in the early stages of the race), he nevertheless covered the greatest distance helped by his uncanny ability to pick the right winds.

In the background was still a third contest—the natural rivalry between the American teams for a civilian, Army or Navy victory. My aide in 1932 was to be Roland J. Blair, who, between balloon races, was a superb Goodyear blimp pilot.

Rising against us were fourteen balloons from Europe. Like the United States, Germany, France and Switzerland each had entered three gas bags, Poland had entered two and Spain, Belgium and Austria one each.

The contest rule to hold the race in the country of the previous year's winner was waved by the victorious U. S. after the 1930 win to help brace sagging European interest. Several countries were unable to finance the transportation and entry fees of sports teams to American soil. They also were having plenty of trouble with our winds. So we conceded the point.

The morning before the start, several of the European entries refused to accept the Swiss Aero Club's method of determining gas capacity. The discussions on the point frankly left Tex Settle and myself bewildered except we made it awfully clear we intended to race no matter what happened.

I also was personally disappointed over the decision of Professor Auguste Piccard to withdraw from the race. At the last moment Piccard telegraphed he would be unable to participate owing to the fact he was obliged to lecture before King Albert on the results of his recent stratosphere flight.

Weather indications before the race were that storms would prevail and that a high west wind would be blowing. It was felt this could prove embarrassing to the contenders for the wind might possibly carry us over Soviet Russia where we did not have permission to fly.

Moments prior to start time, the officials passed out four bottles of champagne per balloon to stave off upper air discomforts. For once we turned them down because we were out to make the best possible run and, believe it or not, they seemed like too much to carry in a racing balloon. I'm afraid it all would have been lost in the storms over the Ricer Mountains in Czechoslovakia, anyway.

We knew the storms were brewing but as we flew along looking at the clouds ahead, we figured they were not too bad. Then we got into them. It was as if a big hand had come from the sky and grabbed our craft. We shook, then went down at the rate of 1,350 feet a minute, faster than a parachute falls. Then up again! We knew there were mountains below and not very far below according to our reckoning.

We thought we were done for and we threw 600 pounds of ballast over the side in that half hour. Finally we came out on the top of the storm. Countering the storm made unnecessary the decision of whether to fly close to the ground, conserving ballast for a long run, or to strike out for the strong winds of the upper air. Trusting to get farther in a shorter time, we had to fly high.

We flew the last nine hours of the trip at a 24,000 foot altitude, sniffing at oxygen bottles. The thermometer dropped to 15 degrees above zero and snow started to drift into the basket. After remaining at such an altitude for several hours, Blair looked at my face. It was blue.

"Do you know, Van," he said, "your face is blue?"

"I don't like to worry you," I replied, "but yours is indigo."

We couldn't get quite enough oxygen out of the bottle to make up for the rarified air. We both shivered and thought of the champagne but said nothing more about it. The sand ballast was gone after the high flying and our bag started down. A ground fog covered the ground. The quacking of ducks could be heard below. We had taken a sighting before and we knew we must be over Lithuania. The sounds we were hearing closely suggested we were over a swamp or a lake.

We figured we couldn't land there so we decided to strew the countryside with sandwiches, goods, shoes, a potpourri from the floor of the basket. Anything to stay up longer. But after remaining in the very cold air for 29 hours, we made a beautiful pitch dark landing in a hayfield 23 kilometers southwest of Kaunas, the capital of Lithuania.

From all directions people came running out of the night, almost stumbling over us and the bag.

"Speak Deutsch? Francais? Russka?" I asked. They shook their heads dolefully. Finally a little girl who could speak German was found. We learned we had almost broken up the Lithuanian potato harvest festival. They found us a place to sleep in the hall where the dancing was going on. Blair and I ate the black bread and drank the milk but decided it was too much to be expected to sleep, even after 36 hours of tense watchfulness, where dancing with wooden shoes was going on. Finally I was approached by one man who seemed to recognize my higher station as the pilot of the *Goodyear VIII*. He beckoned for me to follow him and so I tramped past Blair, leaving him in the hall, on my way to a more appropriate bed and a worthy night's sleep. My guide saluted and departed as I discovered that the pilot's bed was indeed a hayloft full of bugs and ticks.

Blair, on the other hand, awakened in the hall as the party dispersed. He dodged the giggling young master and mistress of the house as they nearly tripped over him, lying where he had been assigned, on the floor next to the open doorway of their bedroom.

In a moment his sleep was forgotten as the soft rustle of the woman's clothing honed his ears to incredible keenness. From inside the room came sighs, entreaties, laughing rejections, then a strange gutteral sound, more entreaties, kisses, a variety of throaty noises, more laughter, a final tearing of clothing, a little shriek—silence.

In the hall, Blair sat frozen in delectable sweat until the rhythm of bedsprings, so close he could with the slightest stretching reach out and touch them, commenced the steady beat which seemed never to stop and which finally, soothingly, lulled my aide to sleep.

For my part, in the hay—the bed of honor for the *Goodyear VIII* balloon pilot—I was eaten by lice and bugs over every inch of my body and enjoyed none of Blair's love music. The sun could not rise soon enough for me, and when a suddenly sneering Mr. Blair disclosed his eavesdropping on the Nest of Eros over breakfast, I resigned myself to despise the man at least for the rest of the day.

We still didn't know precisely where we were upon awakening but the peasants, none the worse for wear, took us to the city of Kaunas in a Goodyear-tired droshky and we learned that we weren't in Russia after all. Although all the balloonists had been warned not to enter Russia, Blair and I really had hoped to get there anyway. We figured that General Nobile, Italian explorer and airship builder who formerly worked for Goodyear but who had since turned Communist, could fix the case for us.

We soon learned that the U. S. Navy balloon had landed close to the town of Wasjule near Vilna on the Polish-Latvian frontier, some 900 miles from the starting point, and had been awarded first place. Tex Settle had beaten us by fifteen miles! Even then he was forced down, the report said, when his balloon cover burst.

All other pilots had landed the previous day, most of them in trouble. The *Polonia* carrying Poland's flag had scored a distance of 1,176 kilometers. The French *Pitmousse* made 1,233 kilometers. The French *L'Adventure* scored 963. The Polish bag *Gdynia* traveled 1,076 kilometers to the city of Bielany, Poland. The *Belgica*, piloted by my old comrade, DeMuyter, had been forced to land near Gorzkowice, Poland, southwest of Germany. A snow storm was blamed. A pleasant surprise was the excellent showing of the Spanish balloon 14 de Abril which landed at Malkin-Dolny, 50 miles northeast of Warsaw—good enough to be third-place winner.

It was a tremendous thrill to arrive in New York harbor and to look up and see the great Goodyear blimp *Defender* flying in salute over the bow of our steamer, *Western Prince*. I thought that was about the nicest tribute anyone could ever hope for, when five minutes later a man on the dock approached Settle and me. He turned out to be George F. Mand, chairman of New York's committee for greeting famous personages. An hour later we found ourselves presented to the great city's acting mayor, Joseph McKee. Much more of the same lay ahead of us in Cleveland and Akron where the turnouts and kind expressions were unbelievable.

I must say in all honesty that I ate it up.

Perhaps the most memorable feature of the whole Basle race experience was the trip in the *Graf Zeppelin* from Danzig to Brazil, a little side treat, courtesy of Captain Lehman. I was no sooner aboard the hydrogen-filled airship, however, when Lehman, knowing too well my chain-smoking ways, took me aside and politely as he knew how, laid down the law.

"No cigarettes," was the message. Very plain. Very clear. "No exceptions." Lehman was a fair and tolerable fellow, however. Following his admonition, he smiled kindly and handed me a small, carefully wrapped package.

"When you get the urge," he said, "open it."

The urge came about thirty seconds after he turned and retreated to the control car to await weigh-off procedures.

I unwrapped the parcel and discovered in my hand a beautiful harmonica which I have and which I play to this day, in public and in private. My nearly uncontrollable urge to smoke never left me that whole crossing. Before we were half way across the South Atlantic, I had mastered *Juanita* on my new German harmonica.

In his Akron, Ohio basement, Van still enjoys relaxing moments with his harmonica, the instrument given to him by the commander of the *Graf Zeppelin*. With the danger of the hydrogen-filled airship in mind, the instrument was to take the place of cigarettes on a transocean crossing.

Before the traumas that befell them in the Canadian wilds in 1933, the flight of Ward Van Orman and Frank Trotter started at this field in Chicago. The 21st flying of the Gordon Bennett classic was Van's last race.

Aide Frank Trotter and a very bedraggled Ward Van Orman (in flying helmet) as they looked when found in the dense Canadian Timagami country after a near-fatal crash landing during the 1933 Gordon Bennett International Race. Both were gravely ill with ptomaine poisoning and fatigue. It was Van Orman's last race. Trotter was later killed while on anti-submarine patrol in an airship in World War II.

# The Race I Didn't Want to Fly

In 1932 I had lost my wife and I had three small children to raise. For that reason alone when Paul Litchfield asked me to compete in the 21st flying of the Gordon Bennett race out of Chicago, I simply said, "No, thank you." Well, I can tell you frankly that you don't get very far with a "no, thank you" with the chairman of the board of a large rubber company.

He quickly trapped me into saying I didn't have enough insurance. Oh, how he jumped on that—"Oh, we'll cover you fully with Lloyds of London!" So there I was—trapped. I did go to Chicago for the race and stayed at the Congress Hotel. I was immediately given two bottles of King George IV scotch, one to take in the balloon and one to save for celebration.

I should have quit while I was ahead.

That year, five foreign teams would battle to break America's six-year winning streak. Three veteran American teams would seek to continue that streak—and, incidentally, to outdo each other. Settle, the present international champion, and I, previous four-time champion, were the bettors' choice.

But Lady Luck and fancy free winds would have the say about a dark horse. Likewise, the excellent showing of Lieutenant William J. Paul and Sergeant John Bishop in winning their first race, the 1932 national, entitled the Army team to consideration as a likely candidate. The European entries also looked good. The Belgian pilot Philippe Querson had competed in six races and as aide had won with pilot A. Veenstra in 1925. His aide this year was Marcel Vinschelle, former Princeton swim star. Ernst DeMuyter, Belgium's most famous balloonist, was definitely out of the race. A report stated he had been unable to keep his aged balloon aloft more than 24 hours in a test flight, despite reconditioning.

Two German balloons were entered. Fritz Von Opel of Germany was in the race after years of thrills, stunting in planes and speedboats and autos and rocket planes of his own invention. He flew with Eric Deku in the *William Von Opel*. The second German balloon was piloted by Dr. Schuetze with Dr. Eric Koerner as aide. Poland was the only nation entered which had never had a previous victory. Her hopes rested on the shoulders of Captain Francis Zekhyn Hynek and Lieutenant Zebigniew Burzynasky. They were better balloonists than they knew.

My eager young aide was Frank A. Trotter who had known victory from the beginning. He and Blair were considered just youngsters by the other balloonists in 1930 in Houston, Texas, when they won a most dramatic balloon contest. Trotter and Blair placed second in the National Race from Akron in 1931 and Omaha in 1932.

For the first time in years, I entered the race without a new gadget or two to help out. I felt I had gone as far as I could go in that direction, and all I did in 1933 was get out my special incremeter and 3-speed vertimeter designed the preceding year and dust them off.

Unsettled weather conditions worsened by stiff southwest winds accompanied our start. All Coast Guard stations in the upper lakes region were asked to stand ready for rescue should any of the balloons be forced down on the water. This real danger existed through the night with several of the balloonists likely scattered over water. The best thrill of the start occurred when the German entry *Wilhelm Von Opel* escaped.

Unlike the American balloon, this foreign craft had no net and the lines supporting its basket were attached to a band circling it at the middle. During the inflation the crew attending the *Von Opel* permitted it to rise from the ground instead of sandbagging it down like the other entries. Hence the gusty ground wind got underneath it and whirled it around considerably. When inflation was nearing completion, exceptionally strong gusts caught the bag and the band to which the basket-carrying ropes were attached started to give way. As the wind whipped about friskly, the band tore loose just as though a giant can opener had been used.

The bag was instantly free and flew to an altitude of some 500 feet before being whipped to earth. The gas hissed out and deflated fabric plopped limply about 100 feet from the starting mark.

Its pilot, Fritz Von Opel, ascribed the break to "too light construction." Even as he saw all hopes of a successful race squashed to earth in front of his eyes, he refused to be bitter or even angry at his crew.

"Better now than later," he chirped.

Well, our destination was Newfoundland. Our plan was to fly north and tap into a high speed current around Lake Superior. A premonition indicated to me that an American long distance record was in the palms of our hands. Trotter and I flew rapidly north on a temperature inversion. But later, over Lake Michigan, we crashed suddenly into the waves, having flown for hours lower than the masts of freighters we passed in the night. Our pontoons were secured in place but all of our sand which we carried on the outside gathered additional weight and there we were, glued to the surface of Lake Michigan!

My aide yelled, "Van, this is a *horrible* way to fly! I hope you know what you're doing!"

"I assure you I know what I'm *doing!*" I countered, "but it doesn't always turn *out* right!"

It took us an hour to hoist the bags high enough so they would drain, so that the balloon would then skip some 50 feet before returning to the waves. Then *more* sand overboard and we would skip 200 feet before getting wet again. Still *more* sand overboard greeted by landings in the water every 500 feet, until ultimate ascension skyward past the Straits of Mackinac, soaring to 15,000 feet into a winging 50-mile-per-hour wind current. By our own calculations we would cover a distance of 1,500 miles, an exciting new American record! All we had to do was sit up there and wait.

We had hoped for another 24 hours in the air and saw no obstacles in our path and were elated. At our present rate, that would have taken us at least to Quebec and likely much further. Oh, it felt good to see the woods and rivers and trees float beneath us and not have a care in the world, now. As we sat gloating, however, I happened to notice to the west of us a nice juicy snowball cloud, a cumulous cloud, and testing with my radio set, it turned out to be a thunderstorm. We tried immediately to find a faster current and you can imagine our dismay when we found we were in the fastest current available and simply could not pull away from the force that was upon us. The most notable thing at first was the darkness. We were flying around 8,000 feet, yet eveything was black as ink.

It got worse and worse. Suddenly the squall came with a roaring rush. When it struck, we had never seen a balloon act as our acted—not even in the Pittsburgh storm. It hit us while we were high and we careened all over, bounced all over. We rushed up and fell and were whirled around—and we were only on the outskirts of it! Had we been in the center of that disturbance, I'm certain we would have been dead at the start. Knocked out. As it was, we figured we were done for.

Somehow, each of us got in our parachutes. Each took a little pocket compass and a flashlight to observe, if possible, where we were going. Every minute the storm seemed to increase in violence. We had done everything possible. For the time being at least, we held on. When I saw we had no ballast left to keep us up in the air, I began to valve out the gas and start down, but was afraid to valve out too much because the lightning was flashing so furiously all around us and had been for hours. We didn't want to be a roman candle. The bridle which held the balloon down at the bottom was torn loose. The crackling yellow bolts were so close we could feel their heat.

We fought the storm for six hours before giving ground. Even then, Trotter screamed at me through the storm, "Van, you CAN'T land! I won't let you!" I said, "Frank, we've got to!" Well, I was in command. Then I remembered an old trick we'd used in training student naval officers in high wind. It consisted of bringing the balloon basket down into the tops of the trees, allowing the foilage to slow it down and ease the fall. In this case, however, approaching at 55 miles per hour, we slammed against the trunk of the first tree, twenty inches in diameter, and knocked it in half, and we saw yellow lights and stars and thought we were finished.

We were thrown head-over-heels in the basket and then we hit the second tree and we saw more yellow lights and we knocked that tree down, too, and we thought *that* was the finish. Then we hit the third tree and knocked that down. More yellow lights. A fourth tree was struck and broke. Still more yellow lights and lovely stars. And then a fifth tree and then our envelope caught on the sixth tree and tore the side out of the balloon and we swung in a circle about the seventh tree.

When the daze wore off, we saw that we were hanging twenty five feet above the ground in a pine tree. Miraculously, the deflated gas bag had draped over the gondola like a tent. The two of us, dripping wet, reached across the basket and shook hands and just thanked God we were still alive. We decided to camp that night in the improvised shelter the freak of the elements had provided for us. For the time being, we might have been tree men in Borneo living in our aerial fortress home high up for protection against man and beast.

We had dinner that night consisting of a can of peaches. Then we curled up for the night and the next morning we crawled down the side of the net and using a boy scout axe, we cleared a square yard of underbrush so we could pile our instruments. The underbrush was up to our chests and we knew we were in for it. We had no idea where we were. There was no farmer to ask, "Where are we?" We could hear the radio reports—knew they were looking for us—but could not respond. Then came the worst news of all. Our aircraft sextant had fallen overboard in the storm.

We did, however, have a tiny marching sextant manufactured by the British, but it required an artificial horizon to note the angle of the sun above the horizon. We filled a peach can with water and obtained the reflection of the image of the sun on the surface of the water, which gave us the angle of the sun above the horizon.

That sounds childishly simple, but every time we would get ready to take a reading, a little breeze would ripple the surface of the water or the sun would move behind the leaves of tall trees. In these conditions, it took us eight hours to compute our latitude and longitude! Nevertheless, when we were finished we knew exactly where we were and exactly where we were was the Timagami Provincial Forest, twenty-six miles from the nearest railroad.

Twenty-six miles may not sound far, but in tall, razor-sharp underbrush, including tens of thousands of fallen tree trunks, we learned that our *best* distance could not better two miles on foot a day. It rained every night with such abandon in the woods during our entire 14-day forced march to civilization that we were not dry a moment of that duration.

At the end of the first week, we both were overcome with ptomaine poisoning. Each day from then on, our progress steadily diminished as overpowering fatigue and nausea nearly conquered us. Frank and I ultimately reached the point where we'd flop on the ground for an hour, then proceed on for a city block. Our meager plan was to measure our diminishing strength against the distance to that damn railroad.

The faces of my children rarely left my mind. Frank and I already had been through high water and more than a touch of hell. I vowed to myself over and over that I would tolerate nothing but return to my children.

Most everything we really needed had been lost overboard in the storm and it was all a bad dream, a strange unreal nightmare sometimes. Water was always a problem. The first we collected from the folds of the gas bag; it tasted of rubber. We had lost our supply of matches which were wrapped in waterproof material. Fortunately we had a few left in our pockets, but they were wet. It took a day to dry them.

On Sunday, September 10th, hope of rescue flared up for a moment in our hearts. It was the tightening suspense that happens in most dramas of lost people. We heard the engines of an airplane overhead. We looked up. The engines seemed to roar almost above us but we could catch no glimpse of the machine.

We had saved our flare gun and some flares from the basket. We fired one flare. No answer. The pilot had not noticed us. He kept straight on. It was pilot Overbury of the forestry branch base at Sudbury making a flight to observe a brush fire burning around Thor Lake. We gritted our teeth and pulled ourselves along. We figured if we kept on going south, we would strike something, even if there was nothing before Sudbury. But we could scarcely walk. Besides being ill from the ptomaine, our feet had given out. We had some bad bruises on our hips.

We rested more and more frequently, recalling faintly the energy and gusto we displayed the first day in the underbrush. We had started salvaging everything we figured we should need for our trip to get us through. We decided we should need a tent so we ripped the material out of the gas bag. It was also obvious right away that we should want knapsacks so we sat down and made them. We didn't have needles. We simply ripped up pieces of the ropes and canvas and used them as thread, cutting the holes with our knives.

We managed to have our first fire the second afternoon. We had our matches dried by then. We made a fire a little way from the wreck and proceeded to get something to eat. When we took an inventory of our supplies we found we had eight tins of pork and beans and four cans of pears and peaches. Five oranges and five apples also were loose in the basket.

Cooking that meal was a great mistake. We thought we would make some pork and beans. We opened the can and didn't take them out, just heated them in the can. It almost cost us our lives! We said very little to each other; were surprisingly quiet. But after Wednesday it was sheer hell. We figured we traveled about fifteen miles altogether. But do you know what it is like in the bush? You never can tell about distance, but we couldn't have made much after that Wednesday. We began to become terribly ill at our stomachs. If we walked only a few steps we had to lie down to get some strength and try to stop the sickness. Then we would get up again and drag ourselves on a little bit further. I was the worst.

We had our gun and axe with us and were on the alert all the time to shoot any game that looked like edible food. We ran across some red raspberries and ate them with the rest of our canned pears and peaches. We had no bread. We got our water from little streams in the valleys. Whatever we thought occasionally about the outcome, we didn't reach the stage of writing our last letters, last wills and testaments. I guess we didn't think of it because neither of us had anything to leave.

And then we fell upon the most beautiful sight I have ever witnessed. To be sure, no artist could gaze on it and see a particle of aesthetic merit. Others could look at it all day and say, "Oh, well, that's nothing but a high tension line!" To us it was life. It was civilization. The high tension line was from Timmons, Ontario, where they generated the power, to Sudbury where they used it in the copper mines.

I must admit I had visions of climbing this 80-foot steel tower and interrupting the flow of current to draw attention to us. Then my better judgment took hold and I decided I didn't know how to do that without killing myself in the process.

But paralleling the high tension line on old wooden poles was a telephone line which I concluded was a discussion line. Trotter and I worked for thirty minutes with a little axe to chop down the six-inch wooden sapling. When it fell to the ground, bringing the wires with it, we severed them, figuring that Canadians did a great deal of talking and would soon be on our backs. Trotter wrote a note explaining who we were, what had happened, and that we would continue south along the hydro line. We went on and only a couple of miles further we struck a shelter hut the linemen used. It seemed like the Drake or the Palmer House! Trotter shot the goddam lock off.

Inside was the height of luxury. There was glass in the windows, a stovepipe coming out the roof. Inside were Hudson Bay blankets and a sack of beans and for the first time in two weeks we got dried out—warm and dry!

Just as I was ready to go to sleep, Trotter said to me, "Man, I don't care whether you're sick or dying or ready to conk out, you just got to get up and look!" I thought, "Gee, if it's that important!" So I got up and looked, and there was the loveliest display of the aurora borealis—just like church lights across the sky. It gave us goose pimples, and while we were not superstitious, we figured it a good omen—those searchlights out there welcoming us back to civilization!

At Sudbury headquarters, meanwhile, orders were issued to find and correct the telephone outage. Finally aware of the approximate location of the short circuit, Superintendent A. H. Skeen instructed Jim Barrett, hydro-patrolman at La Forest to proceed along an eight-mile section.

Next morning, Trotter jumped up, grabbed the shotgun and shot a grouse. In a few minutes time we had grouse stew made in a dirty lard pail. It was the best-tasting morsel I had yet tasted and the only food that stayed down since we landed in the woods two weeks before.

Meanwhile all hell was breaking loose in the states and Cliff Henderson, manager of the National Air Races at Chicago, our starting point, wasn't sitting on his hands. Two balloons were considered lost and potentially destroyed—ours and the Polish. Cliff enlisted the help of the Army, Navy and Coast Guard and was on the horn to the Canadian government. A popular notion was that we had been swept out to sea, knowing our intended altitude was 25,000 feet early in the contest, and realizing that "we could have encountered anything" at that height.

If there was one man in the world who could have freed up the dirigible *Macon*, it was Henderson. Sure enough, the *Macon* received orders to search the Atlantic coast, going as far north as Nova Scotia as soon as weather cleared. Almost as an afterthought Henderson also obligated the state police of a half dozen states, the forest rangers and the Canadian mounties. The FBI had no one more sought for than the two Polish and two Akron balloonists, for soon broad manhunts were underway throughout the New England states, northern Canada and the Great Lakes region. Radio stations throughout these areas broadcasted appeals to listeners to report anything that could be of assistance. Army planes, Navy planes and Canadian forest patrol ships were combing tens of thousands of miles of wilderness and coastal waters.

In particular, Captain Glen Salisbury of the Army was to lead a flight of seven Army planes leaving Boston for Bangor, Maine to base there and cover an extensive area from Bangor to Caribou. Greater concern was felt generally for the safety of the Polish fliers than for Trotter and me for less was known of their ability and equipment carried in the Polish bag, *Kosciuszko*.

We were in the linemen's cabin eating freshly shot grouse, our strength returning in stages, and generally feeling on top of the world when in walked a six-foot Canadian with an 80-pound sack on his back. His greeting was, "What the hell are you fellows doing here?"

It was very nice of him and I said, "Well, we landed in a balloon back in the bush about 26 miles and we're working our way to the nearest railroad." He said, "My God! You're them! Everybody in Canada has been looking for you!" I said, "Oh, that's something."

He went out and put his little portable telephone on the wires that were still intact to Sudbury and in a half hour's time a plane was flying overhead with medical supplies.

I would like to talk a minute about a man who struck me as a tremendous hero of that whole remarkable adventure. He was hardly an impressive fellow in appearance or stature. He might not even have been the best reporter in those parts, but he had one thing—the guts to accomplish what he set out to do.

James Y. Nicol of the *Sudbury Star* beat the world to our balloon crash story with an "exclusive." What made this remarkable was that Nicol was stationed in a town 200 miles from the scene of the crash when he heard the word we were down. About a month later he wrote friend Art Arthur of the *Brooklyn Eagle* how he beat out scores of reporters and the major news services with the scoop. A part of his letter reads as follows:

... I had a lot of fun getting the yarn. While all the boys were yelling about airplanes, I happened to remember that there were freight trains still running through the isolated section where the balloonists had crashed. I beat it by auto 20 miles in 19½ minutes over one of those horrible northern log roads. 'Had to get to the nearest train. I left my own hat at home and stole the boss's. But at the junction where I caught the train—hell! Another reporter came there and got the same idea and was in the caboose ahead of me. When he saw me he looked as pleasant as a guy drinking cod liver oil. He said, "Well, 'guess we'll wait at the Thor Lake overnight and get them when they come out of the woods in the morning." And he was rather patronizing at that.

But when I stepped off the freight at Thor Lake I spied a great big bozo all decked out in high boots, mackinaw, etc.—just a prospector who had come to see the train go by. I said, "Lad, here's $10 if you get me to where the balloonists are tonight," and he said, "Okay."

When the other reporter went into a nearby lumber camp we ran like blazes for the bush and kept on going. About midnight the guide and me pounded on their door. Half-asleep, they opened up and I thrust a bottle of Canadian Club in Trotter's hand and embraced the fellow.

"ANY NEWSPAPER MAN COME HERE YET?"

He said, "No, why?"

"Thank God!" I said, and sat down and copied verbatim the details of the flight and crash of *Goodyear IX* until 4:00 am in the morning. Van Orman and Trotter were a pair of swell fellows. They said I must be berserk rambling through the woods in the black of night, but both opened up like a pair of princes, told me everything. I was wild with excitement. I told the prospector to get me back as fast as he could. He looked a bit surprised as we had just done 10 miles and the going was terrible—but he was game.

He proved to be a real man, too, and I'll never forget the way he behaved—one of those he-men you often read about but seldom see. We started back but in time the groping and stumbling through the brush got the best of me. I wasn't a young man any more. Crossing over a rocky hill, I slipped on a stone and collapsed. Completely winded on the frost-covered ledge, badly bruising a hip in the process, I yearned for nothing but sleep. My reporter's "resolution" and all I had gone through to get that story evaporated from my concern.

My guide turned out to be Syd Fairweather, one of the best bushmen in the whole north. A man of the woods, he gave up a job as telegraph operator to become prospector. For six years he had combed the Thor Lake area. He knew it like a book and he didn't like to see my $10 go for nothing.

While other news gathering agencies were making inquiries about road conditions to Thor Lake and chartering airplanes, he and I had scrambled along the hydro-electric line to the Abitibi Canyon and Tower 738 in the dark. It seemed like weeks ago. It had been hours. But when a trail follows the power line and is "brushed" on both sides, it is almost as wild as a jackpine forest itself.

Fallen trees had strewn the route that traversed hills and valleys, rocks and marshes, creeks and muskeg. Fairweather saw me weakening and remarked rather pleasantly that during the war there were a lot of soldiers shot for folding up on the path, disorganizing the morale of the troops.

202 • *The Wizard of the Winds*

With my hip and scraped rib throbbing painfully and almost delirious with sleep, I whispered, "Okay, lad, get out your gun and shoot. I don't even care."

I did care, though, and in a half-hour we reached Thor Lake and the first interview with the crashed balloonists was put on the wire to the Canadian Press under the banner of the *Sudbury Star*. It was a major scoop and the couple of dozen reporters in the room who hadn't planned seeing Van Orman for another 24 hours, vowed that mutilation was too good for me."

Days later our party had reached Sudbury. Trotter and I were still ill. I could walk only a little way and had to rest. I think we both looked more than a little gaunt and hadn't shaved since Chicago. The long trek by canoe and work train from the cabin had been taxing. Once at Sudbury and the introductions of countless officials was over, the owner of the Sudbury newspaper took us under his wing.

His sister, a trained nurse, put us to bed and kept us both on a bland diet so that in three days we were beginning to approach working order. For the owner of the paper which was already being mentioned for awards due to its exclusive coverage of the Goodyear balloon crash, nothing was too good for us.

One afternoon, as if one cue, his wife left the room and another younger woman entered. She sat down on the bed for several moments talked conversantly in low, soothing tones. She massaged my temples and shoulders with surprising, welcomed firmness, yet gentleness. Then she rose from the bed and removed her clothes.

"Oh, my God, Van, don't!" It was the voice of Trotter in the next bed. Through thick and thin, I had admired that lad for his tested courage, his encouragement when things looked their worst. Above all, for his honest, personal concern for my safety and welfare.

At the moment, however, he was a pain in the ass.

"You'll be with your youngsters in three days, Van! Don't do this thing!"

The young woman sat once more on the bed and cradled my head in her bosom.

Two things became instantly clear to me. I would strangle Trotter at my earliest convenience, and the sickness had drained my body forces more than I had realized. I contented myself with lying on one elbow, admiring the young lady's impeccable character.

Trotter went back to sleep, meanwhile, facing the wall.

In a matter of days, however, Frank and I were reporting our experiences to the world over the combined networks of the British Broadcasting Company and the National Broadcasting Company.

It was finished. I would never race again.

The Polish team of Hynek and Burzynasky, men who had never won a race before, captured the Gordon Bennett title with a distance of 820 miles. Well, they bled for it and deserved it and I couldn't have been happier.

Their experience, one of the worst in ballooning history, well deserves to close this chapter.

The pair left Chicago at 7:19 pm September 2nd with a good supply of oxygen and 59 sacks of sand for ballast. They rose to 500 meters where a northeast wind carried them over Lake Michigan. They skirted the far shore by 3:45 the following morning, having thrown out 13 sacks of sand for altitude.

Later in the trip they were flying high at 4,000 meters with only six sacks of sand left. To preserve that, they threw out empty bottles of oxygen with a small parachute attached to each. They rose above the 4,000 meter mark. Muskoka, Canada was the last sight of land below.

At 1:55 am the following morning, (wrote Hynek) we tuned into a Chicago radio station and by direction, we got our bearings, but then had to throw the radio overboard to get rid of the weight. We had been as high as 9,000 meters during the voyage but steadily dropped. By 8:07 am the final morning we were only 2,000 meters in the air and had only two sacks of sand left. After abandoning our last bottle of oxygen we dropped to 900 meters at 9:15 am. At that point we also threw over our oxygen masks and mouthpieces and our spare ropes.

Still the balloon kept falling. We discarded our coats and fur boots. Our calculations seemed to indicate we had passed eastward to the Atlantic and were over the ocean. There was nothing more left to jettison but our instruments and food supply so we threw over the food, keeping only twelve oranges and a box of forty raisins. Still dropping, we cannot express the joy we felt when we saw below us not a vision of engulfing waves, but the beauty of endless forests.

The beauty soon would become a nightmare and the realization that we jettisoned our food for nothing would return to haunt us many times in the days ahead. The wilderness in which we landed was one of the most extensive on the North American continent. Beyond the habited villages which fringed the St. Lawrence Valley, Lake St. John and the Saguenay Rivers, the big woods began and never stopped. On the new provincial highway which traversed the Laurentides National Park was a stretch of 80 miles without even a one gas pump village.

Our requirement was to trudge 90 miles through the rough country in a week's time using a single pocket compass. We were so fortunate in landing without injury after 40 hours in the air. We divided the oranges and raisins and managed to find a few handfuls of blueberries in the undergrowth. During the last two days, berries were our total sustenance. We had a fair idea of our position. Studying our maps, we made a compass course for the railway. The bush was very dense and we followed trails made by moose or deer. Sometimes we were almost bogged in swamps. We were cold and wet from crossing streams and morasses. Our stomachs were faint with hunger and nausea.

May God be praised, we reached the railway tracks when we did. We could not have held out another day. We were chilled to the bone and almost perishing from fatigue. Nevertheless, we could not help but shout and cheer at the sight of those rails. We jumped about the ground like Indians and carried on so that we attracted the notice of workers who gave us a thrilling ride in their handcar over a dozen miles which separated that place from Revierre a'Pierre, Quebec.

I'm sure these men never made a handcar travel so fast before. I speak French so had little difficulty in explaining who we were. Sleep in a bed was a pleasant change from camping in the freezing open air, listening to the howling wolves and knowing we were surrounded by bears and other wild beasts kept at distance only by a bonfire which must burn all night.

We were quite ready to compete in 1934 if the Polish government ordered it. We were, I suppose, national heroes.

As far as we, personally, were concerned, it was just good not to be dead.

Sad ending to the last race of Ward Van Orman's career saw this entangled balloon (still flying the American flag) which crash-landed in the wilds of Canada's Timagami Bay country. The 14-day search for pilot Van Orman and his aid Frank Trotter involved the air forces of both the U. S. and Canada. The year was 1933.

# · 28 ·

# *Inventions to Serve Humanity*

In the proper perspective of historians, it is doubtful I will be remembered for any of those hair-raising exploits suffered in the Gordon Bennett and Litchfield Trophy Races, no matter how vivid, still, they are to me. Indeed, with the exception of a handful of balloon nostalgics and air historian groups across America, the whole era of international balloon racing long before the miraculous development of the propeller and jet engine aircraft, may already have faded from popular interest into historical oblivion.

The reader therefore can appreciate, I hope, why in the golden hours of my life it is the more lasting contributions of my years—those of the field of invention and development—rather than those of balloonist, to which I look back on with the greater joy of the soul.

Almost all of my years at Goodyear Tire and Rubber Company and the Goodyear-Zeppelin Corporation were connected, directly or indirectly, with balloons, dirigibles and airplanes.

As inventor of the lightning arrester, landing pontoons for free balloons, protective canopy for balloons, a leak-proof, crash-proof and bullet-proof fuel tank for airplanes, a new method of processing balloon fabric, an alarm altimeter, a new-type vertimeter and a special balloon fabric, I believe I contributed something to each of the three branches of air navigation, besides testing some of my own inventions in balloon races. For at Goodyear, the races were never just a sport. They were to our balloon and airship department what the 500-mile auto race at Indianapolis is to automobile builders—a testing ground for new improvements.

Over the years, other inventions included the airtight zipper, an air-conditioned cast for orthopedic cases, a massaging mattress for prevention of bedsores, a self-charging electrostatic filter, a stratosphere pressure suit, discovery of the principle of hyperbaric oxygen as applied to medicine, and a new process in the study of Braille.

Ben Franklin frequently pointed out that laziness and annoyance were superb mothers of invention and how right he was! Early in this book I recalled the unexpected and unscheduled "bath" to which I subjected my pilot students in the frigid waters of Lake Milton while on a routine balloon flight. Not long after, I designed and supervised manufacture of inflated supporting pontoons for future balloon use. Later, these same pontoons led to the manufacture of the life raft.

Though the bullet-sealing gas tank came into prominence in World War II during air combat, I was brought into the picture by the United States Government (through Goodyear) to perfect such a product during the closing weeks of World War I. It had been discovered that in the pitched air battles of that conflict, most American air casualties resulted not from the explosion of gas tanks, but by spillage of gasoline from the ruptured tank over a hot engine, causing fire and frequently fatal crashes. The Government was asking for a tank so "flexible" in construction that when punctured by bullets, it would immediately seal, allowing no fuel to spill on the engine.

The same principle was also ideal for private and commercial airplanes in case of crashes and rough forced landings.

The secret turned out to be a leakproof and fireproof rubber and fabric covering for airplane gasoline tanks which I designed and perfected. While the tank cover was designed especially for combat airplanes for protection against leaks and incendiary bullets, plans also called for equipping all mail planes with the new armor.

The cover consisted of a half-inch rubber blanket especially prepared and vulcanized stretched on top of a thick layer of several piles of cotton fabric. It fit directly over the airplane gasoline tank. Bullet tests conducted by the Government determined that when the gasoline tanks were punctured by firepower, the rubber covering automatically closed and sealed the leak, preventing leakage of gasoline and subsequent explosions in mid-air.

The finished product was no sooner turned over to the military than it immediately became a hot item. In 1919, Major R. H. Fleet at McGook Field, Dayton, Ohio, wrote me and warned me to keep my mouth shut. He said as follows:

October 3, 1919

R. H. Fleet, Major
A S A
Contracting Officer
McGook Field
Dayton, Ohio

Engineering Division
Air Service
Goodyear Tire & Rubber Co.

SUBJECT: Fire & Leakproof Gasoline Tank

Dear Sir:

When in view of the fact that through your efforts a fire and leakproof gasoline tank has been developed which so far as is known is much better than any heretofore in use, either by this or foreign governments, it is of the greatest importance that the details of this construction, as well as the fact that such a tank exists, be zealously guarded, that this information may not fall into the hands of persons who would make use of it against our goverment in case of war.

And, to this end, it is requested that you refrain from giving out information to any outsiders whatever, and that you instruct such persons in your Company as have knowledge of these facts to consider them confidential.

R. H. Fleet
Major

To my knowledge the only other person to whom I divulged pertinent details of the re-sealing tank was another Goodyear engineer at the outbreak of World War II. His assignment was to take my designs and specifications of 1918 and adapt them to World War II planes. I might add, with only passing interest, that he was awarded a Presidental Citation for his work.

Then, somewhere along the line I worked out a method of preserving leaves in self-curing rubber for books on trees and the outdoors for blind readers. The preserved rubber-encased leaves enabled the blind reader to actually "feel" the leaves as he or she read about them. It was only a partial success, I think. The blind have an extraordinary sense of smell. They could be sailing along reading of the trees and their branches and leaves, imagining themselves in the midst of a delightfully fragrant forest.

But then after examining the leaves in ecstasy, they could not help but also smell them and say, "Ah, rubber?"

Perhaps the greatest response from personal friends and the public came as a result of inventing the electric massaging mattress, used today in hospitals throughout the world. The rippling or undulating effect of the special mattress in effect keeps the muscles and skin gently massaged or worked, preventing the earlier dilemma of all hospitals—bedsores.

But I shall always remember quite another invention.

I think the most significant breakthrough—in terms of community life and health—began with a military order in 1942 to perfect a pressure suits for pilots whose planes would fly at 50,000 feet and higher. Using oxygen masks alone, pilots were found to be efficient only as high as 38,000 feet.

We had to pressurize these pilots and it was a crash program. I sat at my desk for two weeks. I'm sure the boss thought I was loafing—until I hit upon the right idea for the pressure suit which was simply a balance of the radial tension against the longitudinal tension, making for superb pilot flexibility.

I had hardly completed the assignment when I suddenly realized that the suit also would make an ideal light-weight Navy diving rig. I traveled to Washington to demonstrate it myself.

I perched on the rim of a 120-foot diving tank. The Navy apologized that they had no air hose for me. What they did have was a cylinder of oxygen.

"Well, hook me up to that," I said. "That'll work."

So up and down I went for at least an hour in the 120-foot diving tank.

Returning home on the train that night, I was aware of incredible physical sensations. I should have been dog-tired but instead felt as fresh as if I'd just vacationed in the country. Completely unexplainable at the time, I literally felt I was Superman! I knew I easily could have worked 23 hours straight with zero fatigue. All this from working with *pure oxygen* for an hour.

Let me hasten to say that the most basic law of physics ultimately came into play—"for every action there is a reaction." Within a very few days I could not even hold my head up and would have relished *sleeping* 23 hours a day. Nature had played its game with me.

There was, of course, much other business to attend to at Goodyear on my return, but I could not clear that experience from my thinking. Yet for what use could it possibly be applied?

Then it happened. Dr. Robert R. Hays, an Akron psychiatrist, called and said, "Van, I've got a patient here who threatens suicide in twenty-four hours if I can't help her. I don't think she's fooling one bit. Do you want to bring that portable gear with you and get over here fast and help me try your 'pressurized oxygen?' "

"I'll be there!" I shouted. In a matter of minutes we had placed the patient in a decompression cylinder which we also developed in the war. She looked horrible. Never had I seen a woman look so disreputable. She was garbed in a filthy blouse, her hair unkempt, no lipstick, no make-up.

In complete despression. The doctor explained she had been exposed to heavy toluene fumes in a nearby factory.

For some time, Dr. Hays had been observing a form of illness among rubber workers which had been alarmingly on the increase since the advent of synthetics. Its cause, Dr. Hays, felt, was the inhalation of toxic substances including carbon tetrachloride, benzol, naptha, carbon bisulphide, di-methyl ketone and alcohol.

The symptoms were, to enumerate the outstanding ones, nausea, vomiting, dizziness and weakness, with the mental findings of confusion, loss of memory for recent events, occasionally also for remote events, difficulty in making arithmetical calculations, emotional depression, vague and ill defined fears, with definite delusional trends which ranged from ideas of hopelessness and despair to poorly systematized ideas of a paranoid character. Delusions of infidelity were rather common.

The patients were unfit for work.

Within moments after placing the suicidal woman in the zippered cylinder and applying gradually increased increments of pressurized oxygen, she started talking like a magpie. Not only was she talking, she was even complaining about the heat in the cylinder. We kidded her along, noticing that her lips were changing from a climactic blue to a lovely pink. She remained in the chamber forty minutes. A second treatment followed soon after.

The woman who came in threatening self-destruction came out of the initial oxygen treatment asking for a mirror and comb for her hair, and fresh clothing. Her whole outlook and sense of status had altered entirely in those forty minutes. Soon after her second treatment, she lost all of her hallucinations and within days had a sufficient sense of calm to see her husband through major surgery in a nearby hospital.

Soon after our experience with this woman, I assisted in similar treatments for thirty-two other patients, all victims of toluene fumes from the manufacture of rubber products. We reasoned that if Hyperbaric Oxygen (pressurized oxygen) worked so conclusively on the effects of toluene fumes, it also could conceivably work on newborn babies with breathing problems, on cases of pneumonia, heart failure, lockjaw, carbon monoxide poisoning, lung disease . . ."

A report of our cooperative efforts entitled "Oxygen Therapy, A Preliminary Report of a New Method," was published in the *Medical Record* in April, 1945.

Not very long after, scientists and doctors from all over the world assembled at New York's Waldorf Astoria to discuss past experiments, significance and potential of Hyperbaric Oxygen. Today, its principle is used widely in many branches of international medicine—all because the

American Government asked for the design of a stratosphere suit!

You do not always know where you are going in science. You prepare for the trip. You consult your maps. You chart your course. And still so much occurs and is learned as the result of pure chance, of random accident, just as the best prepared balloonist strikes a deadly storm current or is becalmed and virtually stopped in his tracks and a year of strategy and calculation goes for naught. And random chance also can save the day. If the Navy had *had* an airhose the day I demonstrated the pressure suit, the whole field of medicine might yet be deprived of a truly miraculous discovery, one which, conservatively, has aided hundreds of thousands of persons since the early 1940s.

It has been a truly marvelous life. I did some very dangerous things in my allotted three score years and ten (which I thank God I have generously exceeded), but always with the eye of the scientist, never the daredevil ... the question, always, of how best, with the equipment I had or could contrive, could I travel farther, stay in the air longer, learn and practice a wizardry of the winds?

Yet for all the satisfaction of the inventor's criteria, the scientist's dimension, it is still, I believe, the flagrant romance of the thing that at times returns me yet again to the sensation of a God-sent wind, a starlit path through the night sky, and the exultation that defies description of a magnificent balloon race in the silence of nocturnal majesty.

High altitude pressure suit for pilots flying in excess of 50,000 feet was developed by Van Orman in 1942. Using oxygen masks alone, pilots at that time were found only to be efficient up to 38,000 feet. "I sat at my desk for two weeks," Van recalls. "I'm sure the boss thought I was loafing—until I ultimately hit upon the right idea for the suit, which was simply a balance of radial tension against longitudinal tension, making for superb pilot flexibility. The project ultimately led to a far more important discovery—the principle of Hyperbaric Oxygen— used in clinics and hospitals around the globe today."

# Introduction to Appendix Section

"... AS A POINTED BOAT CUTS THE WATER"

Ward T. Van Orman was engaged during part of his career in lighter-than-air craft in the development of dirigibles for the United States government under the production of the Goodyear Tire and Rubber Company. This appendix portion of this book was extracted from Ward's manuscript so that the main story would be the autobiography of a free balloonist.

The word dirigible means steerable, not rigid as some mistakenly suppose. It was toward the dirigible that lighter-than-air flight has progressed since the very beginning. Beginning with the first Montgolfier flight scientists of the eighteenth and nineteenth century were researching in order to give direction control to flight.

General J. B. McMeusniar conceived in 1784 the idea of an elongated bag which would cut the air as a "pointed boat cuts the water." Failure upon failure dogged the seekers until 110 years later when Ferdinand von Zeppelin developed the concept of a rigid framework of aluminum alloy to contain the gas cells and to support the skin of the ship. Zeppelin's work progressed through the development of many sophisticated dirigibles, both for peacetime and wartime use, until his death in 1917.

Count Zeppelin had found and developed an outstanding lighter-than-air commander and leader in the person of Dr. Hugo Eckener, a scholar-philosopher who lived in Friedrichshafen. Upon von Zeppelin's death the direction of the development of the dirigible was left in the hands of Dr. Eckener. Under Hugo Eckener's leadership the airship was developed for peacetime use through the commercial company which von Zeppelin had formed, DELAG (Deutsche Luftschiffartag). In addition to the 88 fighting airships which were built for German use in World War I, Dr. Eckener directed the building of the commercial airships *Bodensee* and *Nordstern*. The Allied Air Commission directed that the German airship industry shut down and turn the two commercial ships over to the control of Italy and France.

The United States government was interested through its naval air branch in dirigibles. The Navy ordered the construction of the dirigible *Shenandoah* in 1922 in which the Goodyear Company participated, and as reparation the United States had the *Los Angeles* constructed in Germany under Dr. Eckener's care. The *Los Angeles* was delivered by Dr. Eckener and his crew in 1924.

Until 1928 the restriction against rigid airship construction was enforced upon the German Zeppelin company. In 1928, with the ban lifted, Eckener and his trained staff rushed into construction the familiar and great *Graf Zeppelin*, named in honor of their company's founder. Flight tested in the Fall of 1928 the *Graf Zeppelin* flew on to establish records, conduct research flights, carry passengers and prove that the dirigible was a positive air machine. The great commercial airship *Hindenburg* carried on the tradition of Count Zeppelin until its flaming end at Lakehurst.

Ward Van Orman in his role as balloonist and research engineer of the Goodyear company experienced many interesting and personal attachments to the dirigible as an economic and military benefit to the United States. In the following pages Ward's reports of the various troubles which plagued the United States' effort towards a vital and superior lighter-than-air service arm.

One cannot help but agree with Ward Van Orman's assessment that the Navy had learned little from the many years of research conducted by the free balloonists during the national and international races. It seems certain from reading Ward's reporting of the end of the *Akron* and *Macon* that the Navy knew little about the meteorological phenomena associated with squall lines or hidden thunderstorms. Or, perhaps it was simply the assumption on the part of naval commanders that an airship could operate in forces similar to the old dreadnoughts.

In any event, Ward T. Van Orman's life was closely linked with the fate of the whole lighter-than-air dirigible concept. His tales of rigid airships make for interesting insights into the problems of early lighter-than-air flight.

# Appendix: Section One

## The U. S.-German Dream for an Intercontinental Zeppelin Line

The turn of the twentieth century found Akron, Ohio manufacturers making the change from carriage construction to making automobile tires. The men who were to figure in the American renaissance of lighter-than-air flight were scattered over the earth.

In Europe, Count Zeppelin's experiments had reawakened man's dream to fly. Some of this spirit was caught and returned to America about the time of the first James Gordon Bennett Balloon Race in 1906.

F. H. Lahm, who later became the godfather of American participation in the Gordon Bennett affairs, was a representative of an American manufacturer in Paris. Lahm spent his vacations at Turkeyfoot Lake in Akron.

Walter Wellman, after reaching the 87th parallel "just a little more than 200 miles from the Pole," was seeking new means for conquering the icy wastes.

Melvin Vaniman was in New Zealand making a living by taking photographs and singing with itinerant opera companies when there was no money in picture-taking.

Ralph Upson was going to school in the New England village of Tallmadge. He would later fly the first balloon to cross the English Channel in this century.

Vaniman's life was turned in the general direction of lighter-than-air when the opera troupe with which he left Illinois was stranded in Honolulu and he turned to photography for the best of motives—necessity. To take the kind of pictures he knew he could take with a camera of his own development, he had to be in the air. The balloon was the only device available at that time that could get him there.

But the balloon wasn't too good, either, he found. It would take you up, but not where you wanted to go. Vaniman thought about this in his wanderings and when he arrived in Paris a few years later, his interest in balloons led him to General Lahm who had just seen his son win the first Gordon Bennett Race.

Wellman, it happened, was in Paris at the same time looking for an airship that would carry him across the North Pole. He wanted something with a motor in it rather than the free bag that took the Andree expedition over the ice wastes a few years before and was lost. General Lahm saw Wellman's advertisement in the French paper. He told Vaniman about it. The upshot of it was that Vaniman designed the airship *America*. It was built in Paris and he and Wellman set out in it to conquer the Arctic. The first attempt failed when the 25 h.p. engine failed. The second rebuilding failed with the loss of a stabilizer and all of the expedition supplies.

Then Peary ungraciously succeeded in exploring to the North Pole. Wellman and Vaniman sadly brought their dirigible back to the United States. They were seeking new fields to conquer. Vaniman had an idea that the Atlantic could be crossed by an airship. They set out for Europe, this time in 1910, and thirty miles off the coast, the *America's* engines failed. Members of the expedition were rescued and even as they sailed for shore, Vaniman's plans for a new airship were in his thoughts.

F. A. Seiberling, then president of Goodyear, saw possibilities in Vaniman's idea. He offered to build him a dirigible at the Goodyear Akron plant. So the first ship Akron would build was a 400,000 cubic foot zeppelin. It was Goodyear's first airship and its second aircraft of any kind assembled in Akron. One free balloon had preceded it and Ralph Upson was its builder.

In many ways this first sky vessel to be christened the *Akron* anticipated some of the improvements that were hailed as "revolutionary" in the later *Akron* and *Macon* ships such as propellers that swiveled up and down and Vaniman's principal idea, that of compressing lifting gas to use as ballast.

Vaniman hoped to build a bag using a fabric that was light but strong enough to permit the lifting gas to be compressed by inflating an air balloon inside so its lift could be adjusted in this way instead of by ballast. But the first *Akron's* skin was not of such stuff, even though many experiments were carried out with metal threads woven through balloon fabric. The big envelope was finally stitched together and shipped to Atlantic City. It flew, the first airship ever built in America, and the word went out that a new attempt to cross the Atlantic would be made in the *Akron*.

Then one day on a test flight something went wrong. Some said the bag burst into flames in the air. Others said it burst first, then caught fire. Melvin Vaniman and four others were killed when they fell into Absecon Inlet, a short distance off the Atlantic coast.

There was considerable national speculation about the cause of the accident. The story believed by Akronites connected with the ship was that a sealed main valve caused the tragedy—that Vaniman had sealed a leaking valve several months prior to the disaster was known. That this had not been forgotten or overlooked before the final flight was gathered by expert witnesses who told of seeing the crew of the ship running along the peculiar keel opening some water valves. However, the valves were too small to permit enough gas to escape to prevent the bag from bursting from expanding gas as it rose in the sunshine.

The hydrogen was touched off by sparks from the motors. America's first air disaster brought wide discussion of the practicability of lighter-than-air all over the country.

A notebook filled with the editorial opinion of airships gathered the day after the disaster, is cherished to this day by Willard Seiberling, a youthful witness of the 1912 experiments of Vaniman at Atlantic City. Dozens of papers echoed such comments as the following, predictable after every tragedy:

> Public confidence in the dirigible as a practical solution to the flying problem has never been high, and despite the frequent fatalities that have resulted from airplanes there is far more faith today in the heavier-than-air machines. Transatlantic ballooning has always seemed a visionary conception, being far too hazardous and uncertain to be undertaken.

Goodyear had manufactured free balloons for several years prior to World War I. Then the war in the air over Europe and the zeppelin raids were talked about everywhere. Just before America entered the war, Akron newspaper offices were startled by strange reports.

"An airship is down near Medina, Ohio!" shouted a voice on the telephone. "What airship? Where from?"

It was the first military airship built by Goodyear. It had been constructed secretly, assembled near Chicago, and was being flown to Akron when it ran out of oil and came down almost undamaged in the woods near Medina. Then the war came and the large hangar at Wingfoot Lake was built. The Navy moved into Akron for the first time, training its airmen there.

Goodyear Hall, then under construction, was rushed to completion and was turned into a balloon and airship factory. Blimps, named for the British non-rigid ships, B-type limp, cruised the skies over Akron all day. Strange-eared kite balloons floated over Wingfoot Lake. The military observation blimps with pointed tails and cars like airplane fuselages were turned out in great numbers.

The few Americans who knew anything about lighter-than-air were summoned to Akron to devise teaching procedures for training the military men who came here. Out of such a potpourri came American small airship methods. Such pilots as Jack Boettner and Carl Wollam and builders Upson and Herman Kraft emerged. But the conclusion of hostilities also ended the wild abandon of lighter-than-air construction.

The Navy moved out of Akron. The next few years saw little design or construction advance in airships in a war-tired America. The postwar slump hit Goodyear bringing the company to financial trouble. But research into the stuff of which airships were made continued to make strides. The existence of helium, discovered when astronomers Franklin and Lockyer noted a line of bright yellow in the sun's spectrum, was found in earth in 1907 in natural gas deposits in Kansas, Texas, Utah and Wyoming. It was in such minute quantities and was so difficult to extract by methods of the day that a cubic foot of the gas cost thousands of dollars.

War, of course, hurries everything, and indeed it took a war to break loose the financial backing needed to extract helium in large enough quantities to be used in airships of the line. Distribution headquarters for helium gas were set up at Fort Worth, Texas, and by 1922 all government airships were inflated with the safe new gas. The special significance of helium—one which ironically, if indirectly, would destroy the whole future of lighter-than-air in a very few years— was the fact that America had practically a monopoly on the gas.

In time, due to the stupidity of a handful of American politicians, particularly Secretary of Commerce Harold Ickes, the U. S. would cut off total supply of the gas to Germany. Germany, having no choice but to use flammable hydrogen, would end once and for all the lovely dream of intercontinental airship travel in the crash of the *Hindenberg*.

Persons in 1978 are quite surprised to learn just how close the relationship was between Germany and Akron, Ohio. It was extremely close. By 1931, two separate companies, the International Zeppelin Transport Company and the Pacific Zeppelin Transport Company, had been at work for two years laying the ground work for a commercial zeppelin operation. In fact plans had been advanced to such a point that the year 1934 would have seen international zeppelin passenger service abound if the U. S. government had provided lighter-than-air vessels the same advantage it had in the past supplied surface ships through mail contracts.

Mail contracts, indeed, were the bone of contention.

A bill to provide such assistance, the Parker-McNary bill, also known as the Merchant Airship bill was pending before Congress. Its passage would have insured the construction of commercial zeppelins at Goodyear in Akron. The passenger-carrying airships were to be similarly designed to the *Akron* and *Macon* navy military ships, except that they would have been still larger and would have included accommodations for about 100 passengers and several tons of mail.

Since the end of the war I had served Goodyear as an aeronautical engineer in its Aero Design Division; as development engineer in its Development Department and as director of the Goodyear-Zeppelin ground school. But now I also represented the International Zeppelin Corporation in making studies of possible sites for an east coast hangar for the proposed transocean service. I found the most suitable site, due strictly to meteorological factors, to be located in the areas betwen Philadelphia and Richmond, Virginia, including locations near the cities of Washington D. C. and Baltimore.

The European terminal of this air line probably would have been in the vicinity of Paris. The plan was for the American International Zeppelin Transport Company and the German Zeppelin Corporation to cooperate, using one another's facilities and acting as one line. By 1931, a zeppelin of seven million cubic foot capacity was being built in Germany for the cooperative project. The Pacific Zeppelin Line, meanwhile, would start with a single airship sailing between the Pacific coast and Honolulu, later extending to Manila and Japan, served by additional dirigibles.

On April 7, 1931, congressman John G. Cooper, ranking member of the House Interstate and Foreign Commerce Committee, pledged his support to the international zeppelin traffic legislation. Cooper assured the Congress that Germany was preparing to pioneer an international zeppelin line in cooperation with the Hamburg-American Steamship Line.

"But if the United States is to press forward in the airship industry," Cooper warned, "it is highly important that congressmen act as soon as possible on the necessary basic legislation—the Parker-McNary bill!"

This legislation, as stated, promised the dirigible industry a piece of the U. S. mail contracts necessary for its survival. It also set up a code of air maritime regulation. One section of the bill permitted personnel of the Army and Navy to volunteer and be detailed for service aboard commercial ships. This would facilitate training in airships as a preparedness for war.

The reason the mail question was so critical financially was that dirigible officials knew that full passenger loads could not be anticipated until they demonstrated zeppelin safety and reliability over the ocean to the general public. During this period of educating the public to the possibilities of air travel, they absolutely required the assistance mail contracts would provide.

Yet two years later, the bill on which an imaginative worldwide industry hinged, still lay buried in a Senate committee.

In February, 1933, Redford E. Mobley wrote in the *Akron Beacon Journal*:

The airship bill is still pending in the Senate where its sponsor, Senator McNary of Oregon, expects to bring it up this session if possible. It is my hope that the importance of giving a firm legal basis to this infant industry will lend its hand toward bringing us out of the Depression. The measure, of course, has the airmail feature which has recently been under fire, but I should like to emphasize that it requires no appropriation, not a nickel from the Congress, and places the entire matter at the discretion of the Postmaster General.

When by September of that year there was still no legislation, a concerned Dr. Hugo Eckener, famed skipper of the *Graf Zeppelin*, arrived in Akron for a hurried huddle with Goodyear's P. W. Litchfield. With American progress absolutely stymied and plans for the first U. S. commercial airship hopelessly behind schedule, the marvelous new German airship, the *LC-129*, was to be rescheduled for South American service.

Dr. Eckener urged that the American eastern seaboard terminal be constructed and a crew trained, in hopes that Congress would soon see the light.

In support, Rear Admiral William A. Moffett, chief of the Navy's Bureau of Aeronautics, told the press:

"The commercial airship at present has no legal status as compared with surface vessels. We looked to action by the 72nd Congress for legislation that would put airships on the same footing commercially as surface ships, but it failed in the Senate. We hope for the passage of a similar bill by the new Congress and feel sure that capital will then come forward to then build a much larger commercial airship that will carry air commerce and flag all over the world."

Aside from Moffett, two men had more to do with the American airship story than any others and something more should be said of them.

A newspaperman once said of Paul W. Litchfield, head of the Goodyear Tire & Rubber Company and president of the Goodyear-Zeppelin Corporation, "To tell of him is to seek to portray a sunset with a stick of charcoal."

"Why do you think there is such a great future for lighter-than-air?" I asked him once.

"Because transportation has already paced the world's progress," he said, and he was thinking of Hill, of Vanderbilt, perhaps, or of Fulton and his miserable steamboat.

"This ship you see today," he once said of the mighty *Akron*, "will be an obscure model in years to come, and its accomplishments the Navy views as marvelous today will be outshone in the achievements of this same science in later years."

How did a tire manufacturer, one who dealt primarily in one of the ordinary commercial commodities, rise to such heights of vision?

P. W. was a quiet-spoken man, tall, somewhat stocky in stature, but by manner and inclination reserved and inclined to draw away from display of any kind. He had sat at the tables of great men all over the world and had shared in their insights. He lived and made his home in Akron and his finger had been on the pulse of lighter-than-air since its inception as an infant in the family of industrial enterprise.

Here in Akron where we have seen the miracle of rubber accomplish many things, the translation was not so difficult. Litchfield came to his high office rather well-fitted for the tremendous duties imposed upon him. He was born and reared in Boston and graduated from the Massachusetts Institute of Technology. He earned a Bachelor of Science Degree in chemical engineering. A year or so later he was associated with a famous carriage maker, L. C. Chasen Company in Boston. They manufactured carriage cloth and tires.

But the tire industry was still in its infancy when he was attracted to Ohio. That was in 1900 and Goodyear employed only 176 men. Within ten years he had been made factory manager, then vice-president of the company. Other responsibilities followed as the company plunged forward through its era of tremendous progress under the leadership of F. A. Seiberling.

Litchfield became director of Canadian Goodyear of Great Britain, of the Killingly Mfg. Co., and was vice-president of the Southwest Cotton Co. He was president and general manager in 1926 when he succeeded to the post of chief executive of the Goodyear helm on the retirement of the late G. M. Stadelman.

It was as president of Goodyear and as head of the newly formed Goodyear-Zeppelin Corporation that Paul Litchfield appeared before Navy Department officials in Washington, where he recited the earliest plans and specifications for the two giant dirigibles which Akron would produce. As early as 1926 the same Litchfield appeared before the Naval Affairs Committee of the House of Representatives in Washington and confided that his company—not even organized completely at the time—would undertake to build a giant leviathan of the air that would climb five miles into the sky and fly better than a mile a minute.

He was able to replace the *Shenandoah*, he said, and there were members of that committee who smiled.

The other half of the great dirigible push was Rear Admiral Moffett who had two things going for him—considerable guts and his office as chief of the Navy's Bureau of Aeronautics.

Moffett, who was 68 years old in 1931, had served under Admiral Dewey at Manila in 1898, had commanded the S. S. *Chester* in the capture of Vera Cruz in 1914 for which he received the Distinguished Service Medal, and directed the Great Lakes Naval Training Station at Chicago during World War I.

During the war, Moffett became convinced of the importance of lighter-than-air craft in the Navy. When he became chief of naval aeronautics, he started the ball rolling. First came the construction of the *Shenandoah* at Lakehurst, then the *Los Angeles* as part of the U. S.'s share of reparations from Germany. But these ships were only the beginning. Not until he had fought his way through opposition in Congress did he gain approval for his plan for a lighter-than-air force. In 1931 he still had to answer numerous critics as he had to do as early as 1925 when several congressmen considered him "too progressive."

Litchfield and Moffett seemed unbeatable as a team. And in the thick of the fight, they were.

Since 1911 when Litchfield was factory manager, Goodyear had been interested in lighter-than-air craft. That year, under his personal direction, the Company began designing Army and Navy training balloons. By war's end, Goodyear had built more than a thousand free and observation (tethered) balloons and close to 100 airships.

Then Goodyear acquired the German zeppelin patents for the construction of rigid airships in North America and hired the services of the two great airship engineers in the world in a move to corner the Navy contract for building two 6,500,000 cubic foot dirigibles.

The men were Air Commander Garland Fulton of the Navy's Bureau of Aeronautics and Germany's Dr. Karl Arnstein.

Fulton was graduated from Annapolis in 1912 after two years at sea and took a postgraduate course in naval architecture at M. I. T., making him a naval architect in 1916. He served in the New York navy yard for two years and in 1918 was assigned to aeronautical duty. In 1923 Fulton went to Germany to inspect construction on the *Los Angeles* and on his return was put in charge of zeppelin construction.

Dr. Arnstein, former chief engineer for Count Ferdinand von Zeppelin, builder of the great German dirigibles that at one time threatened to turn the tide of World War I, was the unique talent responsible for the design of the incredibly beautiful, superbly graceful Goodyear ships, the *Akron* and the *Macon*.

When he came to spend his life in Akron, Ohio, Dr. Arnstein was only in his forties. He had already supervised the design of some seventy military and commercial airships in Germany, including the *Los Angeles*. Born in Prague, Bohemia, he accomplished much in his youth besides conceive airships. Among his long list of credits were the design of the great span bridge at Aroza, Switzerland, and the reconstruction work that saved the Strasburg Cathedral when it cracked at its base.

Not only had Paul Litchfield sought out Dr. Arnstein, but he persuaded him to bring to this country a staff of his own experts.

And it was Arnstein most of all who convinced the United States Government and the other American officials that the rigid airship was the fastest and largest vehicle for transportation. When he took charge of construction of the air dock on the municipal airport, it was his advice that prevailed in making the structure large enough to house *two* great dirigibles.

About this time Akron played host to a rather incredible visitor—a tall, lank Briton with an amazing fund of highly technical aeronautical knowledge and a remarkable faculty of expression. He was Captain Hugh Duncan Grant, meteorologist, author, lecturer, balloonist, arctic explorer, weather forecaster and hurricane pathologist. His was the privilege of signing a fair portion of the alphabet after his name, being a fellow of the Royal Meteorological, Royal Geographical and Royal Astronomical Societies of Great Britain. He rated the "captain" by being former superintendent of the meteorological department of the British Navy.

An incredible chap, certainly, he nevertheless came lecturing to Akron as an enemy representative. For he came in all seriousness to sell an incredible-sounding, yet feasible plan for passenger airplanes to play leapfrog across the Atlantic furnishing competition for the Goodyear-mothered proposal for a transatlantic dirigible run.

His knowledge of the subject was intimate and authentic for he was meterological consultant to the Armstrong Seadrome Development Corporation of Wilmington, Delaware, which was not only planning but also financing an incredible venture. Captain Grant asserted that the first of eight seadromes, or man-made islands, which would dot the Atlantic at intervals of 380 miles form the United States to England, would be constructed off the east coast of this country in 1932.

Within a year—or at most two—of the placing of the first seadrome, the other seven ocean landing fields were to be in place and the transoceanic airline in operation. The decks of the seadromes were to be 70 feet above sea level, 1,100 feet long and wide enough to land the largest planes. They were to be contructed as to always lie down wind to allow aircraft to land and take off into the wind.

Rough waters were not calculated to affect the stability of the surface for the center of gravity would be located below the center of buoyancy. Below the turbulent surface of the ocean, stability was further encouraged by an arrangement which allowed waves to pass through the supported assembly without breaking up.

The Armstrong Corporation had gone so far as to name its eight seadromes, giving them the names of aviation leaders. The first one which would be 220 miles east of Boston and a slightly longer distance from New York would be named Langley. Other names: Chanute, Wright, Maxim, Hargraves, Henson, Phillips and Tissandier. The Hargraves seadrome would be just west of the Azores, which would be in line of airflight, and seadrome Henson would be just east of the Azores.

The Armstrong seadromes were to be more than just places to land and refuel. There would be hotels, golf courses, theaters, with 125 resident employees and a floating population of 300 to 500. It was furthermore hoped and supposed that the seadromes would , with a bit of ballyhoo and exposure in the media, turn into flourishing summer resorts with swimming and deep-sea fishing. The latest editions of metropolitan newspapers could be obtained a few hours after publication, it was promised, and mail could be picked up from incoming airships.

If it was a hair-brained idea, it was a shared one, at least. On both sides of the Atlantic, the project received heavy contributions from Canada, England, Netherlands and the U. S. In America, alone, Henry J. Gieow, Inc., New York architects, Black and Bigelow, aeronautical engineers, Belmont Ironworks, structural engineers, Sun Shipbuilding, the General Electric Company, S. Roebling Sons Co., the Baldt Anchor & Chain Corporation, the DuPont Company, the Sperry Gyroscope Company, the Bureau of Standards, the Navy Department, the Sikorsky Aviation Corporation and the Marine Office of America were but a few of a long line of companies and government agencies who viewed seadromes as the only practical answer to flying over oceans.

The visit with Captain Grant was a refreshing and exhilarating experience for me for he was a superb meteorologist, a precise, keen thinker, perhaps bordering on the perimeter of genius. But I do not recall seeing or hearing much of him afterwards. Nor the Armstrong project, either, for that matter. Money matters, most likely.

But the tragic flaw in the thing was not money, it was his certainty, based on supposition and error, that no airplane carrying a worthwhile payload would or could be designed that could fly between the United States and Europe in one jump with safety and practical advantages.

He looked around and saw that few air passenger routes ever sent aircraft more than 400 miles without a stop for fuel. His data verified that the flight range of the present commercial airplane did not exceed 500 miles. He therefore chose to assume—and invest millions of dollars of his and other people's money on the assumption—that a supply of gasoline necessary for an ocean flight forever precluded the possibility of a payload of sufficient significance.

He was dead wrong.

And yet what a romantic, daring, courageous and monumental challenge the Atlantic seadromes *might have been!*

# Section Two

## Shorty Fulton's Folly and Mr. Arnstein's Air Dock with Clouds

A swampy, mosquito-ridden stretch of lowland, bordered by burned-out, down-at-the-heels garden patches with scattered tumbled-down houses here and there had been transformed in seven years into an airport second to none in the world and the development program had only been started.

"Unless one is able to visualize the future in glowing colors," said the *Beacon Journal* in 1931, "it will be impossible to picture in the mind's eye what the future holds for Akron Airport—when the Guggenheim Research Laboratory is built, when Memorial Hall is completed, when the air service hangars are up and occupied, when the playgrounds and other beauty spots are fully developed."

Back in 1924 when "Shorty" Fulton was working in the rubber shop and nuts about aviation, he had an idea he might develop a landing field in a spot along Springfield Lake so hydroplanes could be used in connection with the aeronautics program. He had stored away in the recesses of his mind careful steps to that end but the idea faded away. The practical obstacles encountered were insurmountable and the whole scheme was abandoned. But going to and from work each day, Fulton passed along Massilon Road toward Akron, the low-lying area that was later the airport and the Goodyear-Zeppelin Corporation.

The scene impressed him. Here was a huge tract of land surrounded by hills which he visioned could be developed into an ideal landing field, but even the half-dozen air-minded folks gave Shorty the razz and told him to forget it.

In 1928 he and his wife acquired the rundown farmhouse and two lots which later became the general headquarters for the Akron Municipal Airport and which was abandoned only after the magnificent new air terminal was opened in the summer of '31. From the acquisition of that farm home, its two lots and the small orchard adjoining it, the airport dream that had been distinctly Fulton's for years grew into realization. Fulton Field was a reality.

About the time Shorty Fulton was working on his first airplane, Goodyear-Zeppelin Corporation was negotiating with German zeppelin interests for American rights. Then Goodyear got the contract to build the U. S. S. *Akron* and the *Macon* for the Navy. Work had to be started soon. Goodyear began to look about for a zeppelin factory site. The ships would be built "wherever suitable airport facilities were offered." Goodyear said scored of cities offered facilities. Akron was in danger of losing the factory entirely.

Akron wanted the zeppelin industry. It was up to the city to furnish an airport. Hasty surveys were conducted at a site near Darrowville. Another site near Stowe was considered. Then Shorty Fulton got busy. He had visions of an airdock rising just outside his orchard. He visualized the day when lots of airships and airplanes would fly through the skies over Akron.

He had only one selling point and this he clung to tenaciously. Fulton Field was within ten minutes of downtown Akron. If the city were going to build an airport, why build it so far away from the city that all the time gained by air travel would be lost going to and from it? Besides, argued Fulton, the field was within easy trucking distance of the Goodyear plants where Goodyear parts could be built and trucked to the airport for assembly.

That did it. Fulton won out as he was used to doing.

His flying field was taken over along with the 800 acres surrounding it. This was after Dr. Hugo Eckener looked over the field and pronounced it excellent for an airship base. Shorty went on a tour of American airports and came back with glowing ideas. He rolled up his sleeves and went to work. Hills were mowed down and moved. The field was graded. Steamshovels and tractors clanked over the grounds. More land was acquired to the east of the site. The hills that no one ever thought could enhance an airport were utilized to make the city property an attractive bowl-shape tract.

Massillon Road was moved. Bridges were built. Roads were laid. The Fulton farmhouse, the administration building when the first airlines came into Akron with the mail, was torn down. Over in another corner of the field the Goodyear airdock rose, black and gaunt, bringing inquiries as to "who was building the big barn?"

And finally, out of the mud and sinkholes, rose the airport of Fulton's dreams. He, if no one else, had visualized the project long before the first steamshovel went to work. The plans were constantly being changed with one less hill here and another there, but finally the red and green boundary lights picked out the landing area as it essentially is today.

Shorty Fulton visualized a modern airport as a sort of streamlined public square where all the community activities are centered. It should be sort of an American Templehof—the Berlin airport that was built from the Kaiser's former parade grounds. Fulton would have a swimming pool, skating rink, parkways and amusement park, tourist camps, military barracks, universities and schools on his airport—if they'd let him.

His plan for parkways surrounding Akron Municipal Airport were beginning to take shape two years later. The tourist camps and picnic grounds were already there. Soccer, baseball and football fields could be laid out, making the airport a recreation center with maybe a municipal stadium in one corner of it some day. The city turned thumbs down on the "beer gardens of Templehof," but the administration building opened a roof garden. It didn't take long for Akron to consider "the airport" as a place where something was *always* going on, besides airplanes coming and going.

The new Goodyear airdock was copywriter's dream! Few adjectives were missed in the nation's newspapers. Most were accurate. It was a structure larger than Solomon's temple, larger than the New York Central terminal and the Taj Mahal—a great inverted dish of a building without a single supporting pillar or girder, the largest such structure in the world.

Ten professional football games could be played simultaneously under its roof. Six miles of standard railroad tracks could be laid on the floor area. It could house the aircraft carrier *Saratoga* and *Lexington* together with the Washington Monument and Statue of Liberty.

Its height was built equal to a 22-story apartment building. The Goodyear airdock measured 1,175 feet in length, 320 feet in width, and was 211 feet tall.

Preparing the ground for construction required the removal of nearly 1 million cubic yards of earth and the insertion of 1,300 concrete piles to a rock base. Every precaution was taken to reduce the likelihood of gusts forming about the entrance and interfering with the free moving of the zeppelins in and out.

For this reason the dock was placed in line with the direction of prevailing winds and was provided with "orange peel" doors. These doors derived their name from the fact that they were fashioned like eights of an orange peel, a shape which permitted them to fit snuggly against the side of the building and weighed 600 tons per leaf or 1,200 tons of door weight at each end of the hangar.

Through the length of the building and extending far out into the field there ran a mile of docking rails. Small trucks would ride those rails and the dirigibles *Akron* and *Macon* would be anchored to the trucks as they moved in and out of the dock, further steadying them against cross hangar winds.

A helium storage plant was built underground alongside the dock. It consisted of huge cylinders, each having the capacity of more than a million cubic feet of gas which would be drawn by suction from the storage tanks to the dirigibles gas cells and vice-versa at the rate of a million cubic feet in twenty-four hours.

The building was so large that beneath its cavernous roof actual clouds hung above the construction scenes below when condensation conditions were just right.

A laboratory whereby the effect of line squalls upon an airship could be studied was the ultimate aim of Dr. Theodore Troller, resident director of the Guggenheim Airship Institute, to be constructed in the shadow of this dock facility. The center also would do research along structural lines, concentrate information and make recommendations regarding airship operation, changes in acceleration, velocity in wind direction, effects of gusts of wind on aircraft, etc.

Construction of the institute's 80-ton vertical wind tunnel, rising inside a sixty-foot tower in the annex of the institute building provided almost as much interest as the building of the silvery zeppelins. The vertical wind tunnel, second to be built in the United States, was to produce exact conditions under which the giant zeppelins fly. A powerful motor would send currents of air through the tunnel at velocities up to 125 miles per hour. Suspended within the experimental chamber by delicate wires would be exact models of airships, which, as they tugged at the fine steel wires, engineers would measure precisely the effects of erring currents.

As of 1931 the difficult part of the study of aerodynamics had been measuring the resistence of various parts of the ships while traveling through the air. It had been done in the past by stopping the machinery and then measuring the deceleration of the ship. With a wind tunnel, one of the first studies would be to determine the resistence of parts in the immediate neighborhood of the big airship's hull—such parts as the ventillating hoods and the water recovery rings.

Dr. Troller, graduate of the Technical College of Darmstadt, Germany and the University of Aschen, Germany, and serving in Akron under Dr. Theodore von Karmen, institute director, described one experiment in 1931 which he hoped would eliminate danger to the air dreadnoughts as they landed at the hangar doors.

Envisioning the crews tugging at the cables in fear that the zeppelin would be dashed to the ground and wrecked, Dr. Troller showed that the ever-shunned crosswinds really have an *upward* thrust which is slight but still sufficient to keep the ship from being damaged if full advantage is taken of this phenomenon.

Some experiments with airship cooling systems also were to be undertaken. At the steep sides of a dirigible, looking for all the world like shutters, are located the motor, exhaust, and condensers which act like radiators for the powerful engines. In the construction of the automobile, the radiator could be made large enough to cool the motor without particular attention to size and weight, the scientist said.

"In the airship, these radiators must be as small and as light as possible and still do the work. The exact size and weight best can be worked out in the wind tunnel. We can tell how to build them and where to place them to get maximum efficiency."

Soon came the construction of a "willing arm," an interesting piece of apparatus designed to whirl an airship model around a 65-foot diameter circle to study the forces acting on a dirigible in curved flight and the stresses thereby set up.

The curved flight studies would not require that the air through which the model passed be agitated, but it would be a comparatively simple matter to force air from a point near the ceiling in a diagonal direction across the path and create conditions similar to those existing in a line squall. It was felt such studies would be of great value to the airship builders.

A different kind of experiment conducted there had to do with an X-ray machine designed to find out what happens to the internal structure of metals when they are corroded, fatigued, strained and pounded. With the aid of this equipment, Dr. Raymond Hobrock of the Guggenheim Institute planned to take photographs which would show him how the atoms in various metals and their alloys are squeezed or pulled out of place under varying conditions. The research was planned with a view of determining the capacities of various metals in resisting unusual conditions.

What happens to the atomic structure of metals united in alloys also would be studied. This knowledge was expected to make it scientifically possible to determine what method of producing alloys was best. Little research in this field had been done. It was necessary for Dr. Hobrock to develop methods and equipment for his experiments as he went along. He now had his X-ray equipment completed so that it would direct the rays out through tiny windows in a lead box. The rays would be guided toward the piece of metal being studied. Hitting this metal at an angle, they would be refracted in a manner determined by the arrangement of the atoms in the interior structure of the metal and recorded on a piece of camera film.

Development and study of the fim would hopefully reveal how the refraction varies from that of an ordinary piece of metal "in the best of health," i.e. at its maximum strength.

In another test, a similar study would be made of how the rays are defracted as they pass through the metal. In this case the rays would be shot directly at a piece of the metal.

As more of this work was done, it was reasoned, it would then be possible to determine with considerable accuracy the meaning of variations shown on the photographic film and to work back from this to the scientific determination of which metal best meets certain specific conditions and how best to prepare alloys to meet those conditions.

It would prove a lengthy process.

Another experiment carried on at the Guggenheim Ariship Institute had to do with the feasibility of using sound waves for the purification of helium. Clarence Banton, a student from Brewster, New York, had already crudely applied the principal to the separation of hydrogen and air with considerable success. In the process the impure gas is subjected to sound waves of constant frequency but opposite phase in such a manner than a push-pull reaction is set up.

This reaction occurred in proximity to a metal grid containing very small holes. The smaller molecules of the lighter gas were forced through the grid where the larger molecules could not pass through. By subjecting the helium gas to this reaction several times, a high degree of purity could be obtained, Benton believed. If his experiments proved as successful as he hoped, a much cheaper method of separating helium and hydrogen from air would result.

Maintaining a steady supply of helium was one of the more serious problems connected with servicing the airship *Akron*. Its huge envelope required more than twice as much helium as the *Los Angeles*. As early as 1930 the U. S. Navy began planning for the transportation of helium from Amarillo, Texas to the hangar at Akron. Several special cars had been in the service of hauling helium to dirigible hangars, but it was realized that with the advent of the *Akron*, more would be needed.

Helium for dirigibles had to go through a process of purification about every four months. If an airship was in constant service, it would consume about one and a half times its own volume every year due to leakage and other factors.

The rail cars consisted of twenty-eight large cylinders of special manganese steel and carried as much helium as 1,000 small cylinders of the oxygen carrier type which were formerly the only means of shipping helium gas. Empty, a helium car weighed 100 tons or almost as much as the *Akron* itself.

The helium was pumped into the large cylinders under a pressure of 2,000 pounds to the square inch. The car carried one ton of helium or approximately 220,000 cubic feet.

Thirty carloads were required to fill the Akron!

# Section Three

## Goodyear's Lovely *Akron*: Palatial Fortress of the Air

Oh lovely! Oh beautiful! Mysterious, baffling, glistening silvery shape!

As the *Akron* lifted easily, surely and very quietly into the air Wednesday, it was almost too much to bear! Other airships have launched—other dirigibles have encircled the world—but we have not seen the first breathless moment when they left the ground. Here is the goal of man's dream for many, many generations. Not the airplane, not the hydroscope, man has dreamed of a huge graceful ship that lifted gently into the air and soared with ease. It is come, it is completely successful, it is breathtakingly beautiful!

—The *Akron Beacon Journal*

TO THE *BEACON JOURNAL*, AKRON, MAY 13, 1930—MY HEARTIEST CONGRATULATIONS TO YOU AS THE FIRST TO SUGGEST NAMING THE NAVY DIRIGIBLE *THE AKRON* STOP SECRETARY ADAMS HAS CONSENTED

—CONGRESSMAN FRANCIS SEIBERLING

The congressman's telegram received on the morning of May 13, 1930, told the story. The plan to brand the name of Akron in the skies for years to come and to emblazon it on the hall of the world's greatest airship was inspired and engineered by the *Beacon Journal*.

Congressman Francis Seiberling and attorney Robert Guinther, then president of the Chamber of Commerce, Mayor G. Lloyd Weil, the city council and almost every civic organization in Akron enthusiastically aided in the task. Secretary Charles Francis Adams of the Navy was appealed to and first formal overtures to the Navy Department and to prominent Washington officials were launched in the fall of 1929. From all over Ohio came assurances of whole-hearted support. Cleveland civic leaders were helpful and J. R. Nutt, a director of the Goodyear organization and treasurer of the National Republican committee at the time contributed influential assistance.

Ernest Lee Jahncke, then acting secretary of the Navy, at first responded doubtfully explaining that it had been intended to christen all Navy dirigibles with Indian names, but it was promptly pointed out to him that a departure from the rule was already in evidence with the *Los Angeles*.

At length Jahncke wrote Gongressman Seiberling: "To your request it gives me much pleasure to advise you that after careful consideration and after conference with Secretary Charles Francis Adams, we have decided to name the new Navy dirigible in honor of that progressive city in Ohio that has shown its faith in the future."

Officially, of course, the *Akron* was designated by the Navy as the *ZRS-4* because it was the fourth zeppelin, rigid scout, built for the Navy. The first was the ill-fated *Shenandoah* which broke in half over Cadiz, Ohio, in 1925. The second never was otherwise designated than as the *ZR-2*. It broke in two over the Humper River near Hull, England during a test flight. The U. S. S. *Los Angeles* was the third of a group and was formerly designated the *ZRS-3*.

When the Navy decided that the contracts for the proposed airships were to be let to a private concern, it initiated a design contest. Issuing more complete specifications for an airship than had ever been prepared before the Navy directed attention to the possibilities of definite improvements in design. A total of thirty-seven designs was submitted. The Goodyear-Zeppelin Corporation was awarded first place in July, 1928 and $200,000 was made available for starting construction.

About that time an eastern concern with considerable expertise in the construction of surface craft also became interested and asked for an opportunity to enter its bid. The contest was reopened and the Goodyear-Zeppelin Corporation submitted three alternative designs which were awarded first, second and third place.

The formal awarding of the contract was made in October, 1928, and shortly thereafter work on the Goodyear Zeppelin dock at the Akron airport was started. The assembly of the *Akron* was begun formally on November 7, 1929. Rear Admiral William A. Moffett, cheered on by 20,000 spectators, drove a golden rivet into the master ring during the historic ceremony.

By all comparisons, the *Akron* was the largest, safest, fastest and best airship in the world. She was nearly twice the size of the famous *Graf Zeppelin*, nearly three times as large as the *Los Angeles*, then reigning American sky queen. She was the culmination of decades of accumulated technical knowledge and her eight motors, developing 4,480 horsepower, thrust her streamlined silver sides effortlessly through the clouds.

Persons seeing the zeppelin *Akron* for the first time at its christening had only a faint idea of the great complexity of its construction. A minimum of projecting surfaces were exposed to view and the machine had the appearance of simplicity itself.

Those silver sides themselves involved several separate processes. They were doped to an .8 ounce cotton fabric and put together in several hundred separate panels 74 feet long by either 12 or 24 feet wide. Reinforced eyelets edged each section of the fabric. Heavy cord lacings were passed through these eyelets and drawn tight to the section of the framework. The lacings were tightened three or four times before any dope was applied to the fabric. The small space separating section panels of fabric also was covered over before the doping process commenced.

The prime coat of dope was plain. The second coat was orange-colored so that workmen would know how far they completed the application. The last two coats of dope were treated with aluminum powder. The aluminum gave a silvery tint that deflected the sun's rays, preventing heating of the zeppelin's interior and deterioration of the fabric. Thirty-six thousand square yards of cotton fabric for the outer cover were required.

The framework over which this fabric was stretched consisted of innumerable wire-braced duralumin girders. Some of these were joined in giant rings and others extended between sets of these rings and were known as longitudinals.

The rings were of two classes, main rings (also known as frames) and intermediate rings. The latter were of single girder construction. Main rings consisted of three rings bound into one. Two rings were on the outside and a third on the inside. Transversed and crisscrossed girders joined these three into an inherently strong unit which was further strengthened by an intensive spiderweb of strong light wires. The fact that these rings were large enough to go around a ten-story building but were lifted into place without bracing gives some indication of their sturdiness.

The backbone of every zeppelin airship is its keel and the *Akron* had three of these, one located in the center of the top of the ship and the other two at 45 degree angles from the center line of the bottom. The triple keel more than tripled the strength factor attributable to the framework.

The *Akron's* helium was contained in twelve separate gas cells, the largest having a capacity of 980,000 cubic feet of the lifting gas. The cell was 74 feet long and approximately 130 feet in diameter.

Gas relief valves were arranged so that the airship could rise at a rate of 4,000 feet per minute without causing serious increase in internal pressure.

In the control room were two large handwheels, one on the centerline at the extreme forward end of the room and the other at the left side of the room. The forward wheel operated the rudder and the wheel at the left, the elevators. The steersman at the front wheel was guided by a compass. He was given a course to follow and did so by keeping the ship in lateral alignment with that compass direction.

The steersman at the left hand had an altimeter and other instruments before him. It was up to him to keep the ship at an precise altitude. This he did by moving his wheel in one direction or the other.

Control cables ran in a long series of sheaves from these wheels to the control surfaces. The surfaces were counter-balanced so that a very slight pressure was sufficient to alter their position. A signalling system, much like marine power controls, connected the control cabin with each of the eight engine rooms and with the auxiliary control room in the lower fin. By moving a small pointer to the desired position on the signalling instrument in the control room, the order to stop, reverse or speed the engine was automatically transmitted to an engine room.

It was possible to go from one side of the ship to the other via small walkways provided in the main frames and by means of a walkway above the hangar structure. The hangar was between the crews quarters and below them. Access to the hangar was by means of the longitudinal gangways and staircases. Lights were provided every eighty feet along the gangways. Five fighting planes would be kept in this hangar and could be repaired enroute if damaged in combat. There was a T-shaped opening in the deck of the hangar through which the planes were lowered and raised on a trapeze arrangement in flight.

While the planes were within the hangar they were to be moved about suspended from an overhead trolley arrangement to facilitate moving them on and off the trapeze without contact with the hangar deck. The airplane compartment was about 70 feet long, 58 feet wide and 16 feet high.

A water recovery system was employed by the *Akron* to preserve equilibrium in flight and to avoid the necessity of valving precious buoyant gas. As fuel was burned and the airship tended to become light, the *Akron*'s water recovery apparatus condensed the moisture content of its engine exhaust to water and retained the water so recovered on board the airship as ballast. Theoretically it was possible to recover 135 pounds of water in this manner for every 100 pounds of aviation gasoline burned.

A rather extensive system of piping, principally of aluminum, permitted fuel to be received at the bow or near midships and to be circulated at will. To achieve in-flight trim, fuel also could be shifted in flight from one container to any other container. Lubricating oil was stowed in eight 1,500 pound capacity tanks, one being located near each engine room.

The ballast system comprised some 44 rubber fabric storage bags of several sizes connected by a system of piping. Each of the bags was equipped with a quick discharge valve which could be operated by means of a wire pull leading to the control car. Certain of these ballast bags were located near the bow and stern of the airship and served especially as emergency ballast for correcting the trim of the airship. The remaining bags were located along the length and could have been used in the same way for emergency purposes, but their main purpose was to serve as storage bags for recovered ballast water.

A transverse walk in the aft main frame led to an auxiliary control cabin in the lower fin of the dirigible. This cabin included replicas of the hand wheels found in the main control cabin for the operation of the controls, operating in precisely the same manner, plus two machine guns. It was possible to proceed on aft from there to an observation and machine gun platform at the extreme stern of the airship. This platform was protected by a metal tail cap.

The top gangway was reached by ascending several series of stairs and ladders located in two of the main frames, one near the bow and one near the stern of the craft. Several 50 caliber machine guns were to be installed at various points along the gangway. Together, the sixteen machine guns which were to go aboard the *Akron* would cover all angles of approach or attack. Its fire power was estimated effective at 5,000 yards—nearly three miles.

An observation basket which could be lowered several hundred feet below the airship was contemplated for future installation.

Placing the motors of the zeppelin within the hull was an innovation which was useful for a number of reasons. It enabled the framework to bear the weight of the motors and accessory equipment as a part of the ship. This form of installation reduced the drag or wind resistance. It made possible a roomier engine room and one easily accessible and comfortable. The engineers would experience no difficulty in getting to their motors to make repairs.

Placing engine rooms within the hull of course was possible only because the *Akron* would use the non-flammable helium instead of hydrogen. The use of helium was the greatest single safety factor aboard and would entirely eliminate the possibility of any such tragedy as the crash and subsequent explosion of the British dirigible *R-101* the year before.

Toward aerodynamic lift, stability and controllability, the *Akron* depended upon its eight propellers, its fins and its control surfaces. The swiveling feature of the propellers was important. The propellers could be set at an angle to assist in driving the ship and on the take-off could be used to send a blast into the ground in such a manner that the reaction would help lift the ship.

The fins were the fixed surfaces to which the elevators and rudders were attached. They were the ship's stabilizers. The task they performed was extremely important and they had to be extremely large to satisfactorily do their part. Accordingly, they were built 120 feet long, 35 feet wide at the widest point, and deep enough for a man to walk erect inside.

Several large rooms could have been constructed within any one of them. For ultimate controllability, the airship depended most exclusively upon the rudders and elevators. The rudders were attached to the perpendicular fins and the elevators to the horizontal ones. The elevators were some 15 feet long and as wide as the fins. The rudders were about 35 feet wide and 198 feet tall, second in size only to the Goodyear airdock.

As the *Akron*'s christening drew near, half the town purchased mammoth ads to wish her well (and to get in on the act).

Finally, on August 8, 1931, the day of the *Akron*'s christening arrived. I liked what John Botzum wrote in the paper that day:

> Today's celebration is the last link in the chain of human progress that had its start 104 years ago this summer on the banks of the Ohio Erie Canal when the first canal boat was chistened, launched and started away to make history and make it possible for today's greater event.
>
> How different today's christening from that of 104 years ago. Back there in that candle age of civilization there was not a reporter on the job. There were no newspapers. The story lives in the pages yellowed by time. There was no fancy writing then and no need for such. People were just pioneering the way.
>
> But then as now there were men of vision who thought they saw the coming of today's caravans of the skies. They even talked about such things. People who listened thought the dreamers a bit queer. By looking back to some of those yesterdays, one can better understand the great today. And all along the trail you'll find the men and women, who, in some way or other, have had a part in the great achievements of today.
>
> Old Akron speaks back today to a modern Akron.
>
> The pilot of the canal boat salutes the pilot of the mistress of the skies.

On christening day, downtown Akron got its first big thrill when Lieutenant Commander M. V. Baugh stunted his Navy scout plane, dived at tall building with throttle wide open, looped, did practically everything a plane could do, then was joined by Sherbondy Hill, another Navy flier. Residents were treated to a dogfight. The crowd was thrilled when Baugh went into a vertical bank, just missing the Mayflower Hotel where aviatrix Amelia Earhart was a guest.

Then from all over Ohio and beyond, squadrons of planes came to loop-the-loop, play follow-the-leader, zoom, flip their tails like skiddish two-year-olds—United States Army ships from Wright Field, Dayton, and Selfridge Field, Mt. Clemens, Michigan. After maneuvering their craft, all pilots returned to the airport, but so heavy was the dust kicked up by the constantly moving ships that considerable difficulty was experienced in landing.

A half a dozen Red Cross nurses, a dozen first-aiders spent most of the morning picking bits of cinders and dust out of spectators' eyes. Propeller blasts made the airport look like a miniature sandstorm. The airport drugstore, doing a land office business in dark glasses, had to send to town for a new supply. There was a special guest to town that day. No one less could have overshadowed the presence of the world's greatest aviatrix, Amelia Earhart, who could make anybody's head spin almost anytime.

The large shiny 16 cylinder car that took Mrs. Herbert Hoover from the Union Station to the Portage Country Club was an open job, top down. The thoughtful chauffeur, Forest O. Washburn of Goodyear, moved it to a shady place to keep the cushions from becoming too hot for the First Lady's comfort.

An hour later, thousands of spectators to the mammoth airdock came, saw, but could not hear. Engineers at the eleventh hour gave up as impossible the placing of a suitable amplifying system in the largest building in the world sans internal supports, so the thousands contented themselves with pushing to the front.

That's where Mrs. Hoover stood. And P. W. Litchfield.

Litchfield, the first speaker, stood before the microphone at exactly 2:30. A flash of annoyance passed over his face when his voice failed to penetrate the low hum of thousands of voices in conversation. But he read on, commending the Navy and airship builders for their accomplishment as seen in the U. S. S. *Akron*. The estimated 100,000 to 150,000 persons gathered inside the Goodyear hangar simply could not hear the Goodyear president's voice. Newspaper men standing only 20 feet away strained their ears to hear Litchfield to no avail, Litchfield's voice was lost in the vastness of the building.

A few moments later, Mrs. Hoover's only words were "May the U. S. S. *Akron* leave her moorings always with a cargo of good will and never come to mast without having added to a record of effort and the advancement of international communication and human understanding...I christen thee U. S. S. *Akron*."

Mrs. Hoover's hand pulled on a red, white and blue ripcord at the word *Akron* opening two small hatchway doors just aft of the glistening nose of the great airship releasing 48 white homing pigeons, one for each state.

Then the *Akron* lifted its gargantuan bulk several feet and was pulled back into its position in the middle of the airdock—a salute to the First Lady. The crowd broke and cheer after cheer resounded in the hollow uppper reaches of the great steel shed. Hundreds of people rushed to the east side of the dock where a path had been cleared for the official party, as the pigeons fluttered about under the roof trying to find the exit.

The great orange peel doors had been closed to prevent gusty air from disturbing the big ship as it rested almost on the concrete floor.

The hot, tired, citizens of Akron stood by late that Saturday awaiting to see the newly named U. S. S. *Akron* riding the air. The speeches were over, the crowd was dispersed after hours of honking on roads surrounding the city. The world's largest airship had made its bow to America's First Lady. Within the next three weeks, the sleek, silvery craft, fruit of twenty months' work in the depths of the

Goodyear-Zeppelin corporation's facility would float over the city in its own salute to its builders.

Trying as it no doubt was, they termed it "Akron's greatest day," and it ended with a zeppelin banquet at the armory under the auspices of the Chamber of Commerce. More than a thousand guests were invited and they heard some of the world's greatest aviation authorities tell their version of the day when the *Akron* would be mistress of the commercial airlines of the globe.

Among the speakers was Rear Admiral William Moffett who said something pretty significant for the record:

> We do not lead the world in our merchant marine, (he said), and, alas, we do not lead the world with our navy. But we do, by construction of this great airship, now take the lead in lighter-than-air. But we must now begin to think in terms of rigid airships twice the size of the 6,500,000 cubic foot helium gas capacity. Germany is said to be building a 7,000,000 cubic foot ship and this nation cannot afford to let any other nation take the lead in that regard.

The *Akron Times Press* feature editorial added:

> . . . We in Akron have lived close to the development of airships and we are, in our estimating of their importance, somewhat like a man in a doorway attempting to guess at the height of a building. We live so close to the base that we cannot see the top. But never before in the world's history has a lighter-than-air ship of practical dimensions been constructed.
>
> We have seen the queenly *Shenandoah* and the great *Los Angeles*, the gigantic *Graf Zeppelin*—but as compared to the magnificent ship that floats free in the huge dock at Akron airport today, these predecessors were but experiments. None of them—not even the *Graf Zeppelin*, which has very thoroughly demonstrated the practicality of dirigible airships—had the capacity to operate on the scale which the airship must maintain to be commercially efficient. The *Akron* is big enough, fast enough and stable enough to be of commercial value. It or ships like it can compete with other forms of transportation and find their place in the world's communication scheme.
>
> The *Akron* in a few more days will make way in the big dock for a sister. The next dirigible will be greater than the *Akron* which is, in theory, already obsolete. When its successor floats free, it, too, will be outmoded for the construction of dirigibles proceeds so slowly that the designer is always many steps ahead of the construction man. In any event there are two naval ships. These two naval airships are bids for American supremacy in the air. That supremacy cannot be established by ships of war. It is dependent far more upon the utilization of aircraft in the pursuits of peace.
>
> It is our hope that the mighty *Akron* is to be the first among a long line of dirigibles which will aid America in winning not only supremacy in the air but advancement commercially through that supremacy.

It was soon known that when the "world's mightiest fighting machine" slid out of her hangar in late July and lifted into the northern Ohio skies for a trial run, she would be commanded by a new commander, Charles E. Rosendahl of the United States Navy, hero of the *Shenandoah* disaster, former commander of the dirigible *Los Angeles*, and observer aboard the *Graf Zeppelin* on the German craft's famous flight around the world.

Rosendahl, a strikingly handsome man of thirty-eight, was ordered the day of the christening to leave Washington for Lakehurst, New Jersey to ready the air station and a crew to handle the new $5,375,000 Navy dirigible *Akron*.

Rosendahl was considered one of the best informed lighter-than-air men in America. He had graduated from the Naval Academy in 1914 and saw duty on various ships during the war and commanded a destroyer on the west coast after the war. In 1922 he was detailed to the Naval Academy and was an instructor in physics and electrical engineering. In 1923 a call went out for men interested in lighter-than-air work and Captain Rosendahl was among those who volunteered.

He had gone to Lakehurst as a student officer. Later he was attached to the U. S. S. *Shenandoah* as ship's officer and shortly before that ship's fatal flight he was promoted to lieutenant commander. On the *Shenandoah*'s final flight, he was navigator and third in command. After the terrible break-up of the ship, he directed the free ballooning of the bow section for about an hour, landing it ten miles away without additional loss of life. He was the senior surviving officer.

In the spring of 1926 he took charge of the *Los Angeles* and retained command until 1929, making many long flights and doing much valuable work during the time. He specialized in the study of ground-handling problems and the later development of mooring masts of the stationary and mobile stub mast type were later attributable to him as were better methods of high mast handling both ashore and afloat.

Upon being relieved of command of the *Los Angeles* by Lieutenant Commander Herbert V. Wiley in May, 1929, Captain Rosendahl became commander of the rigid ship training and experimental squadron at Lakehurst. The summer of 1930 he was ordered to the Bureau of Aeronautics in Washington for duty in connection with airships.

When the question of the construction of the U. S. S. *Akron* was first considered in Congress, an important point was made on its behalf when leading Allied naval officials testified that their experience indicated such ships would be capable of scouting an area of 87,000 square miles a day. This, W. C. Young, head of Goodyear's aeronautical sales department pointed out, was considered the equivalent of the work of six scouting cruisers with crews of 550 men and 50 officers each. The cruisers, he added, cost approximately $11 million apiece whereas the cost of an airship was approximately $4 million.

The first trial flight of the world's largest airship was scheduled to take place soon after August 15, 1931, when the last of the *Akron*'s internal fittings had been installed and the test flight crew thoroughly familiar with operation. During the approaching trials, at least 75 hours flying would be carried out in at least five separate flights. Speed trials would be conducted, including a deceleration test. Turning circles would be measured, altitudinal trials would be conducted, dynamic lift would be measured, interior ventilation and pressure equilization would be studied. Fuel consumption would be determined and deflections and strains within the structure measured. Pressure distribution over the hull would be checked and various other scientific data all bearing on the general air worthiness of the airship would be collected and carefully evaluated.

Throughout construction various parts of the *Akron* and her equipment had been critically examined. Step by step, all parts were tested. The first section of the dirigible to be completed, the section near midships, was subjected to a proof test using for this purpose and appropriate gas cell inflated with helium to simulate actual conditions as closely as practicable.

Various loadings were applied to this section and scientific measurements made. Behavior of this critical section of the airship was according to calculations. Hundreds of tests of smaller magnitude were made on girders, joints, fittings, fins, rudders. As the zeppelin approached completion, other ground tests were made including a hogging and sagging test, inclining tests, electrical bonding and insulation tests, testing of fuel lines, control systems.

The *Akron*'s design represented a special effort to stress safety from every standpoint. Structural integrity, accessibility for repairs, insurance against breakdown of any essential operational feature, protection against fire and means for extinguishing fire were but some of the ship's guarantees.

The U. S. S. *Akron* soared aloft at 3:37 pm, September 23rd, on its maiden voyage after being wheeled from the dock stern first. The stern lines were cut loose and the craft veered into the wind with only its prow ring holding it fast to the mobile hitching post to which it was anchored. It began to rise almost perpendicular with two aft motors providing the lifting power plus the lifting power of the helium-inflated container with which the craft was equipped.

At a height of 90 to 100 feet, the propellers began revolving for forward speed. Slowly and majestically with the ease of an immense bird, the great ship nosed upward to a height of 400 feet and flew southwest, coming into view of thousands of Akronites who were perched atop downtown buildings, at windows and in the streets, occupying whatever point of vantage possible to view her.

Earlier, the ship's weighing off process occupied only a few minutes and when the officer forward sang out "600 light!" the command "Up ship!" was given. The dumping of water ballast gave newspapermen, photographers and other observers a thorough soaking. There was a bedlam of noise from shrieking motor horns and other devices to show the public's attitude as the airship soared. As the craft appeared over the business district, the clouds appeared to roll back, permitting brilliant sunlight to flood the dirigible and shroud it in sparkling aureole.

The airport and dock property were surrounded by a fringe of hills and parked everywhere in every cranny and nook, in housetops and trees and motor cars were persons who had come to see the ship fly. It was a picturesque setting for the maiden flight of the aerial leviathan.

It was decided not to take all the passengers aboard inside the dock because it was not known how much ballast would have to be discarded outside to attain equilibrium with the additional passenger weight to be taken into consideration. Goodyear police were stationed at their posts around the airport early on the flight day keeping visitors other than newspapermen, officials and cameramen out of the enclosed area.

Extraordinary precautions were taken by the Navy to guard against stow-aways on the first flight. Guards were stationed at every entrance of the ship and high on the catwalks on the top of the dock to prevent anyone dropping to the ship from above. The first duty of the flight crew was members of their stations was for each man to search a particular area.

On the initial trial flight over the city of Akron, a radio message was received from Mrs. Hoover. It read:

FROM THE WHITE HOUSE, WASHINGTON D. C.
23 SEPTEMBER

TO: COMMANDING OFFICER, U. S. S. *AKRON*

WITH ALL GOOD WISHES TO YOU AND THE OFFICERS AND CREW FOR A SUCCESSFUL MAIDEN TRIP AND YEARS OF EFFICIENT SERVICE.

LOU HENRY HOOVER

The following reply was radioed Mrs. Hoover via the *Akron*'s powerful radio equipment:

TO: MRS. HOOVER

YOUR MESSAGE TO *AKRON* PERSONNEL VERY MUCH APPRECI-ATED. ALL ON BOARD THIS INITIAL FLIGHT EXTEND HEARTY GREETINGS AND BEST WISHES. THIS IS THE FIRST RADIO MESSAGE SENT FROM THE *AKRON*.

CAPT. C. E. ROSENDAHL

Two minor failures affected the motors during the flight. The exhaust man-ifold on No. 7 motor, the forward starboard motor, broke, putting it out of com-mission. A valve spring and cam on the No. 2 motor, the aft port motor, broke when the engineman threw it in reverse too quickly. Lieutenant Commander Bertram J. Rodgers, engineer officer of the *Akron*, characterized both of these failures as unimportant.

"In regular duty," he commented, "we would have had a spare manifold for the forward starboard motor. The breaking of the valve spring was the result of an operating error. This is not uncommon in airship operations. The break was repaired in fifteen minutes. Neither break crippled the ship at all inasmuch as full power is scarcely ever required."

Meanwhile on the field, the refreshment stand at the south end of the dock sold out of sandwiches, coffee, mustard and nearly everything else before the *Akron* returned to its berth. The big drain on the food supply came when the 250 ground crew members decided they were all hungry while standing and waiting and sent details of men to the stand to bring back huge boxes of sand-wiches. While these orders were being filled, everybody else had to wait and after the ground crew men were fed, there was little left for others.

At the gates every fieldglass owner who showed the slightest disposition toward friendliness was besieged by scores of youngsters who pleaded, "Let me take a look, please?" One youngster obtained a long brass telescope from some source and for a time the other children flocked about him but he kept his eye glued to the glass and refused "to give a look" to the others. He finally gave up and turned to the older folk with glasses.

Hugh Allen, Goodyear-Zeppelin's public relations director who successfully carried through one of the heaviest publicity assignments ever loaded on one individual, gave way to justifiable wrath when caught with others and tossed back for a long loss by cops manning ropes and pulling spectators back from ringside views of the mooring.

"Don't go so far and don't go so damn fast!" Allen erupted in volcanic fashion, making for one of the city policemen. The officer made no reply but the hurting game ended right there. Like others, many of those caught by rope were the very persons most entitled to be right on top of the ship.

Mooring of the *Akron* was by far the most spectacular incident of the flight. The sun was just setting in the west when the ship hovered into sight northwest of the airport. As she headed in, her blinking navigation lights were turned on. These added to the beauty of the scene. The two landing lights on the bow and on the stern were white. Spaced along the north side were the two red lights and along the starboard side the two green. Lights in the control cabin and gangway shown dimly.

The sky was still glorious with soft colors as the ship descended. The silvery moon outlined itself with a dimming haze.

On the ground Lieutenant Peck took his post at the top of the mooring mast and shouted orders via loudspeaker. The ground crew was split into groups stationed at proper distances. A long strip of red, white and blue bunting laid out on the ground to indicate the proper direction for the ship's approach.

Lieutenant Peck shouted orders—"Keep your relative positions! Don't get frightened! Stand ready to grab those shoe lines when they come down! Now don't frighten and back away! And don't let those yaw lines hit you when they come down. Remember the starboard yaw line comes down first! The port crew gets the second line. Step lively and obey the orders of the man in charge of your group!"

The lieutenant commanded a smoke candle be lit. It was done. The direction of the smoke indicated the ground crew was much too far to port. Lieutenant Peck ordered a general movement to starboard with each group keeping its relative position. This completed, two more smoke candles were ordered lit. The wind was varying slightly. Peck ordered another slight shift in the position of the ground crew. Motors idling, the *Akron* was drifting slowly into position. Captain Rosendahl had completed his pre-landing weigh-off, shutting his motors and determining to his dissatisfaction that the ship was light.

He nosed her down sharply as he surmounted the ridge east of the port, then allowed her to drift at an altitude of about 400 feet over the path necessary for a mooring. This progress took considerable time.

Lieutenant Peck called for lanterns. Two red ones were placed on the ground hear the flag. The flagman swung two white ones. As the ship approached, the ground crew members moved backward.

The officer stormed at them, "DON'T BACK AWAY! You won't be able to make contact if you do!" This halted their retreat. The ship floated some hundreds of feet, its hulk outlined in the half light of the dusk and beautified by the lights.

"They'll have to darken ship for that baby in time of war," a Navy officer remarked, noting the way the lights shone through the strips of transparent fabric along the gangways.

"HE'S TOO HIGH!" the same officer said. "I presume his yaw lines are about 350 feet. He'll probably circle again."

Captain Rosendahl continued the ship slowly in a circle to the north of the airport. By the time he was back again darkness had fallen. Lieutenant Peck called for the lights on the mooring mast. Airport manager B. E. Fulton turned on the port's eight million candle power floodlight. The moon, now brilliant against the dark blue starry sky, added its glow. The U. S. S. *Akron* lowered slowly toward the mooring mast. It was much lower this time. A loudspeaker bellowed more of Lieutenant Peck's last minute orders to the ground crew. "The starboard yaw lines will be down in a minute. Stand by, now. Keep a sharp lookout and there isn't any danger!"

The *Akron* came in a little to port of the crew and the men on the ground shifted again. The yaw line tumbled out, rolling as it fell and was similarly handled. The bow mooring cable was lowered and coupled to a cable which passed through the top of the mooring mast. A winch on the mast was set in motion. It sped, lifting up the hundreds of feet of cable. As the line lifted, a man in the control cabin kept playing a flashlight on it. As it neared tautness, Lieutenant Peck set off a flare—a signal to the operator to stop and resume action of the winch at a more moderate speed.

The winch began turning again, hauling the airship down. The mooring spindle was guided into place at the top of the mast by Lieutenant Peck and two Goodyear-Zeppelin men. Ground crew members were stationed underneath. Side-handling lines were attached. Official observers and Goodyear-Zeppelin officials disembarked. Ground crew members took their places inthe control car to keep the ship in equilibrium. The celebrities were surrounded by newsmen, announced that they had made official statements and were whisked away in automobiles.

Rear Admiral Moffett was cornered momentarily. He shouted answers to a few questions, brushed his way through the crowd and disappeared.

"It couldn't have been better. No, there was no vibration. Entirely satisfactory" were among his replies as he broke away.

Some additional ballast was taken aboard to replace persons disembarking. The motor on the mooring mast roared into activity and Captain Rosendahl and Executive Officer Wiley went aft, bellowing orders. Flashlight wielders communicated them to men on the mooring mast. The U. S. S. *Akron* took the last half mile of its journey at a speed of slightly more than a mile an hour.

Suddenly Mr. Litchfield was spotted and was mobbed. He smiled good naturedly at the press.

"One of the most amazing things about it is the lack of thrill," he said. "There is scarcely any sensation except change of scenery below. We couldn't hear the motors from the control car. There was no vibration. We traveled most of the trip about a thousand feet altitude.

"Leaving the airport, we went over south Akron onto the Portage Lakes district and back across the city to Cuyahoga Falls and over east Akron and back across the northeast corner of the airport and onto Wingfield Lake. Turning north again we passed over Chagrin Falls and crossed the lake shore line at Gordon Park. We went out over the lake and beyond the breakwater. We came back to the shore over the 9th Street pier and sailed across the Terminal Tower, following Cuyahoga Valley back across Cuyahoga Falls and thence to the airport again. Many passengers spent their time in the control car. As guests of Captain Rosendahl they were served dinner in the mess rooms as the ship was over Cleveland. I was too much interested in the action of the ship to eat!"

Ultimately, of course, the time came to deliver the machine that could cruise 10,580 miles without refueling to Lakehurst as property of the Navy. The U. S. S. *Akron* rose majestically over the city. Factory whistles blew in triumph. Horns of automobiles sounded. Twice Captain Rosendahl sent the new sky queen in sweeping circles over the city of Akron before heading her east. Every Akronite was given a final view of the world's largest and best airship, a triumph of the city's industry. Nothing bigger had ever left the earth.

That's why a lot of Akronites—and citizens everywhere—gasped the next evening when they picked up their newspapers and read:

> Lakehurst flying sailors can make use of some sort of a mammoth shoehorn to help in easing the U. S. S. *Akron* into their dock. The *Akron's* huge fin grazed the top as she moved slowly into the hangar this morning, dwarfing her sister ship, the *Los Angeles*, already resting in the 800 foot structure. The *Akron* is 785 feet long, leaving little clearance fore and aft.

But reassurance rode on the words of Goodyear-Zeppelin Vice-President Karl Arnstein who very soon had a public statement:

> We felt a little sorry to leave our baby down there at Lakehurst, (he said), but I feel reassured now. Rosendahl knows how to take care of her.

By now, Arnstein was practically a folk hero in Akron. Whatever else he was capable of doing, which was probably anything, it was known he wouldn't lie about his airship.

On May 14, 1932, the Navy's new lighter-than-air craft base at Sunnyvale, California, had its first customer, the dirigible *Akron*, swinging from a portable mooring mast, as riveters beat a tattoo on the skeleton of a new airship hangar, the *Akron's* permanent home.

The giant craft was moored successfully the previous night after cruising all day around San Francisco Bay. Circumstances had combined to defeat her contemplated early morning landing on her voyage from San Diego where she had stopped to replenish her fuel supply on flight from Lakehurst, New Jersey.

Circumstances were lack of wind, lack of ballast and a superheated condition of her lifting helium which Navy men blamed on static electricity. While at Sunnyvale, the ship was scheduled to be refueled and its helium supply replenished.

The buffeting of storms across the continent and her frustrated attempt to dock at Camp Kearney cost the *Akron* nearly a third of her gas supply. At Camp Kearney before she was moored, two bluejackets fell to their deaths from mooring lines as the *Akron* suddenly rose. A third was hauled safely aboard after hanging two hours to a landing line as the craft maneuvered.

The two incidents—the storms and the deaths—played easily into the hands of forces forever doubtful of the wisdom of any kind of airship, military or commercial. Much of the *Akron*'s troubles, both real and imagined, hit the newspapers. The *Akron Times Press*, as was its custom, set the matter straight:

> . . . Anxiety over the stress of lightning, fog, sandstorms and high weather encountered on the flight to the coast (it noted), was in existence more in headlines than the public mind and in the control cabin of the *Akron*. The people of a little town in Texas, noting the blinking lights of the *Akron*, believed its skipper was signalling for a landing and sent out a report from which the nation drew the hasty inference that the ship was in distress. The log of the *Akron* will show that while there was much foul weather, there was never a moment when its command was not master of every fortuity.
>
> The *Graf Zeppelin* is making steady trips from its Friedrichshafen base to Brazil and return and the world is never fed with narratives of emergencies met along the way. But when a Navy ship crosses our own continent, every stage of progress is marked with awe and a shade of apprehension. It is time for air-minded America to be of a better fortitude in this matter and acquire the calm that marks the staff and crew of an airship when it sets forth on a trip to a port that it is more than confident of reaching in good order.
>
> The fact that the *Akron* met this latest test is all the more tribute to its airworthiness.

# Section Four

The Death of Our Lovely Akron

### The Akron—In Memorium
#### by Celia Dimmette
#### Published in the Akron Times Press

Unleashed, it rose and crowds
    were there with eager cries
Of might to shame the clouds
    Look! look! The *Akron* flies!
Its helium heart has life
Moves its shining sheath
This drift of silver rife
To quicken dreams beneath.

Its name upheld our faith
And carried wide from cloud to cloud
    our wreath;
The ship was gone; we sighed
    and lived in dreams on it
We, the builders, were the few
    who knew that when it quit the earth in flight
We soared, too.

But there, in cringe at night
The girding ribs were crushed
The broken bodies' flight
    was done;
Its voice hushed;
And in that mighty fall were seventy-three
    who, keeping faith with all
Of us, met death within the sea.

Misfortune seemed to be the lot of the dirigible *Akron* during her brief life as the ranking aircraft of the United States Navy, and, until the *Macon* was built, the largest airship in the world. She was for many weeks the subject of a bitter controversy in Congress. She was alternately criticized and praised. The criticism came generally from laymen, the praise from two of the Navy's most authoritative sources—Rear Admiral William A. Moffett, who quite ironically was lost in the *Akron* crash, and Lieutenant Commander Charles E. Rosendahl, the *Akron's* first skipper.

Sadly enough from the viewpoint of the ship's officers and men, the two major accidents in the career of the *Akron* before her fatal plunge came at moments when the eyes of the entire country were centered on the giant ship. Both were unpredictable and while they in no way reflected on the ship's command, they added nothing to the reputation of the aircraft that had acquired the name of a "jinx ship" even before she left the hangar in Akron, Ohio.

First of these accidents, resulting in injuries to two men, occurred on February 22, 1932, when the ship was being walked from her hangar preparatory to a flight to prove her air worthiness to members of the subcommittee of the House Naval Affairs Committee. A gust of wind lifted the ship, snapped a restraining stern cable and swung her around until she bumped the ground and smashed her lower vertical fin.

That this happened in the presence of the critical congressmen who were getting ready to go on board made the happening even more tragic for the feelings of the crew.

Less than three months after this accident, the *Akron* was turned toward the west coast. She battled a terrific wind storm from the southwest to reach California. There her unhappy fate again overtook her and, as reported earlier, two men on the ground crew at Camp Kearney, California were killed.

The ship received her first baptism of criticism in Akron when it was charged that sabotage had weakened her construction. The idle talk of faulty material, that she specifically was overweight and that eight million rivets were defective came to the ears of the House Naval Affairs Committee.

The Navy conducted its own investigation, found the ship airworthy and so reported.

Then she scraped a fin on her hangar roof at Lakehurst and that news helped little.

Promptly at sundown one evening in the first week of April, 1933, the U. S. *Akron* cast off from her stub mast at the Naval Air Station at Lakehurst, floated silently and moodily into a cheerless sky. One after another the eight engines were started. Commander Frank C. McCord bent a course eastward.

The seventy officers and crew settled down to one more of the *Akron's* routine training flights. This one was to be most casual—a two-day cruise off the New England coast for calibration of the airship's radio compass, a trifling job compared to the 81-hour Canal Zone flight from which the *Akron* had returned the previous month.

If there was any distinction to the present excursion, it was the presence aboard of seven guest officers, most notably Rear Admiral William Moffett, champion of the Navy lighter-than-air program. It was he who had fought and won the airship cause against the stone wall of official opposition raised by the crash of the *Shenandoah* in 1925. Also aboard was Commander Fred Berry, last skipper of the decommissioned airship *Los Angeles.*

At 8:00 pm the Lakehurst radio station received the *Akron's* signal of "all's well." Communication was difficult. A northeaster was whipping the New Jersey coast. The crack of lightning drowned the whine of the radio's dots and dashes. At 10:00 pm the airship again reported her position. That was the last message heard from the U.S.S. *Akron.* When midnight came and the *Akron* remained mute behind a curtain of wind, rain, thunder, Lakehurst tried not to worry.

The *Akron* had ridden worse storms than this one appeared to be. Besides she was at sea where an airship belongs, not over land to be twisted apart by the line squalls, as was the *Shenandoah*—or beaten into a hillside as was Britain's *R-101.* As for her radio, that could easily malfunction with the atmosphere supercharged with electricity. Not until the next day did Lakehurst and the rest of the world know what good cause it had to worry.

At 8:45 pm, little more than an hour after taking off, the *Akron* was nosing above a cloud of fog northeast of Philadelphia. From thirty miles to the south, lightning split the sky. In another hour it was crashing on all sides of the ship. But she continued to ride steadily. By 11:00 pm, the lashing of the wind and rain became severe. When Executive Officer Lieutenant Commander Herbert V. Wiley came on duty at midnight, he altered the course to west.

A half hour later, the great ship plunged from its 1,600 foot altitude. The commander reached for a row of pullcords overhead—yanked at them to release water ballast. Slowly, painfully, the shuddering *Akron* shouldered her way aloft again as a call for "all hands on" brought the off-watch from their bunks. Officers, bosuns, bosun's mates, riggers, firemen groped their way along narrow catwalks to their stations.

Again the storm dashed the great ship downward and this time clawed away a section of her belly fabric and part of her rudder. Again ballast was dumped, but the ship did not rise. Down, down she went-DASH!-CRASH! upon the surface of the writhing sea. For a brief moment the 110-ton hulk floated while its buoyant helium hissed away into the gale.

Then the pounding waves wrenched the airship to bits. Here and there by the occasional brilliance of the lightning flashes, a witness could discern men of the *Akron* flailing about in the water.

And there was a witness.

On the bridge of the German tanker *Phoebus*, butting the storm under ballast stood Captain Dalldorf, taking a turn himself on the second mate's midnight watch. Gazing upward at the ugly sky, he saw to his astonishment the flashing red and green lights of an airship.

"Shortly afterward," he recalled much later, "I saw lights flash on the water. I changed my course to approach the lights and soon heard men hailing me from the water. I stopped the ship, turned on all lights, lowered boats and put them over the side. I saw mattresses and wreckage and pulled one man over the side of the boat. We got four men. I saw some men sink before we could get to them. After this, no more men were found. And no more men were ever found alive."

The *Phoebus's* first dreadful flash of the accident was picked up by the German-speaking operator of Mackay Radio & Telegraph Company in Manhattan at 1:46 am. It simply reported the crash and the rescue of four men. Immediately the Coast Guard sent cutters dashing to the position twenty miles off Barnegat Lightship. The cruiser U.S.S. *Portland* steamed for the scene. Within a few more hours a fleet of rescue ships were circling by sea and by air around the *Phoebus*. They found nothing but small bits of wreckage.

The Coast Guard destroyer *Tucker* took from the *Phoebus* the four men it had rescued and steamed with them to Brooklyn Navy Yard. They were Lieutenat Commander Wiley, veteran of the *Shenandoah*, bosun's mate R. E. Deal, survivor of the *Shenandoah* crash, machinist's mate M. E. Erwin and radioman Robert E. Copeland. When the *Tucker* had the men aboard, its flag came down to half-mast. Radioman Copeland died of injuries.

Of the 73 others, nothing but two dead bodies, as yet unidentified.

In the course of the search, Navy blimp *J-3* crashed in the ocean off the New Jersey coast.

The non-rigid airship had attempted to land after searching for survivors of the *Akron* disaster, but was borne a half-mile to sea where it plummeted into the waves. Two of its crew of seven died. Five of the men were rescued by New York City police planes. Lieutenant Commander David E. Cummins, in charge of the blimp, was scooped up by a Coast Guard plane. He was flown to Atlantic City where, after unsuccessful attempts were made to resuscitate him, he was pronounced dead by drowning.

The body of the seventh, chief machinist mate Pasquale Bettio of Ridgeway, New Jersey, was recovered several hours later by a Coast Guard boat.

Lieutenant Cockell, one of the living, said the blimp lurched over when he pulled a zipper rip in the helium bag to release the gas for a quick landing on the beach and was carried out over the water and crashed. The decision to attempt a landing, he said, was made because of a 45-mile wind which they did not want to buck to return to the Naval Air Station at Lakehurst.

Otto A. Kafke, pilot of the police seaplane, said he noticed the ship was apparently in trouble, and turning his plane around toward it, he saw it "suddenly collapse as though it had been struck in the middle and crash."

"We flew our plane over and landed," he said, "and picked up four men who were in a life ring some 300 feet from the blimp and one who was still 100 feet away. The blimp was all crumpled up. We saw the other two members of the crew swimming but before we could turn our plane around we lost sight of them. My partner, acting sergeant Joseph Forsythe, who had his fingers cut, was a real hero," Kafke reported.

Kafke did not relate how he landed his plane in the choppy seas and then taxied his plane through the heavy, heavy surf to the beach when he found the additional load would not permit it to rise from the water. Both of these feats were highly dangerous.

Another observer of the tragedy was Captain Charles Stoffer who was flying in the vicinity with two Associated Press cameramen, Joe Casneva and John Rooney aboard his plane.

"I saw the Navy blimp *J-3*," Stoffer said, "bucking a hell of a wind about fifteen miles off shore. We flew above and watched the struggle. It seemed to be trying to reach the shore so far as I could make out. It almost made it and was about 300 feet in the air when a sudden gust of wind seemed to catch it broadside and blow it seaward. I saw the gondola rip off and hurtle into the sea. The bag blew on another 200 yards and fell. The crew splashed into the water."

Meanwhile the beach was lined with persons watching the planes and ships searching for *Akron* survivors, as the misfortune befell the blimp. As darkness fell over the cold, black choppy water, Coast Guard cutters continued their struggle to tow the hulk of the blimp ashore.

In the next several days, praise was given by Akron and Lakehurst airshipmen to the crew of the *J-3*. Overshadowed by the immensity of the *Akron* disaster, the courage of Lieutenant Commander David E. Cummins and his men had not received due notice, they felt. Indeed on the evidence it seemed accurate to conclude that the *J-3* had risked everything in the meager hope that a floating sailor might be plucked from the sea alive.

The determination of Cummins and his men to continue their search for *Akron* survivors as long as possible and make it as extensive as possible led to their own crash. Risks unthought of under other circumstances were taken. The blimp started back from her search with just enough fuel to make the shore. There wouldn't have been an accident, it was believed, if winds of storm velocity hadn't sprung up, making it more difficult for the craft to return.

With fuel amost exhausted, the crew reached shore only to be blown back to sea. With any considerable quantity of fuel she could have outridden the gale, but not as she was. It was only a question of minutes until the motors would drain the last drop of gasoline and sputter to a stop. The wind took the ship farther from shore in spite of every effort of the engines.

Lieutenant Commander Cummins was left no choice. He could do nothing but order the rip cord pulled and the ship collapsed into the sea. Riding hopelessly out over the Atlantic, their craft a prey of fitful winds, was the fate facing the crew in the event of any other decision.

And so five of the seven men lived.

Twenty-one hours after the *Akron* crashed with her son, Elmer E. Fink, aboard, Mrs. Hanna Belk of Lawn Avenue, Akron, still awaited word from Washington or Lakehurst, still hoping that when news did come, it would be good news. Fink, 38, was chief petty officer aboard the *Akron*. He had been a member of the crew before the aircraft was launched.

The previous summer Mrs. Belk and her husband Joseph had spent their vacation in Fink's home in Lakehurst, New Jersey, and Fink received permission to take them aboard over the ship. It was partly their memory of the ship which buoyed their hopes that night.

It is an enormous ship," Belk said, choosing the present tense, "and they said it could remain afloat indefinitely. They're hampered now by fog and the storm but maybe they will find the wreckage with some of the men in it alive."

They spoke of chief radioman R. W. Copeland who died after being picked up from the sea. He was a friend of the Finks and they had seen him and his young bride frequently during the three months in Akron preceding the launching.

Will Rogers came on the radio and called Admiral Moffett a "grand soul" of naval aviation. Rogers cautioned, "Now don't fly off and say that aviation is not safe or not practical. There are certain things nature can do to you—whether it's an earthquake in California, a flood in Mississippi, a tornado in Ohio or a drought in Arkansas. When nature enters into it—don't criticize."

Lieutenant Wilfred Bushnell, another of the fallen sky queen's officers, was well known and liked in Akron, both as airship officer and balloonist. His death was a personal blow to Tex Settle. The pair regarded one another as closely as brothers as a result of their long association and their joint competition in balloon races. They together had won the previous year's Gordon Bennett Race at Basel, Switzerland.

From San Diego, Lieutenant Commander Charles Rosendahl, the *Akron's* first skipper and survivor of the *Shenandoah* tragedy, expressed simple bewilderment at the loss of the *Akron*. "Rosy," then stationed aboard a battleship, studied details of the loss as they arrived by radio. They say he just shook his head.

He insisted the aircraft was a marvelously constructed ship and previously had survived the severest test of any airship in history.

Akronites watched the forthcoming investigations of the *Akron* tragedy with considerable anxiety, hoping to find a gleam of light which would indicate ways to improve lighter-than-air construction, if possible. It was terribly unfortunate that only three men should have been saved to tell anything at all about what happened. Lieutenant Commander H. V. Wiley's story of the tragedy seemed to indicate that the ship would have come through it if it had not been forced down to the surface of the sea where contact with the heavier elements smashed her.

He was not positive that lightning did not strike the ship but declared every indication was against that supposition. Ships of that type had passed through electrical storms in the past unharmed. If it could be established that the *Akron* did not break up until she hit the water, that seemed to be the case.

Faith that such a ship was safe as long as it was in its element would not have been shattered. That would mean some gain. At least the *Shenandoah* stage of airship construction would have been past. That ship crumpled in mid-air.

Faith in the *Akron* had been based upon two factors—her inherent strength and her speed. It was expected that she could avoid such a storm as that which caught her off the New Jersey coast. And that, if caught, inherent strength would save her. The *Akron* had outridden many storms before but never had been contended. However, that she was strong enough to withstand being dashed into the heavier medium of the sea was quite another question and a foolish one.

Was it poor airmanship to have her at only 1,600 feet altitude in the face of the stormy conditions? Was it impossible to keep such a craft from being pitched into the sea when she met such conditions? Was the only hope of safety in avoiding them? These and many other questions arose and sought answers.

For two days after the tragedy, thirty women, wives and friends of the airship victims waited at the Naval Station for news. Naval authorities conceded privately that it was a hopeless vigil. Any small boat unequipped with a wireless which might have picked up survivors would have put into port immediately, being but a few miles off shore, it was believed. That any part of the *Akron* substantial enough to bear men could still be afloat was deemed improbable. Besides, the German tanker which rescued Wiley, Deal and Erwin would have seen any other boat in the neighborhood in the abiding lightning flashes which lighted up the sea as the *Akron* crashed down.

Nevertheless, the Navy pressed its search for salvage and the dead. The morning following the crash ships and airplanes scouted off the New Jersey and Delaware shore miles below the spot off Barnegat Light where the *Akron* went in. The body of a lone victim lay in an Atlantic City morgue where the searching craft were ordered to bring all victims found. Another body lay in the morgue of the Naval Hospital at Brooklyn and two men who died on the rescue mission were at Lakehurst, the *Akron*'s home.

Of the airship itself, only a few twisted bits of duralumin and pieces of torn fabric had been found. Atlantic City was designated the center for rescue operations when it became evident that the currents of the ocean had carried bodies and wreckage rapidly south along the coast. The body of Lieutenant Commander H. E. MacClellan was found floating face down 30 miles off the beaches of New Jersey's fabulous beach resort. The Coast Guard cutter #213 reported much wreckage, but all in small bits, near where the body was sighted.

Lakehurst was in deepest mourning. Most of the victims lived near the town and many left widows, babies, parents. In addition to the personal grief of the survivors, there intruded the belief that Lakehurst's days as a busy airport were over. With the *Akron* gone, the *Los Angeles* expected to be sold or otherwise disposed of because of age, and the new *Macon* scheduled to make its home in California, the future of the little New Jersey port town appeared dark, indeed.

On April 5th, Lieutenant Commander H. V. Wiley, second in command of the ill-fated *Akron*, told his own story to newspapermen, first announcing that he would conduct the interview himself and that he would answer no questions regarding his opinions of technical causes of the crash of the airship. Wiley was clad in regulation hospital pajamas as he began his story. He offered to give only an "outline." It was as follows:

> We left Lakehurst about 7:30 pm on a regularly scheduled flight. One object of the flight was to calibrate radio direction finding stations in the New England area. Such calibration could not begin until it was daylight, and as it was foggy, it was decided to cruise inland where the ground could be seen. We were over Philadelphia about 8:10 pm, headed south, following the Delaware River. It was expected that there would be no fog south of New Jersey and that the fog at sea would clear by morning.

> By 8:35 we were 20 miles south of Philadelphia. Lightning was seen ahead and in a few minutes we had reports of a thunderstorm over Washington. We headed east to northeast toward the ocean, flying at about 1,600 feet. The ground was obscured by fog but we knew our position quite accurately and occasionally we would see lights indicating a town which checked our course. The ship was in good flying condition, though slightly heavy. The lightning to the south became quite extensive and also appeared in the west.

> The storm was general—all around the ship. I don't think the ship was struck by lightning as there was no indication of this at any time, although there was plenty of lightning around us. We continued east for about an hour, then reversed the course. When we reached land again, we saw land and identified the shoreline.

> This was about midnight. The course was changed to south. About half an hour later, the ship began to descend rapidly from 1,600 feet. I dropped all the ballast forward. The fall was stopped at about 800 feet. We rose rapidly and leveled off again at 1,500 feet. When we were falling, the engines were pushed to full speed. After we came to altitude again, they were changed to standard speed.

> Three minutes later the air became turbulent all around us and the ship tossed violently. I knew we were near the center of the storm because air in the center is most turbulent. I called all hands to the landing stations so as to have all of them available, not in their bunks.

> The ship took a sharp lurch and the rudder control wires of the upper rudder were carried away. I unclutched the upper rudder and tried to steer with the lower rudder. I was on the right side of the control car and supervising the rudder. Captain McCord was on the left side of the car and supervising the elevator wheel. The elevator man reported the ship was falling rapidly. I heard a report of 800 feet, but this time the nose inclined upward about 20 degrees but the ship was falling quite rapidly.

> In the fog, nothing outside could be seen. I asked for altitude and the answer was 300 feet. I ordered all hands to stand by for a crash. The order was rung up to the engine car and almost immediately we hit the water. We had, as I remember, a list to starboard—to my side of the control car. Water rushed in the windows on my side carrying me out of the windows on the other side of the control car.

> I tried to swim away as rapidly as I could to get from under the ship and finally came to the surface. I saw the ship drifting away as the lightning flashed. Her bow was up in the air and the whole structure was a general wreck. I saw two lights on

what I thought was the stern. On one side I saw the lights of a ship.

I swam toward the ship and after about ten minutes I bumped into a board about three feet square which I clung to the rest of the way. I saw several of the men in the water but none very close. I did not think I could help any of them. I did not see any of the men in the water after I found the board. When I got within 400 yards of the ship, the wind changed, hitting me in the face instead of behind me. The captain put the ship broadside. It floated toward me. I think he must have heard cries of men in the water. I made it easily to the ship and they threw me a life ring and hauled me aboard.

They had boats out and picked up three other men. I did not see the boats until I was on board the ship. As soon as I recovered strength in about an hour, I sent a message to the Navy Department giving the names of the rescued. The German captain is an excellent seaman and did everything he could to save life.

Up to this point, Wiley had spoken without interruption at his own request. He then permitted questions except on the issue of "fault." A reporter asked about Rear Admiral Moffett. Wiley answered that the Navy Aviation Chief had slept until midnight and had then entered the control cabin, but he did not notice if he was there at the time of the crash. Wiley said that there were two enlisted men at the control wheels but that he could be sure what other persons were in the control room. He said he did not know what happened to Captain McCord.

"I was washed out his window," he said. "He may have gone out ahead of me. There was no noise or confusion of any kind," Wiley added, commenting on the last minutes aboard the airship. "Orders were given in a low voice and carried out efficiently. There was no conversation of any kind after I gave the order to stand by for a crash."

Wiley repeated the assertion that there had been no explosion or fire aboard the *Akron*. He was asked if he had any idea of the cause of the crash since he had said that it was not struck by lightning.

"She might have been struck by lightning without our knowing it," he stated. "There was lightning all about but in my opinion she was not struck."

On April 7th, Wiley filled in more details before his superiors at the Navy Department:

> . . . At what I judged to be about 00:30 (12:30 am) April 4th, we struck turbulent atmosphere which up to this time had been remarkably stable. The elevator man reported that the ship was falling rapidly and I jumped over to his side of the control car to assist him. When I first saw the altimeter it read about 1,100 feet and we were going down rapidly almost on an even keel. . . I asked the captain if I should drop ballast and he directed me to do so. The atmosphere became exceedingly turbulent and I realized that we must be near the storm center and I caused the signal to be sounded for landing stations in order to have more men available and not in their bunks should they be needed.
>
> As soon as the landing station signal was sounded, First Lieutenant Calnan appeared and since he is responsible for the trim and loading of the ship, I told him where I had dropped ballast and told him to stand by the ballast board. The engineering officer took his station at the engine telegraphs. The captain was at the port window. These are the usual stations for landing and maneuvering. A very sharp

gust struck the ship. It seemed to be much more severe than any I have ever experienced.

I noticed immediately that the lower rudder control rope had been carried away. I reported it to the captain. My other rudder control broke at this time and the noise made by the sheaves tearing away indicated to me that the ship's structure had been damaged somewhere. The fall continued and I heard a report, 800 feet! I could no longer steer with both rudder controls broken and I hung to the girder alongside the window and looked out to see if I could sight the water. I inquired the altitude and the reply was, 300 feet! At the same time I sighted the waves through the window and gave the order, "Stand by for the crash!"

We descended at a rate I judged to be 14 feet per second. When we hit the water it seemed we hit much harder than I expected. The water surged in my window and submerged me and must have carried me out the port window or port side of the control car. I came to the surface shortly thereafter and started to swim toward the airship which I could see when the lightning flashed. The airship, however, was drifting away from me rapidly and had about 500 yards distance.

I could see the ship entirely on the water, broken in two or three pieces, submerged about one-third of her diameter with bow for a length of about 200 feet inclined in the air at an angle of about thirty degrees. I gave up trying to reach the ship. I looked around, sighted lights of what I took to be a surface vessel or a lighthouse. I saw several men in the water and heard their cries. None was close to me.

I swam toward the surface vessel and after about ten minutes found a board about three foot square which I clung to until I was hauled aboard the tanker. I imagine I was in the water between thirty and sixty minutes. I was very cold and weak when hauled aboard and could not stand. They put me to bed and after about an hour I recovered my strength and visited the men of the *Akron* crew who were on board. I found Copeland, chief radio operator, unconscious and in my opinion he died about that time, which I assume to be 02:30 (2:30 am) although we gave him artificial respiration and worked on him until 5:30 am. The steamer was the *Phoebus*. The agents for this ship are the Standard Shipping Company of 26 Broadway, New York City. I conferred with the captain and found that he was handling the ship in a seamanlike manner, doing all he could to rescue persons and that he had no intention of leaving the scene.

Shortly after daylight the Coast guard destroyers *Tucker* and *CG-23* came close aboard and sent over a pharmacist's mate at my request for medical assistance. Erwin Deal and myself were transferred to the *Tucker* and the body of Chief Copeland was also transferred. We were landed at the Brooklyn Navy Yard shortly after noon and taken to the Naval Hospital before we departed about 08:00 (8:00 am). Two other Coast Guard vessels and the cruiser *Portland* were on the scene.

During the emergency there was no noise or confusion at any time in the control car, and all orders were given and carried out efficiently. The discipline at all times was perfect.

One survivor, Deal, reports that he saw as he lay in his bunk near frame No. 130, port side, two girders above the port corridor at about frame No. 132 bend and buckle. He also noted as he ran forward that the control lines in that vicinity appeared slack but not broken and that nearby fuel tanks had slipped and loosened. He ran forward along a corridor with the idea of getting a pair of pliers so he could cut the fuel tanks adrift.

Just before the ship struck the water he glanced aft and saw the ship still intact as far as he could see, the lights going out just before the ship struck.

It is difficult to synchronize accurately these observations with my own observations in the control car, but apparently the damage to the girders occurred after the very severe gust struck the ship and after the ship had begun its last descent, practically out of control, and which terminated by the ship striking the water with consequent major structural damage.

To be sure, the fate of the boldest American bid for commercial supremacy in the air hung in the balance as the country took stock of the disaster. Mounting determination to end naval airship construction forever spread.

In the Senate, Senator King of Utah, prepared a resolution calling for an investigation of the *Akron* disaster and for consideration of the advisability of spending more than the twenty million dollars plus that the Navy already had invested in lighter-than-air craft. Chairman Trammel of the Senate Naval Committee also was considering a study of the accident. As the House made ready for a separate probe, chairman Vinson of the Naval Committee remained steadfast in his decision that "there won't be any more airships built."

For just eighteen months the U. S. S. *Akron* was supreme as the largest, finest and most complete ship of its kind ever built. She represented the last word, both in German zeppelin building skill and adaptation of Yankee inventive genius to the science of aviation. Even as she fell to her tragic end, however, her sister ship, the *Macon*, marking dirigible construction refinements borne of the building and operating experiences with the *Akron*, waited in the Goodyear-Zeppelin hangar at Akron, Ohio.

The day after the tragedy, P. W. Litchfield declined to comment on the possible cause of the disaster because of limited information. Later, however, Dr. Arnstein said the following:

"News of the *Akron* disaster comes as a profound shock to me and to the entire organization of the Goodyear-Zeppelin Corporation. From the viewpoint of the personnel, it is a staggering loss to the nation. In the absence of anything other than the most meager reports we are at a loss to understand what might have caused the wreck and naturally I cannot indulge in speculation. Our technical staff is ready to render every possible assistance to the Navy Department in the investigation which has been ordered."

That in substance was the comment of Goodyear-Zeppelin Corporation officials who had seen sudden calamity threaten the work of years. They read in the brief account of the *Akron's* plunge into the Atlantic an abrupt challenge to the science and skill that had conceived and built an eight million dollar industry in their city.

The men intimately connected with the zeppelin building made no effort to conceal their concern.

"It will wreck the course of business for a time," said W. C. Young, head of the aeronautics department of Goodyear, but we'll have to carry on." Fred W. Harpham, vice-president of Goodyear-Zeppelin Corporation, declared that the news of the *Akron's* loss "is so shocking that I can't comment." Commander Alger H. Dresel, who would command the U.S.S. *Macon* and who personally mourned the loss of several dear friends among the *Akron's* crew, said quietly that he expected to take the big dirigible now housed in the Goodyear dock aloft at an early date. "These things must happen," he said. "I don't know the facts as yet and it would be foolish to attempt an explanation."

An Akron newspaper said it better:

"Destruction of the U.S.S. *Akron* with its appalling loss of life was a catastrophe that shocked the nation. It was an even greater blow to the city whose creative enterprise had dedicated the airship to the Navy's service and long sustained interest in aeronautics was rewarded by having its first Navy dirigible named in its honor. Eagerly Akron awaits word of the immediate cause of the ship's failure. This is presently shrouded in the usual mazes of doubt and guesswork that attend the first stages of any inquiry into a major tragedy of the day. The three survivors of the 77 persons aboard are presently too shocked to give a coherent account of what happened but time and inquiry will reveal the truth.

"Meanwhile, bowed with its own community grief, Akron's deepest sympathy goes out to the families of the victims. The fact that Rear Admiral William A. Moffett, Commander Fred T. Berry and other officials comprising the flower of the Navy Air Service were carried to death only magnifies the country's loss.

"If it should be revealed that the airship was destroyed by lightning while the stress is incident to a coastal storm unusually severe at this season, it will have an important bearing upon the future of the dirigible industry. It was a storm in which the *Shenandoah* perished and it will be remembered that the hasty judgment at that time, impressed by the heavy loss of life, sighted that disaster as putting a period to any further building of these giant ships.

"But this did not come to pass at Akron or at Friedrichshafen. New dirigibles were built. The *Graf Zeppelin* with its amazing record of round-the-world flight and repeated trips to South America and regular transport, was its own best demonstration of sturdiness and efficiency which the makers had put into their craft. The Navy, by contracting for the construction of the *Akron* and *Macon* expressed its faith in the worth and security of airships as an arm of its service. Only last week, Brigadier General William Mitchell, retired chief of aviation, went before the House Military Affairs Committee to testify that the United States ought to build 50 gigantic dirigibles larger than either the *Akron* or the *Macon* as a preparation of national defense.

"The same day the *New York Herald Tribune*, applauding the Navy for building these airships, hailed the not remote era when such ships in overseas commercial service "with motors roaring and the portholes filled with life will be as familiar a sight in this city as the outgoing steamers are now."

"Time alone will measure the effect the destruction of the ill-fated *Akron* has upon the future of the dirigible industry. This cannot be considered when the nation is in the presence of a great disaster which ever involves heavy loss when an individual airship comes to grief, yet such risks attend every agency of transport. America does not cease building and operating motor cars because they take a toll of 35,000 lives every year. It does not scrap railroad service because wrecks occur. Submarines sink in peace time but their building goes on, nor will it cease the development of aerial transport now in its pioneering stages, but achieving greater safety with every year of effort.

"Because an occasional failure is written in its record of progress, every disaster in the air is of its nature spectacular and no less singular because those of really major status are few and far between. These elements will be considered by the nation after it knows all the factors that caused the *Akron* failure and resolves what future course to take."

On Capitol Hill, meanwhile, Representative James McClintic offered a resolution for a special House investigating committee of seven members, none from either the naval or military committees "because committees are more or less under the influence of the department having jurisdiction."

"At Lakehurst," he told the House, "I saw this ship crash down on a solid railroad track and break some superstructure. I took the position at that time that the entire superstructure was damaged and that so far as I was concerned, I did not want to fly on the ship."

At the same time, Robert Crosser of Cleveland, who with McNary of Oregon had authored the ill-fated Merchants Airship Bill which would have provided the same subsidy for dirigibles as for merchant marine vessels, also urged inquiry by a special House committee, but one whose membership should be divided between the Naval Affairs Committee and others in the House.

"Only a *mixed* committee," he insisted, "could determine fairly whether the disaster was the result of faulty navigation or defects in the ship itself."

On April 6th the Navy Department received a telephone message from Cape May, New Jersey, saying that Coast Guard patrol boats had sighted a large spot of oil on the water about twenty-two miles southeast of Barnegat Lightship. Dragging of the seafloor was planned by a salvage tug. Observers pointed out the strong possibility that this might be the hulk of the *Akron*. The Navy Department also was advised that airplane pilots searching for *Akron* survivors had sighted "wreckage covering a considerable area" about three miles abreast of Barnegat beach.

The wreckage included an empty gas tank, a spare radio transmitting power tube, a life raft from the *Akron's* airplane compartment and bits of wood.

A bumper bag from the blimp *J-3* also was picked up, the message went on.

At about the same time in New York City, dignitaries gathered for a solemn high mass, a requiem for the lost members of the *Akron's* human cargo. The requiem mass was arranged at St. Patrick's Cathedral with Cardinal Hayes presiding in his capacity as chaplain bishop of the United States Army and Navy. Primarily for relatives and friends of the 71 victims, the ceremonies were also opened to the public.

On April 9th, a *joint* congressional investigation of not only the crash but also the feasibility of continuing the United States twenty-plus million dollar experiment in dirigible construction was assured by both Senate and House leaders.

By April 10th there was cause for concern with Lieutenant Commander Wiley's accounts, at least the versions of them which reached the press, of the final moments in the control car of the *Akron*. Discrepancies indicated he was not accurate as to details.

The first news story received, for example, spoke of one section of the rudder controls—the upper—as having been broken. The next story said both sections of the rudder controls gave way. The upper first, then the lower. The most recent official report said both gave way, but the lower first, then the upper. But the testimony of all three survivors agreed that there had been no general failure of the ship's structure before she hit the water.

Much was made of the fact that R. E. Deal and Moody Erwin, surviving crew members, said they saw three or four girders in the ship's structure buckle. To any unprejudiced mind it must appear more important that Deal reported the ship "intact as far as he could see" just prior to hitting the water. From all evidence available, it appeared unreasonable and grossly unfair to describe the *Akron* as "cracking up" in the air.

Talk that airship development should be left exclusively to the Germans was idiotic. They had no monopoly on ability either to construct or to operate them. The U.S.S. *Akron* was a far better airship than the veteran *Graf Zeppelin*, and the U.S.S. *Macon* was better than the *Akron*. Nobody who knew the lighter-than-air business would argue otherwise. But we had *not* developed a Dr. Hugo Eckener or a Captain Ernst Lehman to fly them and the Navy policy of changing airship officers every few months hardly facilitated such development.

Operating an airship wasn't that simple. Rotation of officer personnel was fine for the development of men, but not of airships. You lost experience. Every three years (the length of a Navy tour) you lost all the experience you had and you put in a brand new deal. I should add for the record that Tex Settle, not only a skilled, experienced lighter-than-air Navy man but also a superb thinker, challenged my statement. We argued the point until four in the morning at the Copacabana Hotel in New York. I rarely challenged Tex on any technical opinion regarding meteorology or aeronautics. He was continually, to me, a leader's leader who performed in flight, in the shadow of extreme danger, every bit as brilliantly as he talked, thought, taught and philosophied.

But on this matter of rotation of an airship's skipper, he was, to me, incredibly and irrevocably stupid.

Five days after the tragedy the bodies of Commander Frank C. McCord, the *Akron's* commander, and Commander Fred T. Berry, commanding officer of the Lakehurst Naval Air Base, were found by the *Tucker*. The fact that all bodies recovered to date were occupants of the control car of the ill-fated dirigible gave rise to the speculation that the *Akron*, crashing in the darkness, first lost the control car and ballast. If this were true, it would have been possible for the rest of the big airship to have been carried far out to see by free ballooning.

Some said that the remainder of the *Akron* could have traveled a thousand miles as a free balloon and then might float indefinitely far outside the ship lanes with men aboard. Thus far, no positive proof had been found that the entire dirigible collapsed. In the disaster of the *Shenandoah*, part of the airship ballooned to safety after the rear section crashed to earth. The smallest ring of the *Akron*—132 feet in diameter—exceeded the 90-foot ocean depths in the area where the disaster took place.

It was argued by some searchers that if the entire structure of the *Akron* collapsed, more bodies and records should have been recovered.

On April 11th, a conflict of opinion regarding emergency action to save the *Akron* as the great dirigible was falling to her destruction was revealed before the Naval Court of Inquiry. Lieutenant Commander Wiley testified that swiveling propellers were not used.

"Would it have been desirable?" asked Judge Advocate Ralph G. Pennoyer.

"Yes, if there was time," Wiley replied. "My impression was that no order was given to tilt the propellers," Wiley testified.

"Do you lose dynamic lift in tilting the propeller?"

"Yes, the propellers must be slowed down."

"Then it appears to have been undesirable to tilt the propellers?"

"It depends on the circumstances," Wiley replied. "How grave you consider the emergency. It depends on how you see it at the time."

Wiley testified that on prior occasions the *Akron* had suffered structural damage but that all injuries had been repaired.

"Could these have caused permanent structural defects?"

"Absolutely none. The *Akron* was in fine structural condition."

One week earlier, the Lieutenant Commander reported to Secretary of the Navy Swanson that he thought the shock which wrecked the *Akron* was caused by a sudden terrific gust of wind, but on April 11th, asked permission to change his story.

"I desire to suggest to the court now," he said, "that I am of the opinion that this shock was the result of the stern striking the water."

His revelation was received with surprised silence. The recollection that caused Wiley to change his testimony was that during the descent he felt no air blowing through the control car windows. He was at a loss to explain the day before how a sudden gust of wind could strike the ship and not be felt through the control room windows. The absence of a draft through the windows could be easily understood, however, if the stern was in the water at the time and the bow of the ship tumbled down into the sea.

Wiley said that the two other survivors, Deal and Erwin, agreed with the new version.

"After the rudder control broke," Wiley said, "I was awaiting the shock of the stern hitting the water. That shock never came. I had the impression at the time that the stern must be in the air. This must have been mistaken." Wiley was questioned regarding incidents in the prior day's testimony indicating mistakes had been made in the ship's navigation.

"I know," he said, "that the ship was 50 degrees to the west of its regular course at one time, but that to my own mind was satisfactorily justified. If you're trying to find out if this mistake had any bearing on later events, I can't believe it did, although there is that possibility. To my own mind it was immaterial."

On April 16th, what seemed to me a particularly well thought out statement by a veteran aviator and serviceman was printed in the Akron *Times-Press.* The writer of the letter was Wyndham Bolling Reager and it just seemed to me that he stated the case for lighter-than-air better than any executive, military officer, news reporter or analyst to date. Hence the ultimate power of the citizenry which half the time we forget is even there. Following is Reager's letter for which I could have kissed the man:

"Zeppelins are safe if they are understood. The Germans proved the zeppelin a valuable implement of war as a scout or cruiser and wrecker of morale. They were used on offensive operations, also as bombers. Their carrying capacity for bombs was larger than that of a whole fleet of airplane bombers. On account of their air stability they can practically stop in midair and can easily correct their aim in dropping bombs, insuring a higher percentage of direct hits. They are well protected with their own guns and are capable of carrying fighters in their hold.

"Since the war, the Germans have proved their great commercial value. Their safety has never been questioned in Germany or elsewhere if under German command. But it has been proven that the best naval men cannot handle these airships. England and France have both tried it with the same result. The American Navy is still trying. Now why can the Germans operate these 100% safe when the best navies of other nations fail?

"American zeppelins are 100% safer, using helium gas. The Germans use a highly explosive gas to keep afloat. Helium is non-explosive. These American ships are constructed by German engineers—the cream of the old German company. These engineers supervise all construction. The U.S.S. *Akron* had every known safety device. It was faster than the German ships, had larger lifting capacity and was easily maneuvered.

"Why can't the Navy run them? The Navy does not use men trained in airship navigation! We will start at the top of the aeronautical branch of the Navy with the late Rear Admiral Moffett, a man who spent his life on battleships; an old man at the retirement age who only became airminded after the Admiral Moffett-General Mitchell controversy. Mitchell, as we all know, was a flying general. He had seen service in the world war. As a flier he had downed several German fliers. During the war, Moffett was commandant at Great Lakes Naval Training Station and saw no active service. He was in command of a naval vessel during the Navy's bombardment of Vera Cruz and was an ensign at Manila Bay.

"That was his active service record.

"What did Admiral Moffett know of aviation? Nothing. What did the other captains, commanders and lieutenant commanders of our Navy know of aviation? Nothing. All of the above rank are comparatively old men and almost ready to retire. The Navy system of promotion causes this. When they went to school at their Naval Academy, none of them ever heard of aviation. Their best years had been spent on destroyers, cruisers, battleships and submarines—so why try to teach an old dog new tricks? The commanders and executive officers of our Navy's zeppelins come direct from service on these different type vessels. Why put a submarine commander on a zeppelin as an executive officer or commander with a few weeks or months instruction?

"Would the Navy take a ferryboat captain and put him in command of a submarine with only a few weeks training? Could these officers get a transport license? If so, would Eckener allow them to run his zeppelins? What became of the Eckener trained men of our Navy? Most of them have been transferred to sea duty. Why did not the Navy keep these trained men together and in time we would have had an efficient and safe zeppelin corps.

"Why average intelligence is not used in this branch of the Navy can only be explained by knowing the Navy system. The high officers of the Navy have nothing in common with the aeronautical branch, nor do they have any sympathy for it. It is new to them and they know nothing about it. The nation is airminded and these old sea dogs don't like it. We should put the aviation service on an efficient basis under the control of fliers—warbirds who understand both flying and air military needs.

"Establish an airship school and bring Hugo Eckener back and put him in charge of that school and make him commander of all zeppelins for four years. Let him pick his men to fly our ships according to their airship ability, not because they have married some high naval officer's daughter.

"An Anapolis graduate doesn't learn anything about zeppelins at the Academy because instructors do not know any more about it than the person who reads the newspapers. It has never been clear whether the transfer of an officer to an airship was a promotion, a demotion or vacation. We do not seem to appreciate that Eckener can handle zeppelins better than our officers. He can because he has had 30 years of zeppelin experience. Also, to start with, he had been a sailor. There are no sailors in our Navy now. The present naval personnel would be as lost on a sailing boat as they would if transferred to the moon.

"They do not understand the wind currents as the old sailors did. This knowledge is not needed on electrically-driven submarines. On a zeppelin this knowledge is paramount.

"We will take the record of the *Akron's* log before the fatal crash. During the storm the ship was endeavoring to fly at 1,600 feet—just twice her own length. Would an airplane dare to fly at an altitude of twice its own length? Would an airplane of 30 feet dare to fly at 60 feet above the ground during a storm? An airplane is not safe under *1,000* feet. The wrecks usually come under 500 feet. Zeppelins have been known to drop—or I should say "slip"—over 5,000 feet. That figures only six times their length.

"The *Shenandoah* was wrecked in Ohio through this cause, so one would think from 8,000 to 12,000 feet would be a safe cruising altitude in stormy weather.

"Doesn't the Navy have the data on this wreck? Why should a zeppelin be floating at such a low altitude with its motors idling in a storm?

"After dropping ballast, the nose was raised with the motors wide open. Nothing would have stopped her from gaining altitude if she had been cruising at a safe altitude in the first place. It was only natural that a ship with its nose no higher than its stern, with motors idling, would have begun to slip at such low altitude.

"That crash was inevitable.

"This was not such a terrible storm. These ex-submarine and cruiser commanders either were asleep or afraid to cruise at a safe altitude. We can't blame these poor men. They had not had the proper training. If they had had, we would still have the *Akron* and the live bodies of the efficient service craft's officials.

"The *Akron* log should have read, "Received naval observations of storms over Atlantic seaboard. Training cruise postponed on account of weather conditions." There was no need of taking a training cruise in the face of storms. But if there had been safe altitude, speed would have taken the ship through.

"The deaths of the *Shenandoah* and the *Akron* can be placed as manslaughter, if not murder, at the feet of the politicians and high Navy men, for had Eckener been re-trained to train our future fliers instead of Anapolis steamboat engineers, perhaps we would have more confidence in this safe way of travel.

"Bring Eckener back—or at least put his trained men in as commanders. Don't transfer them to sea duty to conform to antiquated Naval regulations or some pipe-dream of the old seadogs. There's nothing wrong with our zeppelins. They're the world's best and so are our young fliers.

"Give them a chance."

On April 18th, grappling irons from the sea tug *Sagamore* encountered "an object large enough to be the main body of the *Akron*." A message from the tug to the U.S.S. *Portland*, flagship of the searching fleet still in the Atlantic waters, reported that while dragging the floor of the ocean off Barnegat light, it encountered the supposed wreckage.

The message said, "On second trip across between buoys, our grapnel fouled a body heavy enough to part 3/16 chain stopper. Fabric remaining on grapnel contained two sliding round ports about twelve inches diameter. Fabric marked port station No. 18 forward."

A second sea tug, *Falcon*, remained anchored over the spot.

On April 27th, Lieutenant Commander Wiley took the stand for questioning on how the airship service compared to that of wartime German zeppelin commanders. Wiley said that he had approximately 5,000 hours flying time on airships. He also stated that he knew two wartime German zeppelin captains who, in 1928, had told him they had fewer hours than he had. He had met some German commanders generally considered successful during the war, he said, who had fewer than 500 hours.

Wiley said the instruction given airship men at Lakehurst was "as good as could be expected." He said he didn't think it could be improved upon.

Later, Dr. Karl Arnstein, the *Akron's* designer, testified that strength specifications of the *Akron* had been carefully figured out. He said that the lessons learned in all previous airship crashes had been taken into consideration in consideration in constructing the *Akron*. The *Akron*, he said, was intended to excel all previous airships.

Likewise on April 27th, Lieutenant Commander J. L. Fisher, mooring officer, Lakehurst, New Jersey, and officer in charge of salvage and material brought up by Navy search vessels, informed the Navy Court of his belief that wreckage of the sunken *Akron* could be raised from the ocean bed provided weather conditions were favorable. He said he was satisfied the wreckage of the airship was in one piece.

The airship, according to Fisher, apparently was flattened out because divers reported that the maximum height of the wreckage as it lay on the bottom was about twenty-five feet.

Lieutenant Commander Wiley asked whether Fisher believed the control car had broken off from the rest of the airship.

It was, Fisher replied. The control car had been picked up about 100 feet from the nearest point at which the main body was located.

And lastly on this 27th of April, two faded and weather-beaten letters dropped by John Rytell from the dirigible *Akron* over Seattle, Washington, May 24, 1932, were delivered to his widow and mother. Rytell had perished in the recent crash. But while sailing over Seattle a year earlier, he had dropped the letters attached to a handkerchief for a parachute. The handkerchief caught in a tree and was not found until April 25, 1933. The finders mailed the letters.

On May 1, Judge Advocate Ralph G. Pennoyer told the Naval Court of Inquiry, "The cause of the *Akron* disaster must ever remain in the realm of conjecture." Presenting the final argument as judge advocate of the court of inquiry, he said, "The testimony presented in the eleven days of hearings was 'complicated and confusing.' There was no eyewitness to what happened," Pennoyer further said, "and even the testimony of the three survivors is conflicting and difficult to piece together.

". . . In the light of hindsight," he pointed out, "some may say that a certain course of procedure might have saved the ship. It may be accepted in the loss of any craft at a certain place, at a certain time, that any change of action on the part of any individual directly or indirectly connected with the movement of such craft might have averted such loss. In this sense and in this sense only can allegation of direct or indirect individual responsibility for the loss of the *Akron* and the loss of life consequent thereon be supported.

"If any action taken in the light of hindsight be termed 'errors of judgment,' clearly they were without negligence or culpability. This disaster is part of the price which must inevitably be paid in the development of any new or hazardous art. As someone has said, 'the minds of men have projected the fleet of such craft in the air and someday it must fly there.' "

Lieutenant C. J. Maguire, consul for the judge advocate in his summation told the court that information on weather conditions and dissemination of such information on airships was inadequate. Communications on bearing weather conditions while an airship is in flight was described by him as also inadequate. One important lesson has been learned from the tragedy of the *Akron*, Maguire said—

"All thunderstorms should be avoided."

When the congressional zeppelin probers came to Akron, Paul Litchfield told the committee that his company visualized a fleet of vast commercial airships quickly convertible to wartime scout ships with speeds climbing "from the present 72 knots an hour to 100 knots."

He talked of the five million dollar airship of an eight million cubic foot capacity which Goodyear proposed could be built to operate with perfect safety and perfect comfort and make round trips to Europe every week.

"Competition with liner first class passages is possible on a four airship basis," Litchfield said.

How do you hope to offset the rather terrific adverse public opinion?" he was asked.

"There exists in the minds of people the same doubt as there was toward ocean ships when the *Titanic* went down," Litchfield replied. "The building of large liners did not cease."

Questioned on the 4 percent overweight of the *Akron* vs. 2 percent overweight of the *Macon*, Litchfield answered, "That overweight simply cuts down carrying capacity, not safety."

"To my knowledge," Dr. Arnstein said in response to a question, "none of the 113 German airships of World War I broke up in the air. One was struck by lightning and others were shot down in flames after the hydrogen gas had been fired." He emphasized he believed none had been lost through structural weakness.

Asked to account for the *Akron's* apparent fragility, breaking up immediately when it plunged into the Atlantic, Dr. Arnstein replied, "We never endeavored to build an airship that would strike the water at full speed and not break up. I can't see where we can draw the conclusion she was fragile. The *Akron* was built to withstand running full-speed into a 35-mile-an-hour cross wind—the strain believed responsible for wrecking the *Shenandoah*."

On June 1, further government experimentation with lighter-than-air ships was urged by Colonel Charles A. Lindbergh before the Congressional committee probing the crash of the *Akron*. Formerly non-committal about airships, Colonel Lindbergh made his recommendations following the appearance of Rear Admiral King, new chief of the Navy's air service, who made a similar plea.

"I feel it would be a mistake to stop development of lighter-than-air craft at this time," Colonel Lindbergh said.

Lucky Lindy greeted the committee with a shy smile, placed both elbows on the long table and began a low-voiced discussion of the possibilities of aviation.

"Both heavier and lighter-than-air development are new. I don't believe experimentation in a single generation will decide whether either one is impractical or which will be of greatest benefits," he said. "Only about 100 units of lighter-than-air craft have been built whereas thousands of heavier-than-air planes are in use. Lack of numbers has hampered the study of airships. It seems to me we can't expect to reach the maximum development in dirigibles in 25 or 30 years. I have the greatest confidence in the future of aviation," he concluded.

Admiral King was more blunt.

"The Navy has no right," he assured the joint House-Senate investigating committee, "to deprive the country of the services of dirigibles in wartime without knowing what we are doing."

# Section Five

## Prayers Ride With the Macon

Work on the ZRS-5, sister ship of the zeppelin *Akron,* was expected to go forward immediately following acceptance of the *Akron* by the United States Navy. Congress already had appropriated funds to proceed with the second zeppelin which would be built at a cost of considerably less than half that of the *Akron.* The Navy option set the price for the second ship at $2,450,000. Contract price for the *Akron* was $5,375,000.

The cheaper price of the second aircraft was made possible because all of the experimental work applicable to both ships had been done and the force at the Goodyear-Zeppelin Corporation had been trained.

The master ring of the ZRS-5 was raised by David S. Ingalls, assistant secretary of the Navy. He looked on a different scene than was witnessed March 24, 1930 when the first ring of the U. S. S. *Akron* was slipped into the ways. A job that took three days on the first ship was accomplished in 20 minutes after Ingalls blew the tin whistle signalling the start.

Akron civic leaders, two mayors, one retired and one elect, and a handful of spectators stood by as cranes ground out a metallic refrain. Men clung to tackles and the 133-foot duralumin ring rose from a horizontal position on the airdock floor to the vertical position it would occupy in the finished airship. There were no speeches. The master ring of the ZRS-5 had no gold rivet glistening at its uppermost point as had the *Akron,* but it was more perfect from a mass production standpoint than its predecessor.

Ingalls had asked that the new ship be name *Ohio* or for some Ohio city. The names *Cleveland, St. Louis* and *Washington* were strong contenders from the beginning as influential groups far beyond the Buckeye State were quick to get into the act. Then on February 17, 1932, Representative Carl Vinson, chairman of the House Naval Affairs Committee, announced that his committee had recommended the name *Macon* to the Secretary of the Navy and it had been accepted.

This came as a complete surprise. Few Akronites had ever heard of the Georgia city so honored. Investigation revealed that its chief claim to the distinction was the fact that it was the largest city in a portion of the southern state which had been added to Vinson's congressional district not long before.

There was great hope for many weeks of increasing the size of the *Macon* a million cubic feet by the addition of another bay. The late Rear Admiral Moffett had pushed this project persistently and continued to advocate it in his last Akron speech. Sale of the *Los Angeles,* later decommissioned, and various other methods were discussed for raising necessary funds. All these came to nought, however, and the craft remained essentially a duplicate of the *Akron.*

A shrill blast on the whistle of Miss Susan Myrick, Macon, Georgia, newspaperwoman signalled the start of the last operation in the construction of the *Macon's* framework on July 7, 1932. As the ship's nose section was hoisted in place before a crowd of 10,000 persons, guide lines were unfastened and a web of steel wire was thrown around the connecting parts. The ship's bow hung suspended against the giant framework ready to be riveted in place.

Raising the nose had been delayed about a week to permit the Macon group to attend the ceremony. The cone-shaped nose rested on the dock floor like a huge flower pot ready to be lifted at a whistle signal which Miss Myrick blew after distaining instructions on the grounds that she had refereed basketball games for the last five years.

The cone swung upwards.

It is customary to introduce a new ship to her watery element by a bottle of the brine or champagne against her bow. But in the tradition of the *Akron* christening, when Mrs. William A. Moffett christened the U.S.S. *Macon* in early March, 1933, she pulled a red, white and blue lanyard which released 48 homing pigeons from a hatch in the airship's nose. Forty-six of the birds flew out the south doors of the big dock and a few minutes later were at home in an Akron suburb. The remaining two birds circled about, got their bearings and straightened out for a long hop to Macon, Georgia.

A winter wind whipped about the great black cocoon housing the airship *Macon* at the Akron airport. Mrs. Moffett and the U.S. Navy stood by to christen this newest fighting craft with the traditional ceremony. The crowd began to assemble shortly after noon and an increasing swarm of automobiles dotted the parking areas. But the crowd was only a ghost of the enormous throng that blackened the airfield on the momentous day when the *Macon's* sister ship was named.

Among those assembled was J. F. Cooper, general foreman of Goodyear's balloon room. His balloon flying days ended in 1928 when he hurtled 2,000 feet to earth with 35,000 cubic feet of blazing hydrogen over his head when his balloon was struck by lightning in the ill-fated Pittsburgh race.

Interviewed soon after, his comment was he'd just as soon build balloons anyway. On the *Macon's* first flight, Cooper would be aboard inspecting the gas cells, which the crews so carefully installed in the big ship. He'd been with Goodyear since 1913, had worked on the fabrics of eleven free and observation balloons and 130 airships. His most recent job—putting together the seven acres of outer cover of the *Macon*.

He knew more about it than any man in the world.

All of the innovations in airship construction inaugurated with the *Akron* had been retained in the *Macon*—principle among these was the provision of a hangar for five fighting airplanes within the ship, the use of interior engine rooms, and provision of tilting propellers to help push the ship up and pull it down. Both ships had an emergency control room in the bottom fin from which they could be controlled in an exceptional situation.

Only in comparatively minor details did the two ships differ. A provision of seven separate rooms with four bunks each, the crew's quarters aboard the *Akron*, was luxury unknown elsewhere in the Navy. To economize on materials and weight, the *Macon's* quarters, replacing these, consisted of but two rooms— one built for twenty bunks, the other for eight bunks.

This housing style was more nearly in line with general Navy practice. Another weight-saving change was made on the heating system. The *Akron* had heated crews quarters, officers quarters, mess rooms, wash rooms and control car. The *Macon's* heating system did not extend forward to the control car and only the messrooms, washrooms and the wardroom amidships were heated. These and other minor changes made it possible to save about 7,000 pounds of weight.

All of the *Macon's* gas cells were of a gelatin-latex composition developed by the Goodyear-Zeppelin Corporation. They were lighter and superior to every other cell material. Only half of the *Akron's* cells were of this material. New type electric generators and a revised telephone radio power supply system were installed in the *Macon*. The *Macon's* 19-station telephone system was automatic while that aboard the *Akron* was manually operated.

Many improvements in the fuel, water ballast, main engine radiator heating, and control systems had been made possible. To cut down wind resistance, from two to four small helium valve hoods were constructed above each gas cell on the *Macon*, substituted for a single large one above the cells of the *Akron*.

Fewer individual tests were run on the *Macon* since the general characteristics of the type ship had been determined by the *Akron*. However, although the *Macon* was considered an identical twin, more than 100 minor changes had been made in the *Macon's* design, none of which were apparent to the casual observer. The only change that could be noted from the exterior was the addition of pants on the propeller shafts for the purpose and benefits of streamlining.

A new instrument to be used on the initial flight was a gauge that would show with incredible precision the exact stresses of structural members. In the past, gauges had showed the relative stresses, but for the first time the new tool would indicate the total stress in a girder with accuracy. The actual horsepower of the engines on the ship this time would be measured on the shaft with the engines in flight, a test that would show how much horsepower was actually put out in useful propeller thrust and how much was lost in propeller inefficiency.

These new instruments gave exact information in fields that heretofore have been little known.

At the end of the trial flight period, the *Macon* was to be flown to Sunnyvale, California, the new Navy airship base for operations with the fleet. Captain A. H. Dresel was anxious to start the western flight as soon as possible. Not later than May 1, if possible.

There was the thunderstorm season in Texas to worry about.

His pretty red-haired wife talked of the *Akron* tragedy and the cloud of apprehension many felt for the *Mason*.

"Those men and their wives were our personal friends," she said. "We cared deeply for them. But we refuse to allow that calamity to make cowards of us. All the wives attached to the *Macon* undoubtedly feel just as I do. We cannot allow ourselves to become afraid. Indeed, we get used to impending danger. That's one of the things we have always to consider. It's a poor officer's wife who would annoy her husband by talk of fear."

The kinds of thrills most kids find in circuses were pretty close to the emotion my friend Harold Taylor, *Beacon Journal* aviation editor, discovered on those few rare occasions he was actually invited aboard an airship:

"Wonders of the labyrinthine interior of an airship remain wonders," he wrote, "even after you have seen them a few times. A few days ago a half-dozen newspapermen and I boarded the *Macon*. You never stop being amazed at the number of controls there are in an airship. There were the same number on the *Akron*, of course, but it seemed we had forgotten half of them.

"The light on the top of the automatic phone lit up and in a moment it began to whine. Our guide answered it and as his attention was drawn away, we looked around. Yes, that wheel over there operated the elevators and that one up in front, the rudders. The rudder control chain looked sturdy enough. I hoped it never broke. Our man was off the phone now, explaining to us how the whole ship could be operated from where we stood.

"There's the engine telegraph system—four red, yellow and green discs overhead and starboard. The helium content—there's a set of yellow knobs—12 of them.

You can pull on those and release gas. The amount of ballast? There's another group of pretty knobs—red, green and yellow—yank one and out tumbles water. And then there are compasses and altimeters and speed gauges—all aids to the man who would tell the men on deck what ought to be done and when.

"In a second room of the control car are desks for the aerological officer, his maps with his compasses at his elbow. From the room up above, the radio operator would collect all the information possible and relate it to the air officer. In the aft room are machine gun rests as a sort of warning that this was, after all, a man-of-war. Here the personnel could smoke as ashtrays attached to girders testified.

"We ascended to the ship proper. At the top of the stairs, we paused to look around. The maze of girders, wires, control cables was bewildering for a moment. Overhead, the gas cells spread out in all directions. They were bulged tight against the wire netting up above. The lower section floated free, giving the impression of a tent. We passed the officers quarters and on into the bow. Girders cut a triangular path right up to the nose of the ship. Girders, thousands of them, joined and braced by wires, made geometrical designs all around.

"New advances of intricate workmanship were embodied in the *Macon* at every step. For each of those dozens of little control knobs, a wire zigzagged its way via the pulleys to the valve to be controlled. We mounted a staircase which followed the contour of the ship's body to the starboard gangway. A series of ladders stretched to the very top of the ship where, our guide pointed out, men are constantly on watch to see that nothing happens to damage the gas cells. It looked interesting up there but it was off-limits to us.

"So we traveled aft on the gangway. Gasoline tanks of varying sizes were fastened on the port side of the gangway and along its length. We stepped down from the gangway into the crew's quarters. Four sets of bunks were provided here and the dining room tables and chairs were ready for use. The galley looked crowded for the preparation for meals for more than one hundred, but we passed on quickly for a glimpse of one of the ship's engine rooms.

"There was a giant 500 horsepower Maibach engine occupying nearly all available space. We wondered how a man could get in there to run it, let alone repair it, but the odor of gasoline fumes reassured us that they did. All eight of the motors had purred perfectly in a test earlier in the day."

Like the sensitive whiskers of a cat, tiny wires of an instrument located outside the control car of the *Macon* could tell which way the wind was blowing and how hard. The tool was a hot wire anemometer, the latest gadget added to the airship, now ready for its maiden flight. Perfected after months of calibration, it was based on the principle known in electrical engineering as the wheatstone bridge.

The same principle had been used before in measuring wind velocity but the present instrument was the first of its kind designed to detect directional changes. Conceivably, the instrument could be used to permit the wheelsman on the big dirigible to trim his course to offset a gust of wind registered at the bow before its full effect is felt at the stern.

The sky was just turning bright blue at 6:00 am, April 21, 1933. Maiden-flight day had finally dawned. The U.S.S. *Macon* quivered on her mooring mast, silver grey in the morning half light. Lieutenant C. W. Roland lifted his yellow megaphone and blared, "Stand by to up ship!"

Silence—deep silence—after the excited chatter and bellowing of orders—fell over 200 Navy wives, reporters, ground crew. Lifting his megaphone again, Lieutenant Roland yelled, "All ready, aft!" The faces of the crowd were strained. A man tore his copy paper in shreds. Another sank his teeth into the soft wood of a pencil.

"Cast off forward!" Lieutenant Roland's order came, reverberating over people so deathly still they could hear the sharp hiss of their companions' excited breathing.

"UP SHIP!" There was a fraction of a second while shooting chills palsied the spine and the knee cap. Then came the rising roar of four motors and triumphantly, gloriously, the U.S.S. *Macon* rose, swinging away from earth in a movement so swift and sure that it brought exultation to every heart. The zeppelin turned and headed east. The sun came from behind a cloud and shone brilliantly, turning the beautiful ship resplendent silver.

Unafraid, with courage and with knowledge, man had sent another great ship into the air, this time with understanding born of tragedy. It was a touching and a mighty moment. That was the climax of the U.S.S. *Macon's* first take-off. That was the poetry and the beauty of the maiden expedition.

The crowd that wished the *Macon* her first bon-voyage was small, probably the smallest that had been on hand since the Navy ordered that the ship should fly. The Navy wives were there, newspapermen and photographers and city and Goodyear-Zeppelin officials made up most of the crowd.

Too often had interested Akronites risen before sunrise only to have the weather call off the flight. So today they slept—and missed the take-off.

Everything worked smoothly. The *Macon* was in the air twenty-eight minutes after the bell had sounded through the airdock for the walkout.

\*   \*   \*

By 6:00 p.m., June 24, 1933 at the airdock, the familiar crowd was gathered to see the *Macon* leave for good . . .the same faces of the officers' wives who dropped in for every flight—Frank Petrie, Mark Felber and Hugh Allen from the Goodyear publicity staff—sweethearts of the sailors . . . They were all there. There were always plenty of children and that night David S. Ingalls, former air secretary of the Navy and candidate for governor, was there with his youngster as was Dr. Karl Arnstein, the ship's designer, proud and touched. His two daughters and son and wife accompanied him.

As usual the wait seemed endless, and as usual, much speculation among the amateur zeppelin experts added to the excitement.

"Super heat" according to one of the gentry, held back the ship. Some people waited standing up. One mustached man stolidly ate his sandwich. A mother put her baby to bed right on top of an official-looking blueprint. They turned the motors on for a while to fan the perspiring crowd. Finally the hangar doors opened a crack and the light traveled up to the top of the dock.

Outside the sun was just going down and the field was still warm with color. Natty in his panama hat, tennis shoes and leather jacket, Rear Admiral Ernest J. King led the procession out, striding along, looking stern and taking big steps, Captain Dresel walked in front of the control car, his scarf, his badge and identification mark to the crowd, floating in the breeze.

Outside, P. W. Litchfield's car was driven right to the mooring mast. Looking jovial, Litchfield boarded the ship and they started weighing off at once. No hesitation or ceremony marked the farewell. Ten minutes after getting her out, they were ready to leave. The sailors inside were leaning out every available porthole, four or five to a single window, and they waved and waved.

The police, this last time, mellowed by the farewell, let people push closer. The inner circle stood by the mast to listen for the last time to the weighing off.

"Twelve hundred pounds light!" reported a husky voice from the stale dark. Then quickly it was gone, gone over the city where craning thousands wished it a hail and farewell. But more than anything, Godspeed.

The wives, the sweethearts and the children of the crew in light clothes against the dark hangar waved handkerchiefs and the white arms and the white handkerchiefs were a swift moving pattern against the dusk of the hills in the background.

"I hope," said a newspaperman, "that it never makes anymore news and dies from old age after a long life."

"There goes our baby!" said one of the ground crew.

In groups the publicity men—aviation reporters, photographers, the other professionals who witnessed every flight, who had "covered" the *Macon* since the first rivet was put in her, stood together craning upwards—looking once more at the ship.

"We shouldn't be sentimental about this one," Hugh Allen, head of Goodyear-Zeppelin publicity, said solemnly. "We've seen it plenty often enough. *Look* at it, though!"

Everyone looked up. There it went, enough to make you catch your breath. It seemed almost miraculous that men could create such a thing. That's the way the people who saw it that Friday night would always remember it—the shiny silver thing, sailing, sailing, floating in the heart, touching beauty in the lovely evening away from the city of its birth.

Somebody said, "God take care of it."

And all around the field as people went quietly away, they said to each other, "Please don't let it go like the *Akron*. Take care of it. Take care of it."

* * *

Clear, warm weather with light winds was reported in the area off Point Arguello, California, on November 14, 1933, where over 100 ships of the Navy were to concentrate the next day in a spectacular event of the Navy maneuvers. Naval strategists, particularly those of the "Brown Fleet" whose mission it was to defend the coast on this large-scale maneuver, anxiously scanned weather maps.

The U.S.S. *Macon* would join in the maneuver, the key pawn of the offensive forces. The "Blue Fleet's" mission was to effect a landing party in the San Diego region. It was the "Brown Fleet's" job to stop the landing.

With some indignity, to say the least, in her baptism as a unit of the United States fleet, the world's greatest sky ship was theoretically destroyed in maneuvers off the California coast. The *Macon*, early in the games, found herself above the scouting force and promptly was put under theoretical gunfire of six light cruisers.

Then heavy, squally weather stirred up by a northwester chopped the Pacific Ocean south of Point Arguello, seriously hampering aerial arms of a hundred Naval vessels engaged in the games. Observation was nil. Land-geared planes from the carrier *Langley*, after battling against high winds, dropped into the sea in distress and the lives of all eight naval fliers were saved only by the prompt action of the cruiser *Cincinnati*, the battleship *Colorado* and the tender *Wright*.

Even with the *Macon* theoretically destroyed and of no further use, the "Blue" or attacking fleet obtained its objective of landing an expeditionary force on San Nicolas Island, north of Catalina Island, winning the day.

That was November, 1933, and it was a game.

The night of February 12, 1935, wasn't.

The two and one-half million dollar dirigible *Macon* lurched out of control and plunged 2,500 feet and sank into the Pacific. Eighty-one of the eighty-three men aboard were saved. The fate of the two men who remained aboard the fallen ship, her radio operator, Ernest Edwin Daily, and the mess attendant Florintino Edquiba, was not determined. First reports said an explosion occurred aboard the giant craft. Commander Herbert W. Wiley, skipper, reported that the stern had crumpled suddenly.

He said the ship fell slowly, giving the crew sufficient time to don life jackets and take to rubber lifeboats.

Wiley, only officer to survive the *Akron* disaster, was picked up by rescue ships which were on maneuvers with the airship. The scene of the disaster was thirteen miles southwest of Point Sur, rocky promontory 110 miles south of San Francisco.

The Navy Department received from the commander of cruiser division number 3 the following information transmitted by Wiley:

> "Wiley off Point Sur, course north, all engines standard speed 63 knots, altitude 1,250 feet. Air squally at time about 5:18 Pacific time. Casualty occurred in stern. I thought elevator control carried away. Ship took bow up inclination and rose properly. Ordered all ballast and fuel tanks dropped aft of midships. Received prompt word No. 1 gas cell under fin was gone, the stern was crumbling and finally the No. 2 cell was gone.
>
> Tried to land ship near cruisers off Point Sur. Could not see surface until shortly before landing. Ship planted stern first (no speed ahead at 5:40 p.m.). Discipline excellent. All hands at alarm in time to don life jackets. Sixty-four survivors picked up by the cruiser *Richmond*. The *Concord* took 11 aboard and the *Cincinnati* saved six in thrilling rescues. A number of lifeboats carried by the *Macon* made the rescue of the crewmen possible. Without the rubber boats a heavier loss of life might have resulted.

The airship was observed cruising through the skies, its giant bulk outlined above lowering fog, and the lighthouse keeper at Point Sur, indicated the passage in his log. Then when something went wrong aboard the craft Commander Wiley flashed the first SOS. It called for immediate assistance, indicating that the big Navy air cruiser was falling and adding ominously that there had been a bad casualty. Then came the word "wait"—while the Navy vessels over which the *Macon* had been flying on its return to the Sunnyvale base already had thrown over their rudders and were headed for the spot.

The last SOS call then came from Commander Wiley. It said, "Will abandon ship as soon as we land on the water somewhere 20 miles off Point Sur, probably 10 miles at sea." From all directions the gray Navy ships sped to the fallen sailors.

Apparently the ship remained afloat only a short time after striking the water. Reports saying, "The *Macon* floated three hours" no doubt were garbled in receipt. Whether the dirigible broke in two before crashing into the water was not known.

Fog overhung the sky when the *Macon* was stricken and after it hit the water, night closed down rapidly concealing the wreckage and survivors until searchlights pierced the gloom and the red glare of rockets directed the rescue ships. The first rocket, fired by the men of the *Macon*, was observed by the flagship *Pennsylvania* at 6:32 pm and about the same time the battleship *Maryland* sighted the wreckage of the *Macon*.

By February 13, 1935, President Roosevelt was said authoritatively to have tossed the entire problem of airship continuance or discontinuance to the Naval Committee. The Navy itself was divided on the lighter-than-air craft question. While the administration had approved a thirty-eight million dollar program for new naval construction projects, an airship was not so much as mentioned in the Navy's priority list from which the projects were taken. The crash of the *Macon* was the end of the rigid airship, the zeppelin, for America.

# Section Six

Rendezvous at Lakehurst: The Dream Destroyed

"If there should be a fire . . ."

That was the question asked, mostly to himself, by R. H. Ekins, editor of the United Press wire service, seated in the serene and luxurious "fireproof"smoking lounge of the palatial German dirigible, *Hindenburg*.

The date: October, 1936.

Ekins was on the first stage of a record-breaking flight around the world by commercial airlines—which he would complete successfully in 18 days, 14 hours, 56 minutes, 50 and two-fifths seconds.

"We were a carefree crew and a merry list of passengers," recalled Ekins. "We thought little of fire. I asked the question purely in fun.

"*Every* precaution had been taken to protect the vast silver airship—the most comfortable conveyance I have ever used for travel—from flames. They took our matches and cigarette lighters from us as we boarded the ship. We could smoke only in the insulated lounge. Elaborate contrivances were used to keep the highly inflammable hydrogen gas from penetrating the room."

It was due precisely to the recognized dangers of unstable hydrogen that *Hindenburg's* owners had done everything possible to make the largest airship in the world, 803 feet long, nearly as safe as a floating cradle.

The smoking compartment, for example, was separated from the rest of the ship by guarded double doors. One of these doors had to be closed whenever the other was open.

There were other safety precautions. The crew wore asbestos suits and sneakers whenever they worked near the hydrogen-filled gas cells. The airship's catwalks and ladders were covered with rubber to prevent sparks or static electricity. Only wet-cell batteries were used on board.

Not that the German builders had not preferred helium. The *Hindenburg* was *designed* for helium and only helium. Considerable work already had been done to pool German and American ships and docks into one magnificent airship line when World War II interrupted. The only helium in quantity came from America. We at Goodyear-Zeppelin who knew the situation strongly urged that enough safe helium be sold to Germany to at least serve the *Hindenburg's* needs. I personally urged this because, first of all, the world looked to that magnificent airship as an example, as a *last great chance*. If anything disastrous happened to *this* ship, everyone in the industry, the Congress, and Wall Street knew the jig was up.

World War II would be over some day. The little batch of helium in question for the *Hindenburg* was nothing. What is more, the Germans were convinced the airship would not make an offensive weapon. One man and one man only in America was responsible for that barbaric denial of helium. It was not Roosevelt. It was no one in Congress. It was Harold Ickes, American secretary of the Interior. Ickes alone was the stumbling block. His super fears and *super judgment* was alone responsible for multiple deaths. Roosevelt refused, for reasons of his own, to override Ickes. The decision stood, no helium! Germany *and* America's destiny in lighter-than-air was ended by Ickes' departmental order.

"I had met the *Hindenburg's* skipper, Captain Max Pruss, before," H. R. Ekins recalled. "I felt close to him, a gallant gentleman and an able commander. He and every member of his crew made every effort to assure our safety and comfort."

One of the first men in the country to be notified of the *Hindenburg's* dreadful incineration at Lakehurst, New Jersey, the night of May 6, 1937, Ekins, in semishock, let his mind wander over the probable scene:

"I can picture the gay passengers aboard the airship," he said, "as they soared over New York City in the sunlight before today's electrical storm. I can imagine that some chafed at the delay caused while soaring around Lakehurst waiting favorable landing conditions.

"I can see them as the *Hindenburg* nosed to the mast. The companionways were filled with baggage ready to be discharged. The passengers were dressed in their finest and chatting animatedly of the landing, the swell voyage behind them and the good times ahead.

"None dreamed of the fire which was to roar over the ship and send it crashing, a mass of molten metal and smouldering fabric. I remember my first farewell to Captain Pruss as I left him on the green field at Frankfort a year ago: 'I shall never travel any other way if I can help it, Captain.'

"Throughout that earlier voyage," sighed Ekins, "we had known that potentially we were an inferno. The *Hindenburg* was inflated with hydrogen, a gas inflammable beyond imagination. Though the Germans had sought, but were cut off from the safer helium, all aboard had faith in the Germans who had established a magnificent record for operating lighter-than-air craft in both military and commercial service."

As to the disaster's effect on the future of world airships, Ekins said, "I am afraid it will add further discouragement. . . The *Shenandoah*, *Akron* and *Macon* disasters, followed by those suffered by Britain, Italy, France and Japan, may well cause virtual abandonment of the American lighter-than-air program."

Ekins talked of the major escape route through the *Hindenburg's* belly:

"Through a square opening at the foot of a companionway leading down from the salon and dining room, they were about ready to thrust a stairway to the ground.

"I can imagine that as the passengers waited for the arrival of immigration and customs men, they were clustered around that opening. The steward, the beloved "Max," at the first indication of impending disaster, would have opened the exit and urged the endangered passengers to jump to the drenched earth below.

"Crew members in other parts of the ship would have used emergency exits to jump for their lives."

The afternoon of May 6 was balmy in Cleveland, a fresh spring wind blowing in off the lake shore.

Mrs. Emma Latin sat on her porch reading a newspaper story that said the *Hindenburg* would probably be a little late getting into Lakehurst because of headwinds.

Her mind wandered back to the previous June when her lifetime dream had been realized. She was thinking about the indescribable thrill she had experienced when she traveled on this gigantic airliner from Lakehurst to Frankfort, Germany. She wondered whether today's passengers were as thrilled as she had been, whether their trip would prove a golden recollection as hers had been.

"I had waited two years for the trip," Mrs. Latin recalled. "For two years my name had been on the application list and for two years I hoped and prayed that I could someday make the trip.

"It was just as if a gorgeous hotel had been picked up and was floating away with you inside. No noise, no vibration, no sea sickness and not a passenger had any fear."

Mrs. Latin said the only instructions issued the passengers when they embarked were not to keep any matches about them and not to throw out any paper because it was liable to go into an engine.

"We spent most of our time on the upper of the two decks," she continued. "On this deck was a large dining room where everyone ate at one time. There were 57 passengers on the trip I took and 25 staterooms, two passengers sharing a room. There also was a beautiful social room with a writing compartment at one end.

"On the lower deck were the smoking rooms in which there was a bar, and the bathrooms. The crew also had quarters on the lower deck."

Mrs. Latin described the ship as "so steady that a fountain pen would stand on a table."

"Although the Hindenburg was slightly behind schedule because of headwinds," she said, "not a passenger felt the wind or knew of the delay until the ship landed."

Another Ohio Hindenburg proponent was Frederick G. Folberth, president of the Automotive Development Company of Cleveland. Reached for comment the fateful night of May 6, 1937, Folberth, inventor of the automatic windshield wiper, said, "This catastrophe was not an accident. It was planned by somebody. It might have been a bullet shot from a high-powered gun. I am certain it was planned. It couldn't have happened any other way."

I feel I must interject to state this was not my personal opinion. To be sure, there was conjecture about sabotage. Robert Wise, producer of the Universal Studios film "Hindenburg" (1975) followed the sabotage theory to its fiery end for the most obvious box office reason. To quote the producer, "You can't make static electricity very dramatic." As someone who knew a bit more about airships and was not strapped with the burden of drawing movie patrons, however, it was my strong conjecture that Lehmann, knowing he was somewhat light on his landing approach, commenced to valve hydrogen. This, I believe, ionized the air which made it more conductive, so that a stray bolt of lightning followed the ionized column of hydrogen directly to the ship, setting it ablaze at the valve.

Calling the Hindenburg "a masterpiece the whole world admired," Folberth assured that "other ships would replace her because this system of transportation is here to stay."

He added that no safety instructions were issued the passengers on his trip "because there was no need of them."

"It was so safe," he said, "that even if the four motors failed, the ship could be sailed to its destination. Why, it was safe enough for a blacksmith forge to be operated in the smoking room. No," he again repeated, "this whole thing was planned."

The night of May 6, "Shorty" Fulton, manager of Akron Municipal Airport, recalled that Paul Litchfield, president of the Goodyear-Zeppelin Corporation where airship building had been an industry in Akron since 1913, had been the foremost critic of the hydrogen-filled dirigible.

Litchfield's own fleet of semi-rigid airships had flown an aggregate of approximately three million miles without serious mishap, while carrying 700,000 passengers.

As had been stated, the fight for air mail subsidies which would have put the American flag over the seas on regular airship runs had been carried on in Congress by combined American and German interests. Accordingly, Dr. Hugo Eckener, grizzled skipper of the incredibly successful Graf Zeppelin on a visit to

Akron in 1936, proposed his willingness to come here and aid both in the construction of the first Akron-built commercial airship and in the training of the crews. He planned also to lease a huge new German-made ship then under construction at Friedrichshafen, Germany, for the common dream of a U. S.-German intercontinental line. Eckener already had piloted more airship trips across the Atlantic than any other man.

As director of Germany's zeppelin company, he was reportedly in the bad graces of the German government because, it was averred, he had failed to agree fully with Nazi policies.

The reports were denied, but after the third trip of the *Hindenburg* in 1936, he turned over command to his veteran lieutenant, Captain Ernst Lehmann, afterwards confining himself to the Company's financial operations, away from the public eye.

After World War I, when the *Los Angeles* was ordered for the U. S. Navy as part of the war reparations, Eckener personally piloted the craft to America. That was in October, 1924, when he already was considered the leading airship pilot in Europe. His reputation grew with the round-the-world flight of the *Graf* in 1929. In 1931 he piloted that ship over the polar ice cap and in the following year inaugurated the first regular transatlantic schedule with flights to and from Brazil.

The *Hindenburg*'s disastrous 1937 voyage marked the first time that Captain Max Pruss had skippered the Germany to New Jersey run. He had had a quarter of a century and more than a million miles of airship travel to his credit; had flown over five of the six continents and crossed six of the seven seas.

In 1924, Pruss had spent five months at Lakehurst, New Jersey, as an instructor, teaching U. S. Navy officers the rudiments of lighter-than-air craft, including navigation and maneuvering.

When the *Hindenburg* burned, the *Los Angeles*, then moored at the U. S. Naval Air Station, was the Navy's sole surviving dirigible. It had been retired, however, from active service because of fear that obsolescence had weakened her metal structure beyond the safety margin.

Captain Ernst A. Lehmann, advisor on the *Hindenburg*'s death flight, had been its commander before 1937. He had received the German "Iron Cross" for his flight achievements during World War I, particularly in the Baltic Sea area. After the war he became identified with the Zeppelin Company at Friedrichshafen. He had helped Eckener pilot the *Los Angeles* to Lakehurst in 1924.

Regular trips to South America on the *Graf* soon became such a matter of routine that Eckener seldom went along, but left Lehmann in command. It was hardly a surprise, therefore, that the world-reknown *Hindenburg*, completed in 1936, also was placed in Lehmann's command.

During this period, so linked were the mutual airship and scientific interests of Germany and Akron, Ohio, that from 1923 to 1927, Ernst Lehmann resided in Akron as vice-president of the Goodyear-Zeppelin Corporation.

The date "May 6th" played a double role in the brief career of the airship. On May 6, 1936, the *Hindenburg* left Friedrichshafen, near Berlin, on its maiden voyage to the United States. A year to the day later, it lay in an inferno on the wet New Jersey earth.

Such symbolic coincidences, it would be said, often tickle the fancies of assassins and plotters.

The next day, newspapers appeared on Berlin streets with bannerlines on the Spanish war and other news. Nothing on the *Hindenburg's* demise. The regular morning editions, according to reports, went to press too soon to include the story. Ascension Day and holiday schedules also hampered news distribution. None of the German papers carried the disaster bulletin even five hours after the crash.

The official Nazi news agency ultimately declared, "A new dirigible, now building at Friedrichshafen, will continue to carry the German flag across the Atlantic in the *Hindenburg's* place. The nation is horrified, but still looks with pride at the honorable record of the *Hindenburg* and her crew."

Reichsfuehrer Adolph Hitler, called early from his bed to receive news of the worst disaster to German air transportation in history, refused formal comment.

A report of the catastrophe was telephoned from the ministry of propaganda to the Chancellor and propaganda minister Joseph Goebbels. They were told, erroneously, that the 39 passengers and 61 crew members all had been killed.

The propanganda ministry understood that the explosion was due to "a flash of lightning."

On Ascension Day, a legal holiday in Germany, an official declared simply, "the whole Zeppelin crowd is away from town."

At the same time an Ohio editorial urged "some international arrangement for the use of helium in all passenger dirigibles. As the latest of a long list of heartbreaking accidents," the newspaper conceded, "it strikes a discouraging note. The feeling of many will be to abandon dirigibles altogether. But so much progress has been made in recent years that it *cannot* be thrown away! Man must go on to capture the skies, though the lessons are costly in the extreme."

If men were to capture the skies, however, it was soon evident it would not be in dirigibles.

Congress, nearly as a body, was quick to shout, "I told you so." Wall Street seconded the motion.

Typical was Congressman Hill, of Alabama, Chairman of the House Military Committee. "The accident," he said, "should have the effect of confirming and crystallizing sentiment in this country opposed to the use of dirigibles. . ."

Hardly had Congress spoken when a sudden Hitler communique ended any shred of hope for the future. He ordered all German airships to fly only inside the borders of Germany. No more transatlantic flights without helium—helium the U. S. wouldn't sell.

In 1940, he further ordered all German airships grounded and reduced to scrap.

The *Hindenburg* was all people talked about that 7th of May.

Agency upon agency ruled on the tragedy's cause.

The U. S. Bureau of Air Commerce issued its view and closed its books forever.

"St. Elmo's fire," they said ". . . an electrical discharge from a tall object, such as a mooring mast."

The phenomenon occurs when the air is full of static electricity after a thunderstorm. And there *had* been a thunderstorm over New Jersey prior to and during the huge liner's descent.

Most, however, chose to believe the words muttered by Ernst Lehmann before he died of his burns: "It must have been an infernal machine (time bomb)."

Though not many today may remember anything else about Herb Morrison, a strange twist of fate would spiral the little known radio reporter to journalistic fame that early evening of May 6, 1937.

It all began placidly enough. The *Hindenburg* had made Frankfurt-to-Lakehurst runs nine previous times. It no longer was hard news. Reporter Morrison must have spent extra time wondering how to make his commentary interesting.

Eventually, through the darkening mist, the silvery giant slid silently into view.

"Here it comes," he told his American radio listeners. "And what a sight she is. The *Hindenburg* is riding majestically toward us like a feather. . ."

Then the panicked quick sentences still remembered by millions: "It's burning, bursting into flames!"

As fire spouted like a fountain from the *Hindenburg*, people were falling and jumping from the blazing airship and landing all around Morrison and other newsmen.

"This is terrible!" Morrison sobbed. "I can't talk, ladies and gentlemen. This is the worst thing I've ever witnessed!"

Others who never were in position to jump were trapped on board, their screams drowned out in the white-hot inferno. The crumpling, blazing holocaust collapsed in two minutes, leaving nothing but charred and melted metal framework. But the fuel tanks burned for hours. Some passengers were so gravely injured, among them Captain Lehmann, that last rites of the Roman Catholic Church were quickly administered to them.

An explosion of the No. 2 gas cell toward the stern of the ship was named as the initial cause of the disaster by State Aviation Commissioner Gill Robb Wilson, who termed the blast "strange."

Another account said the ship had angled her blunt nose toward the securing tower, the spider-like landing lines had been snaked down from her belly and the ground crew had grasped the ropes from the nose when the explosion roared out, scattering ground crew and spectators like frightened sheep.

As the flames raced forward along the fabric toward the passengers' lounge and control car, the Navy men of the ground crew "dove into the flames like dogs after a rabbit," Commissioner Wilson said in voicing high praise of the rescue heroism.

The tail, with its swastika emblems of Nazi Germany, sagged downward immediately after the first rending explosion. The nose hung motionless for a moment in the air, then slumped earthward, the split sections telescoping as they fell, and pieces of the silvery fabric fluttering down, some in flames.

Screams and cries of injured in agony were "terrible," the hardened sailors and marines who did the rescue work reported. Clothing was completely burned off some. Others were blown clear through the envelope.

Three blasts ripped the ship as if she were made of paper.

Ground crew member Harry Wellbrook, directly under the exploding stern, dragged three victims into the clear. None of their features were recognizable, burned away. One of them was still breathing twenty minutes later.

Paul Kimball Hospital at Lakewood, New Jersey, was quickly over-filled. The facilities of all others in the area were taxed. Some victims were flown out by plane to Newark, seventy miles away.

A temporary morgue was established back of the Naval hospital. In time, the first weeping group was brought into the small hangar for identification purposes.

Reporter Patricia O'Malley, on location, came up with her own version of what had sparked the macabre tragedy:

> I saw smoke, (she said) trailing out from the left rear engine and then several minutes later, flames burst from this motor. It is a practice of dirigibles to reverse their engines on landing, and this may provide an explanation of the disaster— sparks flying from the motor coils when the engines were thrown into reverse.

George Willens, owner of a Detroit printing company, had booked passage on the midnight *Hindenburg* return flight.

> I was running like hell, (he said) to get some movies of the landing when it all happened over my head. From a distance of 300 feet, I saw a man hurl himself from a window of the ship, drop to the ground, get up limping and brush himself off. I was taking a movie of it, yet I could hardly believe my eyes.
>
> I ran over to the spot and introduced myself to Joseph Shahs, a German acrobatic jumper.
>
> "How on earth did you do it?" I asked.
>
> "I don't know," he said, feeling his legs and arms and neck, assuring himself he was all in one piece. "Whew, am I lucky? Not a scratch!"
>
> Then, (Willens said) I saw a young woman running toward the inferno. "My father is in there!" she screamed.
>
> A German in a leather jacket rushed toward her. They embraced, laughed and cried. The German—I did not get his name—was a passenger on the *Hindenburg.* The flames had burned the back of his jacket off, but he was unharmed, only singed.
>
> These were cheerful notes among all that was horrible.
>
> The explosion and the succeeding metal-melting flame was the worst sight of all. I saw several bodies blown into the air as that vast gassy interior burst with a force that shook the earth under my feet.
>
> I and my son Harvy, 17 (Willens said) were to have gone back on this ship to attend the Coronation. That is off, now and so is any trip in any zeppelin. I thought them about the safest way to travel, once, but after seeing this, I'll never set foot in one again.

Lastly, one unidentified passenger, moments after the tragedy, recalled packing in his cabin in the forward section of the *Hindenburg* in preparation for the landing.

> I first felt a slight tremor shaking the ship, (he recalled). I learned later it was the explosion that rent the tail of the airship, the first of three that tore the craft apart, but its effect, where I stood, was no more than that of an air pocket.

Hearing people run past my door, I joined them to find the cause of the tremor. As I walked toward the promenade deck, a second tremor occurred.

There was very little confusion among the passengers, no screaming, hardly any noise. Nobody knew what had happened and people were just curious. When I reached the promenade deck, the nose of the ship was about twenty feet above the ground. Although I wasn't alarmed, I knew something was wrong and I decided to get out as fast as I could.

I climbed to the sill of a window, planning to jump to the ground. Suddenly the steel sill under my feet buckled and virtually catapulted me to the ground. I rose uninjured.

In front of me, Captain Lehmann had reached the ground after jumping from the ship. His hair and the back of his coat were on fire. I rushed up and beat out the flames, getting pretty badly burned myself.

Even after the blasts had broken her, (said the passenger) the great airship settled slowly, almost majestically, down. Even in breaking up, the *Hindenburg* was gentle to its passengers—those who lived.

Time of the blast was 6:23 pm (EST).

At midnight the big ship was to have sailed away, but instead a curl of smoke drifted to the sky—where the *Hindenburg*, homeward bound, had expected to be.

# In Memoriam

## 1894—1978

### WARD T. VAN ORMAN

In a recent issue of *Case Alumnus* magazine, editor Grant Anderson announced that two graduates of Case Institute of Technology had been selected to receive one of the nation's most prestigious honors, the Case Alumni Association Gold Medal Award for 1977.

One was Dr. Elmer Hutchisson, Class of '23, a distinguished teacher and scientist. The other: Ward Van Orman, Case Class of '17.

Wrote Anderson, "When scientists were more concerned with flying across the Atlantic than rocketing across the solar system, Van Orman was one of the glamour boys of the American skyways. His craft was a balloon. His venture was racing.

"World War I interrupted the sport, but in 1919 balloon racing regained popularity and captured the imagination of the world. That year Ralph H. Upson won the National Race in a Goodyear Tire and Rubber Co. balloon. His aide on the trip was a young fellow from Lorain, Ohio, who was to become the best known name in ballooning during the 1920s and 30s—Van Orman.

"In 1924 as chief Goodyear balloon pilot, Van Orman won the National Race, covering 1,072 miles from San Antonio, Texas, to Rochester, Minnesota. That was the beginning of an extraordinary string of victories for Van Orman. In all, he entered 11 National Balloon Races and was aboard the winner five times. He finished second twice and third once.

"Van Orman went on to compete in 10 International Races," concluded Anderson, "winning three and finishing second once and third twice. This is the greatest record a balloonist ever compiled in international competition."

Joining Goodyear as an aeronautical engineer in 1917, Van Orman qualified as a free balloon and airship pilot the next year. During World War I, he was a civilian instructor at a Naval Air Station near Akron, Ohio, called Wingfoot Lake. Van was one of the first men to employ radio in balloon racing. He invented several devices to aid balloon navigation, including a lightning protective shield. He developed the shield after his hydrogen-filled sphere was struck by lightning and crashed like a plummeting torch in the National Race from Pittsburgh, Pennsylvania, in 1928, killing his aide and companion.

From the skyways, Ward Van Orman became head of physical testing and in charge of air filter research at Goodyear in Akron. Another of his achievements was the development of terminal sites for zeppelin transports when plush lighter-than-air travel between continents was believed a certainty in the days before the tragic demise of the *Akron*, the *Macon* and the *Hindenburg*, the largest airships in the world.

This man's list of inventions surpasses the most far-fetched Horatio Alger saga:

1918: Inventor of what is now the popular life raft used on overseas flights of aircraft.

1919: Inventor of bullet-sealing fuel tanks used on military aircraft and crash-proof tanks used on transport aircraft.

1928: Inventor of the fabric process.

1933: Inventor of a new method for measuring vibration of the front wheels of automobiles.

1938: Inventor of the air-conditioned cast for orthopedic cases.

1942: Inventor of the airtight zipper.

1942: Inventor of the stratosphere pressure suit.

1943: Inventor of Hyperbaric Oxygen Therapy.

1947: Inventor of a breathing machine for heart patients.

1947: Inventor of a new process for Braille study for the American Red Cross.

1947: Inventor of the pulsating pressure pad for the prevention of bedsores.

1949: Developed the self-charging electrostatic air cleaner.

Goodyear was already in the airship manufacturing business for 12 months when Ward Van Orman joined their ranks in 1917. It was already well-known that the Navy blimp was an extremely effective submarine hunter and the lighter-than-air Goodyear machines were used nearly exclusively for convoy patrol. The Akron tire manufacturer also turned out "kite" balloons (tethered balloons) for observation, and free balloons for airship pilot basic training.

"I worked with Lee DeForest," Van Orman recalls, "on his radio transmission signals from a kite balloon. At that time, transmission was via wire built into the center of the cable which was fragile and uncertain. But with this radio transmission, one of course could talk freely to the ground, and that was the beginning of aircraft transmission. It was a superb pleasure to work with DeForest who was the inventor of the vacuum tube for radio."

When World War I came to a close, Van was assigned to the aero design department as Goodyear continued to build the giant airships for two more years.

"But then the airship field became quite limited," Van recalls, "and I found myself designing passenger tires until 1924 when the whims of fate shifted again and Goodyear reorganized for the building of the *Akron* and the *Macon* dirigibles, the largest dirigibles ever made by man."

He transferred into the Goodyear-Zeppelin Corporation and worked on the zeppelins from then until 1932 during which time he was also the organization's meteorologist and headed training for civilian airship pilots.

In 1939, Van Orman was called to Cleveland by Dr. George Crile, Sr., to work on a pressurized pilot suit with oxygen which would enable men to fly higher than 30,000 feet. Out of a freak accident during the investigative procedure, the Akron researcher stumbled upon the principle and marvelous properties of Hyperbaric Oxygen, yet considered by the medical establishment as an important breakthrough in the areas of heart disease and depression symptoms.

In 1945, Van Orman became head of the physical testing department of Goodyear research. He retired in 1962. He still sings the praises of Goodyear Tire & Rubber.

Ward Van Orman turned international free ballooning into a command post for science experimentation.

# Balloon Racing
## INTERNATIONAL RACES
### (FOR JAMES GORDON BENNETT CUP)

| Year | Winner | Country | Starting Place | Distance Miles |
|------|--------|---------|----------------|----------------|
| 1906 | Lt. Frank P. Lahm | America | Paris, France | 402 |
| 1907 | Osker Erbsloh | Germany | St. Louis, Mo. | 872 |
| 1908 | Col. Oberst Schaeck | Switzerland | Berlin, Germany | 753 |
| 1909 | E. W. Mix | America | Zurich, Switzerland | 696 |
| 1910 | Alan R. Hawley | America | St. Louis, Mo. | 1,173 |
| 1911 | Hans Gericke | Germany | Kansas City, Mo. | 471 |
| 1912 | Maurice Bienaime | France | Stuttgart, Germany | 1,334 |
| 1913 | Ralph Upson | America | Paris, France | 384 |
| 1914-1919 | Cancelled, War | | | |
| 1920 | Ernest DeMuyter | Belgium | Birmingham, Ala. | 1,098 |
| 1921 | Paul Armbruster | Switzerland | Brussels, Belgium | 476 |
| 1922 | Ernest DeMuyter | Belgium | Geneva, Switzerland | 852 |
| 1923 | Ernest DeMuyter | Belgium | Brussels, Belgium | 717 |
| 1924 | Ernest DeMuyter | Belgium | Brussels, Belgium | 444 |

### WINNERS OF THE SECOND JAMES GORDON BENNETT CUP

| Year | Winner | Country | Starting Place | Distance Miles |
|------|--------|---------|----------------|----------------|
| 1925 | A. Veenstra | Belgium | Brussels, Belgium | 836 |
| 1926 | W. T. Van Orman | America | Antwerp, Belgium | 585 |
| 1927 | Edward J. Hill | America | Detroit, Mich. | 745 |
| 1928 | Maj. W. E. Kepner | America | Detroit, Mich. | 460 |

### WINNERS OF THE THIRD JAMES GORDON BENNETT CUP

| Year | Winner | Country | Starting Place | Distance Miles |
|------|--------|---------|----------------|----------------|
| 1929 | W. T. Van Orman | America | St. Louis, Mo. | 341 |
| 1930 | W. T. Van Orman | America | Cleveland, Ohio | 542 |
| 1932 | Lt. Cdr. Settle | America | Basle, Switzerland | 921 |

### WINNERS OF THE FOURTH JAMES GORDON BENNETT CUP

| Year | Winner | Country | Starting Place | Distance Miles |
|------|--------|---------|----------------|----------------|
| 1933 | Hynek | Poland | Chicago, Ill. | 848 |
| 1934 | Hynek | Poland | Warsaw, Poland | 808 |
| 1935 | Burzynski | Poland | Warsaw, Poland | 1,025 |